Philosophy for Girls

Philosophy for Girls

An Invitation to the Life of Thought

Edited by

MELISSA M. SHEW AND KIMBERLY K. GARCHAR

OXFORD
UNIVERSITY PRESS

OXFORD
UNIVERSITY PRESS

Oxford University Press is a department of the University of Oxford. It furthers
the University's objective of excellence in research, scholarship, and education
by publishing worldwide. Oxford is a registered trade mark of Oxford University
Press in the UK and certain other countries.

Published in the United States of America by Oxford University Press
198 Madison Avenue, New York, NY 10016, United States of America.

Library of Congress Cataloging-in-Publication Data
Names: Shew, Melissa M., editor. | Garchar, Kimberly K., editor.
Title: Philosophy for girls : an invitation to the life of thought /
edited by Melissa M. Shew and Kimberly K. Garchar.
Description: New York, NY, United States of America : Oxford University Press, 2020. |
Includes bibliographical references and index.
Identifiers: LCCN 2020018924 (print) | LCCN 2020018925 (ebook) |
ISBN 9780190072919 (hardback) | ISBN 9780190072926 (paperback) |
ISBN 9780190072957 (oso) | ISBN 9780190072933 (updf) | ISBN 9780190072940 (epub)
Subjects: LCSH: Philosophy.
Classification: LCC B21 .P95 2021 (print) | LCC B21 (ebook) |
DDC 108.2—dc23
LC record available at https://lccn.loc.gov/2020018924
LC ebook record available at https://lccn.loc.gov/2020018925

For Kayla Murphy, with love

Contents

Acknowledgments

We thank Oxford University Press, especially our editor Lucy Randall and her assistant, Hannah Doyle, for providing this avenue through which girls may find and love philosophy. We are grateful for the anonymous reviewers whose comments helped hone our project. We are beyond thankful to Michael Neubeck for his expert initial editing of this book, which required countless hours of reading and rereading at a microscopic level, not to mention a firm belief in this collaborative project.

As first-time editors, we are thankful to know and have learned from Deborah Barnbaum, Kevin Gibson, John Lysaker, and James South, all of whom generously offered advice in the early stages of publishing. We also thank the Fund for Diversity and Inclusion of the American Philosophical Association (APA) for the grant that allowed us to work together in person at important points. We are so very appreciative of Hyo Won Seo, a graduate student of philosophy at Kent State University, for her diligent work. Hyo Won created a robust and thorough index that insightfully interprets and frames this text for our readers. We thank the Kent State University Division of Research and Sponsored Programs for providing the funds with which were able to hire Hyo Won. We are grateful too to Lily Pickart, who transformed the original symbolic image of a pomegranate into a beautiful cover for this book, and to Peter Beck, for digitizing her art.

Our hearts are full of gratitude for our contributors who worked diligently and as a labor of love to complete this project in a life-giving and dialogical way. Finally, we are thankful for our readers and those who support them. We imagine them reading and exploring their ideas everywhere this book can find them.

✳✳✳

Melissa

In truth, this book was born fully formed as a concept a decade ago. It hit me all at once, but life circumstances and academic jobs being what they are, I never finished it, though I tried. Two years ago, I realized that this book needed to exist more than I needed to be the one to write it, so I asked Kim

Garchar, my dear friend and now excellent coeditor, to help fulfill the initial vision in another way by turning it into a multiauthored volume. There is no one else with whom I'd have wanted to learn all of the very many steps of publishing and editing. I am entirely grateful for her friendship, smarts, devotion to justice, and extremely hard work, all of which helped make this book as strong and worthy as it is.

When developing and communicating the pitch, tone, and scope of this book, many sensational young women remained in clear view. Najah Buck, Tamia Fowlkes, Nicole Fuschetti, Mia Gates, Jackie Gehringer, Jordyn Gonzalez, Maggie Hensien, Christina Keyser, Jenna Nordness, Brooke McArdle, Tess Murphy, Meghan Quadracci, Nora Reynolds, Jasmine Rodriguez, Sophia Romero, Maia Salameh, Alissa Trepman, Grace Tallmadge, Elizabeth Whelan, Kal Yelle, and so many more: I see you and hear you. Also, a chorus of support has pushed me and this idea along for a very long time, including Tricky Burns, Curtis Carter, Alexandra Crampton, Julia DuBois, Katie Egan, Charlie Gibbs, Owen Goldin, Joshua Kramer, Stephen and Mary Neubeck, Jane Powers, Dominique Reid, and Elise Span, whose own lives reflect deep philosophical commitments. The team of women educators at the Marquette University Child Care Center allowed me to spend a beautiful and humbling morning at a retreat with them in Fall 2018, where Persephone's story was first read aloud.

My parents, Archie and Nancy Shew, encouraged an important curiosity in me from an early age and are utterly supportive of their daughters. My thoughtful sister, Maryanne Shew, actively empowers women, including me, while also being the best "Aunt Punk" to her nephews. Michael Neubeck's insistence on vivid prose and love for the written word make me weak in the knees. Without his steadfast belief in me, this book would still be lingering on the Oregon coast. Finally, to Sebastian and Gabriel, my bright and curious stars: I love painting pomegranates with you.

***

Kim
I first thank my dear friend and philoso-sister Melissa, who dreamed this project for many years and invited me to join her in breathing life into it. I am grateful for her husband, Michael, who has supported us and this project in countless ways and who generously contributed his expertise. I thank my mom, Diane, who still carries the resilience and strength she learned as a farm girl, for showing me that girls could do absolutely anything: tough

things, grimy things, beautiful things. I thank my dad for regularly reminding me of the same. I thank the many enthusiastic teachers I had in primary and secondary school, including Mrs. Templeton and Mrs. Moore, who fed my curiosity and cultivated my love of reading, art, and science. I thank my mathematics professors, Drs. Ron and Marilyn Loser, for teaching me discipline. I thank my professors and mentors at the University of Oregon, especially my advisor Dr. Scott Pratt, who continuously challenged me and encouraged me when I floundered. I thank the cohort of outstanding women philosophy graduate students who led me into feminism and the examined life, which is so very worth living. I thank my many, many students who have inspired me and energized me, who have helped me think and made me a better philosopher. I thank the many strong, super women whom I count as friends and who make me a better person; they are too numerous to name but include Mansi, Shelly, Sarah, Deborah, and Deb. They are wise and wonderful, all. I lastly thank Kent State University for the support I've enjoyed throughout my career.

Contributor Biographies

Elisabeth Camp is professor of philosophy at Rutgers University in New Brunswick, New Jersey, specializing in language, mind, and aesthetics. Her research focuses on forms of thought and talk that don't fit the standard philosophical model of a propositional calculating machine. In the realm of communication, this includes phenomena like metaphor, sarcasm, slurs, and insinuation. In the realm of minds, it has included maps, nonhuman animal cognition, imagination, and emotion. Along with Elizabeth Harman and Jill North, she is a co-organizer of *Athena in Action*, a series of workshops for mentoring women graduate students in philosophy.

Myisha Cherry is assistant professor of philosophy at the University of California, Riverside. Her research interests are at the intersection of moral psychology and social and political philosophy. Cherry's work has appeared in such scholarly journals as *Hypatia* and *Critical Philosophy of Race*. She has also written for the *Los Angeles Times*, *Boston Review*, Huffington Post, Salon.com, and *New Philosopher Magazine*. Her books include *The Moral Psychology of Anger* (coedited with Owen Flanagan) and *UnMuted: Conversations on Prejudice, Oppression, and Social Justice*. She is also the host of the UnMute Podcast, where she interviews philosophers about the social and political issues of our day.

Shanti Chu is a full-time instructor of philosophy at the College of Lake County, a community college outside of Chicago, where she coordinates Philosophy Club. She holds an MA in philosophy from Miami University. Her courses and research focus on feminist theories of embodiment, postcolonial theory, and plant-based eating. She makes philosophy palatable through two blogs, one on ethical, affordable, and vegetarian eating in Chicago, chiveg.com; and a Tumblr blog on race, culture, and gender. Shanti runs Coffee/Tea with a Splash of Philosophy tours in Chicago as a means of making philosophy more accessible while sampling coffee and tea.

Julianne Chung is assistant professor of philosophy at York University. Her primary research areas lie in epistemology, philosophy of language, aesthetics, and philosophy of mind, and she is particularly interested in how comparative and cross-cultural philosophy can shed light on a variety of topics. She is associate editor of Oxford Studies in Epistemology and president of the American Society for Aesthetics, Rocky Mountain Division. In addition, she serves on the American Philosophical Association's committee on Asian and Asian-American Philosophers and Philosophies.

Meena Dhanda is professor of philosophy and cultural politics at the University of Wolverhampton in the United Kingdom. She migrated to the United Kingdom from Punjab, India in 1987 with an award of a Commonwealth Scholarship for doctoral work in philosophy at Balliol College, Oxford University. Meena has taught moral, political, and feminist philosophy in the United Kingdom for over twenty-eight years. Her scholarship is wide-ranging, from caste discrimination in Britain and philosophical foundations of anti-casteism to problems with racism in academic philosophy and more. A socially engaged philosopher, Meena pursues philosophy with practical intent. She is placed on Amnesty International's Suffragette Spirit Map of Britain (2018) in recognition of her long-standing commitment to anti-discrimination research and practice. Her books include *The Negotiation of Personal Identity* and *Reservations for Women* (edited). Her most recent project is called "Freedom From Caste: The Political Thought of Periyar E. V. Ramasamy in a Global Context," funded by Horizon 2020 Marie Skłodowska Curie Actions Independent Fellowship (with Karthick Ram Manoharan), commencing in fall 2020.

Kimberly K. Garchar is associate professor of philosophy at Kent State University and associated graduate faculty at Northeast Ohio Medical University. She specializes in American pragmatism, ethics, and clinical ethics, especially death and dying. Her current project is an investigation into human suffering, what it means, and how we might respond. She came to philosophy through mathematics and has been focused on issues of gender and gender equity throughout her education and career. In the summers she can be found in her garden, on her kayak, or searching for the perfect swimming hole.

Lori Gruen is the William Griffin Professor of Philosophy at Wesleyan University. She is also a professor of feminist, gender, and sexuality studies, science in society, and the coordinator of Wesleyan animal studies. She is the author and editor of eleven books, including *Entangled Empathy*, *Critical Terms for Animal Studies*, and *Ethics and Animals: An Introduction*. Gruen's work lies at the intersection of ethical and political theory and practice, with a particular focus on issues that impact those often overlooked in traditional ethical investigations, such as women, people of color, incarcerated people, and nonhuman animals.

Serene J. Khader is professor of philosophy at the CUNY Graduate Center and Jay Newman Chair in Philosophy of Culture at Brooklyn College. She is the author of *Decolonizing Universalism: A Transnational Feminist Ethic* and *Adaptive Preferences and Women's Empowerment*, as well as a number of articles. She also coedited, with Ann Garry and Alison Stone, the *Routledge Companion to Feminist Philosophy*. When she isn't philosophizing, she can be found engaging in political activism, lifting heavy weights, and discovering the world with her toddler.

Tabatha Leggett has an MA in philosophy from Birkbeck College, University of London, where her thesis examined issues of consent as well as the parallels between consciousness-raising groups of the 1960s and 1970s and today's #MeToo movement. She also has a BA in philosophy from Cambridge University, where her thesis focused on the relationship between pornography and art. Tabatha has a background in digital media, having worked at the Finnish public broadcaster Yle, British GQ, and BuzzFeed UK, where she held the position head of buzz for five years. In addition to philosophy, gender, and digital media, Tabatha is interested in languages and literature. She is currently working as a literary agent in Helsinki, Finland.

Patricia M. Locke is a senior Tutor at St. John's College, Annapolis, Maryland. Since St. John's has an all-required curriculum, she has taught almost every subject and learns something new every day. She especially likes the philosophy and literature seminars, and enjoys lab sciences. In addition, she is an MFA critical theory advisor at the Marchutz School of Art in Aix-en-Provence, France. Dr. Locke received a PhD in philosophy at Boston College, with additional studies in art. She loves to paint and does tai chi as a martial art. She is writing a book on night phenomena in Proust, and has published articles in phenomenology of art, literature, and biology. Her big questions right now are "What does it mean to be a self?" and "How are we intertwined with others?"

Claudia Mills is associate professor emerita of philosophy at the University of Colorado at Boulder, specializing in moral and political philosophy, especially issues involving the family. She has published articles on such questions as: What do grown children owe to their aging parents? Are there morally problematic reasons for having children? Is the rise in prescriptions for behavior-altering medications for children ethically troubling? She is also the author of dozens of books for young readers. Her two careers intersect in fruitful ways: she uses examples drawn from children's literature in her university courses on ethics, and her children's books often feature children who face ethical dilemmas in their own lives.

Monica C. Poole is professor and chair in the interdisciplinary Department of History and Social Sciences at Bunker Hill Community College in Boston, MA. She teaches and learns from her students in philosophy and religious studies. She earned an AA degree from a community college and an MA degree from Harvard University, and she takes equal pride in both. Current projects in progress include a chapter exploring how Biblical narratives of community responses to the resurrected Jesus can provide lessons for community responses to contemporary survivors of trauma; a chapter on solitude, imagination, and chronic illness; and an essay about reclaiming righteousness.

Gillian Russell is professor of philosophy at the Dianoia Research Institute in Philosophy at Australian Catholic University in Melbourne, Australia. She is the author of *Truth in Virtue of Meaning* and the editor of *New Waves in Philosophical Logic* (with Greg Restall) and the *Routledge Companion to Philosophy of Language* (with Delia Graff Fara). She is currently working on a book on Hume's law—the thesis that you can't get an *ought* from an *is*.

Devora Shapiro is associate professor of philosophy at Southern Oregon University, where she also serves as co-coordinator for the Healthcare Studies Program and Affiliated Faculty for both the Honors College and for the Gender, Sexuality, and Women's Studies Program. She holds a PhD in philosophy from the University of Minnesota, an MA in clinical medical ethics from the University of Tennessee, and her BA from Johns Hopkins University. Her research covers areas of feminist epistemology, philosophy of science, and the philosophy of medicine. She has written on such topics as experiential knowledge as well as the failure of objectivity as an epistemic ideal. Her current work, "Intersectionality and the Medical Subject," focuses on the intersections of medicine, knowledge, and justice in the context of diagnosis and treatment, through an intersectional lens.

Melissa M. Shew is visiting assistant professor at Marquette University. Her expertise and interests are wide-ranging from ancient Greek to contemporary philosophy, philosophy of literature and the arts, and pedagogy. In her scholarship as with her students, she usually finds her way back to authenticity, dialogue, chance, and understanding the power of a moment. Melissa has taught at the university level for fifteen years and also taught for five years at an all-girls college preparatory high school, living out her firm belief in empowering young women and girls through education. She came to philosophy through literature, music, myth, politics, and the arts.

Subrena E. Smith is assistant professor of philosophy at the University of New Hampshire. She is a philosopher of biology whose work focuses on human behavioral variation and conceptions of human difference, methodological problems with evolutionary explanations of human behavior, and the concept of the organism. She received her PhD from Cornell University.

Karen Stohr is associate professor of philosophy at Georgetown University, as well as a senior research scholar in Georgetown's Kennedy Institute of Ethics. She writes primarily in ethics, with a special focus on the moral dimensions of social conventions. She has published two books, *On Manners* and *Minding the Gap: Moral Ideals and Moral Improvement*, and is currently working on a third book on Kantian ethics. If she couldn't be a philosopher, she'd like to be an advice columnist or a professional gardener. Obviously she is a Jane Austen fangirl, but she also adores Harry Potter, Hamilton, and The Good Place. She lives in Maryland with her husband, two teenage daughters, and a very exuberant golden retriever.

Shannon Winnubst is chair and professor of women's, gender, and sexuality studies at the Ohio State University. She has written two books, *Way Too Cool: Selling Out Race and Ethics* and *Queering Freedom*, as well as many articles and essays spanning feminist theory, queer studies, and twentieth-century French philosophy. She has served as an editor of several projects, most importantly of *philoSOPHIA: A Journal of transContinental Feminism* (2013–2018) and of *Reading Bataille Now* (Indiana 2007). She is currently working on the figures of personhood, white death, and the transhistorical force of the Door of No Return.

Charlotte Witt is professor of philosophy and humanities at the University of New Hampshire. She is interested in social ontology, feminist theory, and Aristotle. Her publications include *The Metaphysics of Gender* and *Feminist Metaphysics: Explorations in the Ontology of Sex, Gender, and the Self*. She received her PhD from Georgetown University and lives in Maine with her family.

Robin L. Zebrowski is associate professor of cognitive science at Beloit College. She has spent the last two decades specializing in the metaphysics of mind and artificial intelligence, with a focus on embodied cognition. Her work also deals heavily with the philosophy of technology and cyborg studies, overlapping with tech ethics. She is deeply committed to philosophical education and is excited to share this volume with her students and her own child as soon as possible.

Prologue

Persephone: The Invitation

Melissa M. Shew

γνῶθι σεαυτόν[1]

As most good stories do, this one begins with a girl. We meet this girl as she crosses a threshold that transforms her life. Through her initiation into a strange world that morphs into her own, the girl becomes who she is. This girl is Persephone.

Here are the contours of her story. Like Europa, Oritheia, and other mythical flower-plucking maidens, Persephone is but one girl in a catalogue of tales about old men who prey on young women. In the original ancient myths, Persephone is abducted by Hades, the god of the underworld, though the specific details differ among those accounts.[2] Nearly all versions of the Persephone myth follow the same trajectory after the initial abduction, however. We know that Persephone becomes Hades's spouse and that she is given shared rule of the dead. We also know that after she grows fully into herself, she figures in subsequent myths as an elusive yet determinate figure whom Greek heroes and heroines encounter in their own lives and journeys.[3] We know these basic aspects of the myth, but in truth, we know few details about Persephone and her story, especially not from her perspective.

We know much more about Demeter, her powerful and devastating mother. Demeter's emotions and perspective are evident; she holds nothing back. For instance, when her daughter goes missing, she grieves and rages, confused and alone. She shouts into a void, tearing at herself. Panic sets in. Her anger is limitless, terrifying. Even the grass trembles at her rage. Unknown to her, there were witnesses to the violent act, but those who heard dared not tattle on Hades. Demeter thus wanders the wrong realm, scouring the earth for her daughter when she should be seeking beneath it.[4] At one point, Demeter unleashes the full awesomeness of her powers and begins to kill everything that grows, hardening the earth and starving its creatures, bereft as she is by her daughter's absence. When the gods understand the extent of the horror unfurled by Demeter, they order a reunion between mother and daughter so that they can regain their playthings, mortal human beings. In the end, powerful goddesses tend to get what they want, if not how they want it.

This eventual reunion between mother and daughter gives us a tiny glimpse into Persephone's perspective, especially about what she thinks her mother might want and need to hear. Persephone tells her mother that she was abducted while she was playing with friends, that she became a ruling queen, and that she ate some pomegranate seeds in the underworld. When she heard about the seeds, Demeter gasped and recoiled. She knew immediately that they were filled with a potent secret because they would keep her daughter tethered to both realms, away from her more than she could stand. Thus, mythically, we come to experience seasons through this separation and reunion, inaugurated by the pomegranate seeds, with autumn and winter representing time that Demeter punishes the world for her daughter's absence. Spring and summer, of course, then represent the joyful bounty that Demeter gifts the world in having her daughter returned to her once again.

It's a complicated story of opposites. Demeter unleashes her fury and sorrow on the world, killing all that grows in the sudden absence of her daughter, while Persephone simultaneously grows *into* herself in her new domain as ruler. Demeter feels life slip from her grasp in a world filled with life. Her daughter conversely discovers her life and becomes who she is in a realm replete with death. Above ground, when playing with friends, Persephone was simply called girl or daughter (in Greek, *korē*); as queen, however, she is called by her name, which is nearly always preceded by the Greek words for thoughtful, circumspect, noble, wise, and holy.[5] She is no longer just a goddess's daughter but a complex divinity with powers of her own. Tellingly, Persephone omits these details and her own stories when talking with her mother.

She Wakes Up

Think'st thou I am that same Persephone
   they took from thee?
        —Persephone to Demeter in "The Pomegranate Seed," Edith
                Wharton (1912)[6]

As noted, little is written of Persephone in Hades, but we can imagine her. The newly ordained chthonic goddess wakes up in the underworld a little scratched up and more than a little scared. The world as she knew it is gone. Her friends are gone. Her mother, whom she loves but who is more than a little overbearing, is gone. Where before there were flowers and play and light, now there are roots and caves and darkness. At first, the smell is what hits her most. It's like an old, musty library born from eternity. All is a little damp, even her robes. Primordial cries without origin echo in the caverns. She is alone. She thinks to herself that this cannot be her new home. She refuses it. She finds an ornate bed crafted for her and goes to sleep.

When she awakens, she stands on clay and feels the stone beside her bed. It's cold and damp like everything else in this place. She curses her luck. There are torches lit with orange fire. She sees a figure crouching in the corner, a shadow wrapped in shadows, watching her. He looks familiar. She can make out a table lit darkly by candles dripping wax on food and drink set on violet and crimson tapestries, which she will discover are the unofficial colors of this place. She has heard stories of Hades and knows it to be ruled by Zeus's brother, who is also her mother's brother. She has been told that ruling one of the three great realms—the heavens, the earth, or the underworld—is a high honor, but it's an honor she doesn't want and with a deathly life she refuses. She glances at the shadow again. It must be him. She kicks the walls, traces shapes of flowers and rivers in the clay. She goes to sleep again.

She wakes up to the same dirt, same smell, same place. She's restless, though. A girl can sit still for only so long before her mind and body want to wander. She is a little curious and more than a little hungry. If this is to be her fate as she's been told, this girl is going to learn it and know it. She thinks about her mother and how worried she must be. She knows her temper and her desire for control. Above ground, her mom rarely called her by her name, instead saying things like, *Daughter, come here*, and *Where is my girl?*, almost always in relation to herself and her desires. But still. The new queen of the third realm feels terrible for her mother and could not begin to imagine what it's like to raise a girl only to have her disappear.

But *still*. Here she is with no one to tell her what to do or how to be or where to play or how to dress. She stands and stretches, releasing a low hum to hear her voice among the echoes. Surprised, she likes the sound—resonant and fitting, more lyre than flute. She walks to the table and surveys the food, taking what she wants and filling herself with olives, figs, and cakes with honey. Someone had prepared her a regal feast, another surprise in the land of the dead. She pats her hair. Her mom would not be pleased, she knows, with its tangled mess. She takes the one big knot and shoves into a bun at the nape of her neck. That'll do for now, she decides. Maybe she'll chop it all off tomorrow.

The girl has time. Indeed, all she has is time. Above, she was busy with this and that, playing the role of dutiful daughter to a powerful goddess, which certainly had its perks but didn't always make room for her and her own desires. Here, she has some time to herself, to explore her world, to think. She wouldn't have known to choose this path, both unruly and forbidden, in transgressing that world to this. She has a curious nature, however, which is a trait that removed her from her mother's watchful eye in the first place. She decides to see what's possible for her in this world. After all, no one else can give her knowledge, and she knows it's up to her to make sense of this world and the other. She must feel it, learn it, and live it for herself.

She spends her days exploring, mapping the rivers, meadows, caves, and entrances, noting each with their own function and design. She makes charts and keeps track. There is no one around to tell her the reality of her situation or of her life. She thinks about the differences between this world and the other, speculating on the ways that they fit together and don't. Each day, though the memories of a pleasurable world in which she could feel largely irresponsible still ache in her, she also begins to notice a different kind of pleasure in feeling her mind make sense of her world and in developing her judgment to be sound and admirable. She grows into her name, Persephone.

Even the king of the underworld, who has many names, calls her only Persephone, though as noted at the beginning, sometimes this name is preceded by what the world will come to know her as: thoughtful Persephone, circumspect Persephone, holy Persephone. Her reputation for sound judgment tinged with wildness will lay the groundwork for rituals and mysteries that mortals will enact to pay respect to this goddess and her mother, both dreaded and revered, in the world above. People often fear those who have and seek knowledge, especially if those who seek knowledge are young women or goddesses who transgress their conventional place in either world. The Host-to-Many recognizes the uncanny insight and renegade spirit of his powerful bride. He too reveres her in her steadfast resolve to find her own place in this place. To tell the truth, he is a little afraid that she will leave.

She Becomes Who She Is

They say
there is a rift in the human soul
which was not constructed to belong
entirely to life.

— "Persephone the Wanderer," Louise Glück (1943)[7]

In the Homeric version, Hades learns of a plot by Zeus and others to reunite Persephone with her mother—for the gods' benefit, of course, in their wanting to stop Demeter's killing spree. Hades thus takes action and devises a plan of his own. Just before the planned reunion between Persephone and Demeter, Hades reminds his spouse that she "will have power over all that lives and moves" and also "will possess the greatest honors among the gods,"[8] for she has become thoughtful Persephone imbued with power and demanding respect. He is not wrong in his praise, for Persephone knows that she has indeed become this goddess with these powers. She has grown fully into herself and her divinity. Persephone will return not as an unnamed girl to be told what to do or how to be or how to act. She will return as a full goddess replete with capabilities.

The god's speech also deceives, however, for though his words are true and she does have these powers, Hades also tricks her to keep her with him. After praising his holy bride, he furtively offers her some pomegranate seeds, which seem innocent enough but which contain secrets. They keep her from returning fully to the earth. The powerful seeds thus dictate a return to the underworld after she is to reunite with her mother. From her perspective, however, the ripe fruit is a welcome addition to the daily offerings on the table, and she happily eats the crimson seeds not knowing the secrets they secrete. This eating both seals and releases her fate. For the rest of eternity, she will indeed remain in the underworld as its powerful coruler, but she will also have a share in power over the living world as well. Indeed, this twofold power over the living and the dead brands her as most unusual among immortals in being the only one to rule over both. The secret plot to contain her unleashes her instead.

In Ovid's version, while walking through an orchard in one of the underground meadows, Persephone is driven by her own desire and curiosity to pluck a pomegranate from a tree and avail herself of its secret chambers filled with bittersweet juice. She eats it greedily and without regret. She doesn't know, of course, the curse that comes with eating in the underworld. When she eats it, she unknowingly dooms herself, for she learns that she is forbidden to return permanently to the world of the living. In this case, her desire both seals and releases her fate. She becomes a liminal figure, the "only divinity common to both realms."[9] Again, the curse that should doom her frees her instead.

A pesky pomegranate. Much has been made of its power. Taken as a symbol of deception like a warning akin to shunning a drink prepared by a stranger, one lesson learned is vigilance and caution, especially for young women. Other times the fruit is taken more generally as knowledge forbidden to young women, as it so often is, with the likes of Pandora, Psyche, and other would-be sisters about the threat of women and the importance of staying in their place. Still others take it as a symbol of death, for it is this fruit that prohibits Persephone's full return to the living realm. It therefore also represents regret, lamentations, melancholy.

These interpretations and more are all viable, and there's much to be made of what this fruit "objectively" represents. There is no one idea, of course, to which the pomegranate absolutely refers; rather, we must consider it in context. In the context of this story told in this way here, of a young goddess finding herself in a place she didn't ask to be and with powers she didn't ask to have while growing into both, let us contemplate it as an enticing pomegranate. After all, we have learned that she is curious and prone to adventure.

It is an open question regarding the degree of autonomy that Persephone has when eating the seed in addition to what the seed represents. After all, we have learned that she desires, that she transforms into a ruler, that she misses her mother but not as much as Demeter yearns for her, that she enjoys her power, that she is unafraid of a little transgression, and that she is confident in who she is becoming in this strange place. Let us remind ourselves that the story began with a girl on a threshold, as many of us have found ourselves in our own ways, and let us remind ourselves that we too desire to know the full extent of our (human) condition. When Persephone gobbles the pomegranate seeds, we can see her desire culminating in an acceptance without resignation. In the myths, the acceptance comes in recognizing fully her indebtedness to and power in the realms of the living and the dead. Symbolically, for our purposes, this recognition comes in our fully recognizing our own powers to know, at least to some extent, about ourselves, our world, each other.

The pomegranate, then, marks a second threshold in the story. It is a symbol of the degree to which Persephone must take up the task of her own life in two realms as it is a symbol to us as we take up our own learning. It emblemizes a rite of initiation that is seldom pleasant even when driven by our own curiosity, for through eating its seed, we cross a threshold into a knowledge that excites and thrills while also obligating us to see what we can know and how we can know it. That knowledge can be daunting, for paradoxically, it reveals how little we know while also mandating that we throw ourselves into its pursuit.

Thankfully, like Persephone, we have some time. To be sure, Persephone's path is sometimes lonely. As she crisscrosses from realm to realm, she wonders if anyone really understands her, if she is up to the expectations in both realms, if she can love her mother while carving a space for herself, and if she can exist as an oddity in two worlds that are hers but not fully. As we have imagined her in Hades, she is a wanderer not unlike her mother, though with a notable difference: Persephone is intent on understanding where and who she is rather than searching for what she has lost. Certainly, through her violent abduction, much is lost forever—her life as girl, maiden, or mere daughter. Certainly as well, through developing autonomy in her underground explorations and eating the seeds that both bequeath knowledge and obligate her to the consequences of that knowledge, Persephone cannot return to a point before she started to grow into herself or before she entered into knowledge of the extent of her condition. There's a sadness sometimes in knowing that her return to a former time or to relative unconsciousness is impossible, but there's also great strength in knowing who she is becoming and what she can know.

Most, if not all, of us can relate to Persephone on these grounds, whether we ask our own questions about ourselves, how to meet expectations that present themselves to us, how to think about those who care for us, and how to navigate different spaces of our existence: work, home, school, vocation, relationships, passions, and more. Thus, in a formidable and real way, Persephone's questions that she asks herself as she wanders in and across her worlds, moving first this way and now that, are also our own. After all, her way is a philosophical way: thoughtful, circumspect, curious.

She cuts her hair and stuffs it under her bed. Her mother won't be pleased. She sets out again to her orchard, wondering what she will find this time.

Her name is Persephone.

In our own way, we are all Persephone.

You are Persephone, and you are invited in.

Notes

1. This phrase, which translates to "know yourself," was written atop the Delphic oracle in ancient Greece. The suggestion is that any oracular wisdom received from the gods, if it's to be understood as wisdom, requires that mortals take up the task of self-knowledge, a lifelong philosophical journey.
2. The "original ancient myths" are primarily Homer's and Ovid's. In Homer's version, Zeus, the most authoritative of all the gods, commands her theft while she's playing with flowers and friends. Zeus bequeaths Persephone to Hades, the god of the underworld, who is also known as the Host-to-Many. In Ovid's version, Venus, the fickle goddess of love, is threatened by other women's power and so commands her son Cupid to facilitate the abduction of Persephone through the use of one of his arrows. In that version, one of Persephone's nymph friends tries to stop Hades, throwing her arms open and making her body wide to block the Host-to-Many from taking her friend. The friend fails, however, and the Host-to-Many's own power is unleashed in turning the crying nymph into a puddle. Powerful gods tend to get what they want.

   Though Persephone is called "Proserpina" in Ovid's version, for the sake of coherence and clarity, she is called by her Greek name, Persephone, in this prologue. To read these original myths, please see Homer, *The Homeric Hymn to Demeter: Translation, Commentary, and Interpretive Essays*, ed. and trans. by Helene P. Foley (Princeton, NJ: Princeton University Press, 1994), and Ovid's *Metamorphoses*, especially Bk. V, lines 341–642, Ovid, *Metamorphoses*, trans. by David Raeburn (New York: Penguin Putnam, 2004).
3. Persephone is an important figure in several ancient myths and stories not explicitly devoted to her. Among the most notable are the following: Persephone cares for Aphrodite's son, Adonis, in Hades; she gives song-filled Orpheus a chance to reunite with his dead wife, Eurydice, though the story ends in tragedy; she escapes another abduction intended by Theseus and his friend, who are turned to stone for a while by Hades in the underworld; she lets Sisyphus return to the living world to see his wife; and she helps Hercules complete one of his many impossible tasks. In nearly all cases, Persephone dispenses wise judgment and an ability to see clearly the problems and challenges facing mortal and immortal beings alike.
4. The clever goddess conceals her divine nature to appear as a mortal and sets off on a quest to find her. She ends up caring for the son of a king and queen—a replacement, as it were, for her own missing child. In the palace one night, Metaneira, the child's mother, spies on the goddess and sees Demeter dipping her own son into a fire as an act of divine initiation. Understandably, the mother lunges to stop the act, not knowing that the caretaker is a goddess.
5. See, for example, Homer, *Hymn* ll. 337, 348, 359, 370.
6. Edith Wharton, "The Pomegranate Seed," *Scribner's Magazine* 51 (Mar. 1912): 284–291.

7. Louise Glück. Many poets and authors, mostly women, have honored and continue to honor Persephone and her story through poetry. For example, please see
   Alice Ostriker's poem "Demeter to Persephone"; Alice Ostriker, *The Book of Seventy*
   (Pittsburgh: University of Pittsburgh Press, 2009), 37.
8. Homer, *Hymn* ll. 365–366.
9. Ovid, *Metamorphoses* V.566–567.

Introduction

Melissa M. Shew and Kimberly K. Garchar

When we, the editors of this book, sought contributions for this volume of essays written by expert women in philosophy for their younger counterparts, we provided this directive to authors: "Consider yourself when you were roughly eighteen to twenty years old. What kind of book, with what kinds of chapters, do you wish had existed when you were discovering your own questions and growing intellectually? This is an opportunity to write that chapter."

The book you hold in your hands results from the efforts of twenty women in philosophy who took the spirit and rigor of that question to heart, producing a richly diverse set of essays on major philosophical topics from their areas of expertise. Nearly every field in philosophy is represented in this volume, from metaphysics and epistemology to existentialism, social and political philosophy, ethics, and more. In their chapters, authors cite mainly women philosophers to highlight women's original thought and scholarship in these and other philosophical fields. Moreover, the contributors in this book represent a snapshot of the diversity of women philosophers today. Coming from distinct kinds of philosophical training, working at a variety of colleges and universities and at different stages in their careers, having their own diverse backgrounds, and drawing on their own experiences and interests in philosophy, all have participated in this volume with a singular vision in mind: to let you know that we are thinking about you and are wanting you to explore philosophical ideas with us.

You, reader, might be told that you "think too much." Perhaps you were given this book by a relative or friend who knows that you're curious and tend to ask questions that dig beneath the surface of life. You might be reading this book as a requirement in a university or high school class, and as your finger traces down the table of contents, you note a chapter or two that call to you, thinking maybe this book won't be so bad. You might be in an upper-division philosophy seminar, preparing to give a presentation on one of the book's

Melissa M. Shew and Kimberly K. Garchar, *Introduction* In: *Philosophy for Girls*. Edited by: Melissa M. Shew and Kimberly K. Garchar, Oxford University Press (2020). © Oxford University Press. DOI: 10.1093/oso/9780190072919.003.0001.

chapters on epistemology. You might have come across this book in a bookstore or online and are intrigued by the opening anecdotes, some of which ring a bell but are told in a different way than you're used to. You might not identify as a girl or young woman (or boy or young man) but are reading it because you know that good philosophers are not limited by gender. You might be in a philosophy club or book club and have chosen this volume to generate lively discussion and dialogue. You prepare to make notes in the margins and write your own questions in a notebook.

However it is that you come to this book, know that we know this much about you: you are a curious creature, and we have written this book for you.

In the four sections that follow, we briefly flesh out the vision of this book, address the status and meaning of gender in philosophy, explain how this book helps close the gender gap in philosophy, and provide ideas for reading and discussing topics in this volume.

I.1 Vision

This book invites and encourages girls and young women to think philosophically. It is a snapshot of philosophy expressed through a range of essays written by academic women philosophers for their younger counterparts. The essays welcome readers to reflect, inquire, and analyze in philosophical ways. The goal of the book is to equip girls and young women with a sound introduction to philosophical thinking in a way that explicitly includes and speaks to them and their lives in the book's examples, anecdotes, scholarship, and overall layout. Thus the book has both epistemic and ethical ends. We want girls to embrace their existence as thinking agents and make the world better in the process.

We titled this volume *Philosophy for Girls: An Introduction to the Life of Thought*, with forethought, completely aware that the moniker "girl" has sometimes been used to infantilize, demean, and dismiss women of all ages. Nevertheless, we've specifically chosen this term and this title because this book has moxie and is written for readers with moxie. Further, we believe there is nothing inherently problematic in the term "girl" and stringently resist the idea that being called a "girl" is necessarily insulting. We worry that those who do believe being labeled a girl is necessarily demeaning are replicating misogynist cultural norms. We submit that the term "girl" is being reclaimed by women of all ages as a title and identifying point of pride in the same way that "queer" has been reclaimed as a powerful label by those whom it had previously been used to shame and silence. Indeed, phrases like "you go, girl!" and "get it, girl!" are heard regularly, and spoken by people of various genders. This reclamation and shift is palpable in the many uses of the term "girl" in contemporary movements, including "#likeagirl," Girl Power, Guerilla Grrrls, Amy Poehler's Smart Girls, the US women's national soccer team's "play like a girl," and so on.

Not only do these movements reclaiming "girls" empower women of all ages, they empower in ways that do not simply reproduce masculinity. Women have, historically, often adopted traits typically associated with masculinity, both good and bad, as both a means of survival and a viable form of competition. On the contrary, "girl" is meant to demarcate a new region and locus of power, one that does not rely upon norms of masculinity for definition. We insist that girls deserve to be able to find positive representations of their identity in the field of philosophy and they deserve the opportunity to philosophically wonder, reflect, and think about themselves and the world in which they live. They deserve to find a book that speaks to them directly.

I.2 Gender and Philosophy

Women and girls have been, historically, widely excluded from the Western philosophical tradition, both in representation and participation. If there were gender equity in philosophy, we would expect roughly half of students at all levels and professors at all levels to be girls and women. Such is not the case, however, for girls and women are grossly underrepresented in the classroom and professionally. We refer to this imbalance as the gender gap.[1]

Before discussing the potential causes of and strategies for addressing the gender gap, it's worth making a few preliminary notes that will be further developed by many contributors to this volume. First, women and girls are not the only persons excluded from Western philosophy. Philosophy is no different than other fields in that historically, the people doing it have been privileged in certain ways. Many were men, many were white, many were wealthy; many identified as Christian; and many were heterosexual. We recognize there are numerous, interwoven axes of exclusion and oppression in philosophy.

Second, gender has historically been assumed to be a binary category. A person is identified as feminine or masculine, woman or man, girl or boy.

Gender has also historically been assumed to map onto binary biological sex differences of XX or XY chromosomes, vagina or penis. We now know that biological sex differences are *not* binary, as there are numerous genotypical and phenotypical variations among human beings. There are a number of genetic conditions[2] that evidence the assumed binary between XX and XY chromosomes is untrue. Further, intersex persons are born with various combinations of primary and secondary genitalia such that the supposed binary between vagina and penis is untrue, too.

Third, if the assumed binaries of biological sex have been undermined, then the concept of gender supposedly mapped onto the binary biological sex is nonbinary, too. Gender, rather than being a strict binary, is a fluid and complex set of sociological and personal identifications, actions, and expectations. It is true that "woman" and "man" are still the dominant gender categories, but we now understand that persons can express or embody an array of gendered identities beyond woman or man, such as queer, androgynous, transgender, and so on.

We emphasize the fluid nature of gender identity and acknowledge the ongoing academic exclusion of many people. In this volume, though, we focus on gender and work to address the underrepresentation of those who identify as women and girls in philosophy, for there have indeed historically been two primary genders in our world and one of those genders has been systematically excluded and oppressed in the field of philosophy.

I.3   The Gender Gap in Philosophy

Bearing in mind these complexities of gender and exclusion, we now turn to the pervasive gender gap in philosophy. There are several places that the gender gap worsens in the pipeline from undergraduate education in philosophy to success as a professional academic philosopher. Much attention (although not enough) has been paid to the gender gap in academic philosophy, as well as the gap that occurs between earning a PhD and procuring a position in academia. With this project, though, we want to increase the number of girls who study philosophy before, at, and through the baccalaureate level.

There are a number of theories about *why* girls and women do not participate equally in undergraduate philosophy. Some have suggested that women are not good at philosophy, or at least not as good as men, simply *because* they are women. Empirical evidence does not support this claim, however;

there simply is no measurable difference between the sexes in the capacity for abstract thought. Moreover, this claim is false in other ways. We can, for example, look to the excellent contributions contained here and the regular outstanding performances of our students who are girls. Additionally, the idea that women are somehow "naturally" less able to do philosophy assumes that are there are only two genders, which we've critiqued, and that there are immutable skills and characteristics associated with those binary genders whereby men can do this and only this, women can do that and only that. As Charlotte Witt argues in her chapter, we have no more reason to believe there are innate gender traits than we have to believe there are only two genders.

It's also been suggested that perhaps the *way* philosophy is done is itself gendered, that there is something distinctly male about philosophical methodology. This hypothesis has more merit, since we understand that human institutions take on the characteristics of the humans working in them. Subrena Smith, in her chapter on science, claims that we should perhaps be looking to change disciplines themselves (science in her chapter, philosophy in this larger project). Attending to methodology alone, though, will not correct the gap in the practice of philosophy as a discipline.

We believe that there are a number of socialized factors that come together to cause the gender gap. Louise Antony refers to this as the "perfect storm" (Antony 2012). Two of the most visible and powerful of these factors are implicit biases and stereotype threat, both of which are grounded in gender schemas. Gender schemas are foundational social constructs that decide and dictate which behaviors are appropriate for gendered people. Schemas are slippery creatures, though. They tend to shift, invisibly, from dictating which behaviors are socially acceptable to asserting that those socially expected behaviors are inherent or occur "naturally" in the given genders. For example, it has been the case that labor has been divided such that women are tasked with caring for the young, the elderly, and the sick, while men do other things to contribute to the society (anything from hunting to working on an assembly line). Fair enough. The problem occurs when we begin to believe that women are "naturally" good caretakers and can be only caretakers and that men are "naturally" good hunters or workers and be only hunters or workers. This is patently untrue. One need only think of a caring father or Rosie the Riveter for evidence that illustrates the fictive and tricky nature of the gender schema. Gender schemas reveal the *chosen* values and priorities of a given society rather than immutable, biological characteristics or capabilities.

Nonetheless, we must admit that there are certain gender schemas operative in our Western culture. Implicit biases are the beliefs and actions grounded in our gender schemas, as well as many other schemas, including schemas of race, religion, class, and so on. They are implicit because we do not readily perceive the biases as a *biases*. We have been trained to assume that schemas are "true" and thus actions grounded in those schemas are "natural." The bias at issue here is the assumption that girls are not good at philosophy. If we, as a society, believe that girls are "naturally" incapable of doing philosophy, it would be unsurprising—that is, "natural"—that there are few girls studying or working in philosophy. According to this schema, the gender gap is both predictable and unproblematic. Implicit biases lead to stereotype threat that cause girls and women to fear actually confirming the biased assumption that they are incapable of doing philosophy. The girl studying philosophy must demonstrate not just that she is a good philosopher, but that she is a good philosopher *for a girl*. This cuts both ways. First, it denigrates women because it assumes that men are the normal, good philosophers, and second, it presents an exceptional pressure to somehow "beat" the stereotype.

The question then is how we counter the perfect storm of implicit bias and stereotype threat, both grounded in constructed gender schemas, such that we encourage girls to study philosophy. First and foremost, we can invite and *welcome* girls into the field. We can encourage them. We can legitimate their presence and participation. As Latham notes, the "next time a young lady is in her room studying philosophy for hours on end, let her know she can and she should. Leave her alone, she's in training and she's spending her time well" (Latham 2018, 143).

There are, of course, additional strategies, some of which come from the efforts to bring girls into STEM fields. We can work to provide female role models, although this requires addressing the gender gap in academic philosophy, too. We can work to help girls identify with philosophy by providing examples that include them and are relevant to their lives. We can diversify course syllabi to include women philosophers. We can work to be aware of gender schemas and how they affect the methodology of philosophy, the texts we choose as canonical, and the kinds of philosophy that we believe to be legitimate and important. We can also rethink pedagogy, curriculum, assignments, and evaluative measures to counter the gender schemas at work in doing philosophy.

Finally, we can encourage young women think philosophically about their lives. This volume is an explicit invitation to girls, asking them to engage in the challenging but invigorating intellectual work of the examined life. Thus an additional strategy to help bring girls and women into philosophy is to talk with them about their ideas, perhaps starting with this book.

I.4 Pathways

This book is divided into four sections, with each section associated with a topic of sustained concern and questioning in philosophy: the nature of the self, what constitutes knowledge and how we pursue it, the ways that social structures and power relations shape our realities, and the ethics of our actions and attitudes. Each chapter in each section addresses its correlative topic from its own distinct vantage point, resulting in a plurality of responses and approaches to big ideas in philosophy.

We want to note, though, that the section headers and their corresponding chapters do not exhaust philosophical thinking about the topics addressed here. Indeed, they indicate and sketch starting points for further exploration and questioning, even among chapters themselves. For instance, considering the section on knowing broadly, we might ask ourselves whether knowledge gained and experienced through art is similar to the experience of knowing as mediated by technology. We might also consider the arguments made in the science and logic chapters critiquing "objective knowledge" that might challenge or upend our typical way of thinking about both fields as immune from sociopolitical concerns, which is a question that arises elsewhere in the book as well. We may even wonder whether we can attain knowledge at all or whether we're destined to lapse into radical skepticism, as explored in the chapter on doubt. Taken together, the five chapters in this section approach the topic of knowing from a plurality of perches while also inviting readers to consider the philosophically rich similarities, differences, and questions among them.

All chapters in all of the sections work in this way. We invite readers to see how ideas cross-pollinate—and don't—from one chapter to the next in each section. The book contains many more pathways for exploration across and within the sections, however, some of which are indicated in the following sections. Whether weaving and challenging goddesses like Arachne did or picking up Ariadne's threads with a tremor of uncertainty tinged with wild determination, readers should be open to possibilities for making and remaking their own paths through the ideas in this book.

I.4.1 Thematic Pathways

Voice: Several contributors allow girls and women from myth, history, and religion to speak and be heard when tales about them tend to obscure their genius or marginalize their powers. For example, Persephone, Cassandra, Venus, Jael, and Medusa are all imagined in their own right, with chapter authors tending to them beyond the ways that the characters are typically maligned and viewed with suspicion. Consider the importance of hearing their stories as well as the stories of the other girls and women who begin each chapter.

Empowerment: While all chapters seek to empower readers through encouraging and building their intellectual confidence and ability, some chapters explicitly address ways that girls and young women can be and are empowered both individually and collectively. Though there's no firm distinction that should be made between individual and collective empowerment because each involves the other, the following chapters highlight individual empowerment specifically, in the ways that we can individually grow in our capacity to know ourselves and the world with greater clarity, acting in accordance with that knowledge: Autonomy, Pride, Self-Knowledge, Questions, Doubt, Art, Logic, Technology, Tzedek, Recognition, Anger, and Courage. Other chapters, including Identity, Science, Credibility, Language, Race, Gender, Consciousness-Raising, and Empathy, address individual empowerment but also the ways that we can be empowered through our communities, even with nonhuman animals, and can participate in and motivate collective social change for a more equitable world.

Questions: This book is filled with big juicy questions of all kinds. Indeed, many chapters close by saying that there is much more to be asked and answered about individual topics, which is how philosophy works. Sometimes in philosophy we learn that topics we thought were clear are not as simple as initially presumed. For example, issues of justice, agency, freedom, good and evil, and more may appear obvious on the surface, but like a single grain of sand, reveal whole worlds of detail and color when examined under a microscope. Philosophy relishes the nitty-gritty in the sediment, calling on experts from different fields in philosophy to address aspects of what appears to be a unified grain of sand. Consider the kinds of questions asked in the different chapters to see what they have in common, like how art relates to knowledge, how technology informs our senses of self, and how all of the chapters in Section II address knowledge on a large scale. For all of the chapters within sections and all of the sections within the book, consider what perspectives they bring to bear on a topic, how philosophers from different fields approach their topic, and what kinds of questions should still be asked at the ends of chapters, sections, and the book as a whole.

I.4.2 Pathways of Questions

Here, we list several examples of overarching questions implicit in the book's content. We ask that readers consider the "what," "how," and "why" of these topics as they appear in various ways throughout the chapters, each one a different strand of Ariadne's threads or bit of sediment in the sand.

- **Identity**: Who am I? Who are we? What does it mean to have or be a being, anyway? How do we become who we are? Consider how abstract metaphysical and logical principles as well as sociopolitical questions and embodiment address issues of identity.
- **Justice**: What does it mean to treat others and ourselves well, and why should we do so? What kind of world or worlds should we work toward in light of the multiple inequalities and injustices present? How can we face the problems we encounter and know exist in our communities and around the world? Consider the nature of justice, the conditions that can prohibit a person's full being and expression, and how we can better empower each other and ourselves in creating a more equitable world, becoming freer individually and together by doing so.
- **Wonder**: Why do philosophers ask so many annoying questions? How does wonder initiate philosophical questions and connect to curiosity, leading to doubt, speculation about the future of technology, the nature of reality, metaphysical and ontological questions, and more? Consider the relationship between wonder, curiosity, and knowledge. Of special interest may be the philosophical sticking points, tensions, and questions within individual chapters themselves, which often reveal a philosopher's own sense of wonder.

- **Virtue**: What characterizes a good action or habit, making it distinctly ethical or virtuous? How might cultivating specific virtues like courage, empathy, tzedek, pride, and anger be important in our lives even if they fly in the face of social norms and expectations? What challenges might we encounter in cultivating these virtues, and why? Consider not only the virtues themselves but also other ethical and ontological questions raised about the necessity of these virtues. Consider too how these virtues connect to ideas from other ethical theories as well as to themes of empowerment, justice, identity, and self-knowledge in this book.
- **Reality**: What is real? How can we know? How are our ideas about reality shaped by claims about objective knowledge, subjective experience, and issues in between? Consider how different ideas regarding technologies, human rationality, science, aesthetic experiences, knowledge itself, and more inform our understanding of the nature of reality.
- **Deliberation**: Are we free to make our own choices? Can we grow in our identities over time through intentional self-reflection? What role does deliberation play not only in our understanding of ourselves but also in how we act? Consider how reflection plays a role not only in our own contemplation but in action.

Of course, we know that you, reader, will generate your own pathways of themes and questions, adding your voice and philosophical reflections to those who advocate for your intellectual growth and development by giving you this book. We expect that you will engage in philosophical dialogue both with others and yourself, agreeing with some aspects of what you read here and disagreeing with others. We want you to listen hard, and think harder, considering which questions and which approaches to topics resonate with you. We hope that you will respond. We are your Chorus, and we hear you.

Notes

1. Enrollment of girls in BA and PhD programs hovers around 30% (Garry 2009; Crasnow 2009). This is the lowest proportion of women in the Humanities (Ma et al. 2018, 68; Crasnow 2009, 8) and the only majors with lower proportions of women are engineering, computer science, and physics (Ma et al. 2018, 68). Further, the percentage of women majors in other fields has increased during the same time that the number remained flat for philosophy (Crasnow 2009, 9). It doesn't begin that way. We

see that girls constitute roughly have of students enrolled in introductory philosophy classes but their participation atrophies between the introductory course and declaring a major (Thompson 2017, 2). At the professional level, the British Philosophical Association puts the percentage of women professors at 19% (Latham 2018, 132). The American Philosophical Association (APA) notes only 21% of professors were women as of 2011 (Ma et al. 2018) and Sally Haslangar, former President of the Eastern Division of the APA, notes that data collection is lacking.

2. For a concise discussion of genetic variability and contemporary examples, see The World Health Organization's work on genetics and gender: https://www.who.int/genomics/gender/en/index1.html.

Bibliography

Antony, Louise. 2012. "Different Voices or Perfect Storm: What Are There So Few Women in Philosophy?" *Journal of Social Philosophy* 43, no. 3 (Fall): 227–255.

Crasnow, Sharon. 2009. "Women in the Profession: The Persistence of Absence." *The APA Newsletter on Feminism and Philosophy* 9, no. 1 (Fall): 8–10.

Dodds, Susan, and Eliza Goddard. 2013. "Not Just a Pipeline Problem." In *Women in Philosophy: What Needs to Change?*, edited by Katrina Hutchinson and Fiona Jenkins, 143–163. New York: Oxford University Press.

Garry, Ann. 2009. "What Is on Women Philosophers' Minds?" *The APA Newsletter on Feminism and Philosophy* 9, no. 1 (Fall): 4–7.

Goguen, Stacey. 2018. "Is Asking What Women Want the Right Question? Underrepresentation in Philosophy and Gender Differences in Interests." *Dialogue* 57, no. 2: 409–441.

Haslanger, Sally. 2013. "Women in Philosophy? Do the Math," *New York Times*, September 2, https://opinionator.blogs.nytimes.com/2013/09/02/women-in-philosophy-do-the-math/.

Hutchinson, Katrina, and Fiona Jenkins. 2013. *Women in Philosophy: What Needs to Change?* New York: Oxford University Press.

Holland, Nancy J. 2014. "Humility and Feminist Philosophy." *The APA Newsletter on Feminism and Philosophy* 13, no. 2 (Spring): 18–22.

Latham, Sally. 2018. "It's Not Brains or Personality So It Must Be Looks: Why Women Give up on Philosophy." *Think* 48, no. 17 (Spring): 131–143.

Leuschner, Anna. 2015. "Social Exclusion on Academia through Biases in Methodological Quality Evaluation: On the Situation of Women in Science and Philosophy." *Studies in History and Philosophy of Science* 54, December: 56–63.

Ma, Debbie, Clennie Webster, Nanae Tachibe, and Robert Gressis. 2018. "21% versus 79%: Explaining Philosophy's Gender Disparities with Stereotyping and Identification." *Philosophical Psychology* 31, no. 1: 68–88.

Rooney, Phyllis. 2014. "An Ambivalent Ally: On Philosophical Argumentation and Diversity." *The APA Newsletter on Feminism and Philosophy* 13 no. 2 (Spring): 36–42.

Schouten, Gina. 2015. "The Stereotype Threat Hypothesis: An Assessment from the Philosopher's Armchair, for the Philosopher's Classroom." *Hypatia* 30, no. 2 (Spring): 450–466.

Schouten, Gina. 2016. "Philosophy in Schools: Can Early Exposure Help Solve Philosophy's Gender Problem?" *Hypatia* 31, no. 2 (Spring): 275–292.

Thompson, Morgan. 2017. "Explanations of the Gender Gap in Philosophy." *Philosophy Compass* 12, no. 3: 1–12.

World Health Organization. n.d. "Gender and Genetics," accessed September 13, 2018. https://www.who.int/genomics/gender/en/index1.html.

SECTION I
SELF

1

Identity

Being-in-the-World and Becoming

Meena Dhanda

As the planks of Theseus's ship needed repair, it was replaced part by part, up to a point where not a single part from the original ship remained in it, anymore. Is it then still the same ship? If the discarded parts were used to build another ship, which of the two, if either, is the real Ship of Theseus?

This statement of the famous paradox of identity over time, noted by the ancient essayist Plutarch (45–120 CE), and developed by Thomas Hobbes (1588–1679 CE), forms the epilogue of the film *The Ship of Theseus* (2013). The paradox challenges us to think about what anchors the identity of a human being insofar as the film is about human beings, although the ship is given as metaphor for a person in the epilogue. The film tells us the stories of three people, with the link between them revealed only at the end. The three stories are of Aliya, a blind photographer; Maitreya, a Jain monk; and Navin, a stockbroker, all based in India.

We will find our way through the puzzle of identity by first acquainting ourselves with these stories. We will then discuss the problem of bodily identity as posed in the analytical tradition of philosophy (Williams 1973) in search of an objective answer to "what matters in identity?" and consider criticisms internal to this tradition (Wilkes 1988). We will then propose an alternative conception of bodily being from the Continental tradition of philosophy (Merleau-Ponty 1945/1962; Beauvoir 1952/1989) and discuss its deployment by contemporary feminist philosophers to explicate a kind of female bodily identity (Young 2005; Alcoff 2006). The Continental tradition takes up identity often in terms of what being-in-the-world means. With

Meena Dhanda, *Identity* In: *Philosophy for Girls*. Edited by: Melissa M. Shew and Kimberly K. Garchar, Oxford University Press (2020). © Oxford University Press. DOI: 10.1093/oso/9780190072919.003.0002.

reference to the stories, we will thus ask the question: If *lived body* is the pivot of identity, then which changes can be sustained without a threat to a person's identity?

1.1 Three Stories

The first story is of Aliya, who takes up photography after losing her eyes to a cornea infection. She uses sound to guide her to the subject of her photographs and a hand-held scanner that "speaks" out the color of the object it scans. Curtains are bright orange and yellow, the sari blouse of an aunt she playfully touches with the scanner is red. Orlando, her partner, sometimes narrates what's in the picture she has taken. Together they edit the photos. Sometimes there are arguments. She complains, "I have to draw opinion and assurance about my own art from what others say." She does not, however, see lack of vision as a limitation of her art.

After a corneal transplant, Aliya's vision is restored. One might have expected her to become an even better photographer, but that is not what happens; in fact, her photographs become nondescript. She no longer captures the essence of her subjects. To become again the photographer she once was, she resorts to blindfolding and prefers the results of her resumed, blind artistry. She has become herself again.

The second story of Maitreya, a Jain[1] monk waging a court case against experimentation on animals, takes us to the busy corridors of a High Court with ceaseless footfall around a centipede trying to avoid being crushed under heavy boots. Maitreya comes to its rescue offering it safe transport atop court papers, out of the traffic of booted feet, on to the safety of a green leaf where it can continue its life.

Maitreya is diagnosed with liver cirrhosis and his life will be in danger if he does not accept a liver transplant. His circumstance means he must give up his fundamental guiding principle of compassion and consume medicines whose production has involved the "torture" of animals. Since all the medicines prescribed to him are from companies that have not pledged to end animal testing and thus torture, he refuses treatment. His condition worsens dramatically and in the face of death, despite his heroic resolve to live a life of integrity, his body pulls him back from the ultimate sacrifice. He finally agrees to get the transplant.

The third story is of Navin, a stockbroker and a recipient of a kidney transplant who accidently accosts Shankar, a needy worker, from whom a kidney has been stolen. After an initial panic Navin is relieved quickly to find out that his kidney is not the stolen one, but drawn into the intriguing drama of illegal kidney transplants, he resolves compassionately to help the poor man find the thief of his kidney. The investigation takes Navin to the house of an old man in Stockholm. When the truth is placed before this old man that he is the recipient of Shankar's stolen kidney, he pleads: "Maybe my family was protecting me emotionally by not telling me it was a stolen kidney. Maybe the doctors felt they will lose a client. But what could I have done even if they told me the kidney was stolen from somebody?" Navin wants the old man to return Shankar's kidney for the sake of justice, but the old man uses money to buy his way out. Shankar agrees to accept the money he is offered as an out of court compensation because he does not want to be caught in court battles. Navin argues on the point of principle, saying, "We'll get your kidney back . . . We'll get justice." Cramped within the constricting walls of a slum, Shankar cries: "What will I do with the kidney? The [black] market rate for kidney is 30,000. He has given me 650,000 . . . Leave it. I am getting fixed for a monthly payment. Why are you messing it up?"

This story illustrates the gap between two ideas of integrity. Integrity means one thing to Navin, a stockbroker who can easily make money and can afford to not compromise his idea of justice narrowly conceived as seeking compensation for a wrong. We might wonder how Navin can possibly uphold justice when trading with companies who are blatantly unjust. Indeed, his socialist grandmother in the film initially chides him for his choice of career as a stockbroker. Given his privileged background and his apolitical experience of dealing with power structures, his idea of integrity is to stake all to get back the kidney, so he is unable to sympathize with the pragmatic choice Shankar makes. Had the kidney been actually sold in a legal transaction, Navin would not have seen any fault in it. The taking of the kidney without consent makes it unjust for him. Integrity for Shankar, who lives a precarious existence, is not tied to Navin's idea of seeking justice, a path too onerous for him. If personal integrity means being true to oneself, then from Navin's privileged point of view, Shankar's integrity has been compromised. From the point of view of Shankar's lived reality, his choice is the rational one, based on possibilities realistically open to him. In Maitreya's story, legal cases get dragged in courts and wrongdoers are not

brought to justice. For Shankar, seeking undeliverable "justice" is point-
less. Instead of committing to a fruitless exhausting court battle, Shankar
chooses to lead the remainder of his incapacitated life with some financial
security. His wholeness as a human being, his identity, is threatened no
matter what he chooses. In accepting out of court compensation from the
person responsible for the theft of his kidney, Shankar makes the more live-
able choice.

At the end of the film we learn that the three protagonists, Aliya, Maitreya,
and Navin, are linked to each other through the body of one donor, a cave
explorer. They belong to the lucky set of eight people of different ages,
ethnicities, and genders, each having received a body part from one man
who died from a head injury while on a cave exploration.[2]

1.2 Personal Identity and Bodily Identity

In light of the trajectory of the film, then, we may ask a few questions about
the nature of the identity of a person. If body parts change, is it the same
body? And if it is not the same body, can it be the same person? Aliya's life
is changed remarkably when she loses her sight. We can wonder whether
Aliya remains the same person through her many bodily transformations.
Perhaps Aliya becomes a different person when she loses her sight. When
she regains her sight, does she return to being the same person she was before going blind, or does she become yet another new person? Is Aliya, the
blind photographer who uses a hand-held scanner to "see" color, the same
as Aliya after her vision is restored? One way to answer the question is to
say that since we are describing the change as it has happened to Aliya, it
follows that Aliya is the same person to whom these remarkable transformations occurred. Additionally, because Aliya remembers how she was before
the change and looks back at the photography as *her* photography, it can be
argued that she must remain the same person. We might ask, however, "Does
she understand herself as the same self?"

Maitreya's story illuminates questions about what is essential to identity
in normative terms. Is Maitreya still the same Jain monk who once dedicated
his life to protecting animals from suffering *after* he has become a beneficiary
of violence against animals by accepting medical treatment? At the end of the
film we see him dressed in ordinary clothes and not the garb of a Jain mendi-
cant, indicating that he thinks the answer to the question is no.

Navin's story is about ownership and trade of one's body parts. If we conceive of a person's identity in a way that the body is merely a possession, then it appears that like other things we "own," the parts of a body can be traded without detriment to identity. This conception of identity has specific application in cases where the sale is not of a body part but of the *use* of parts of the body.

Analytical philosophers after John Locke have also raised and answered the question of identity of persons but instead in terms of reach of memory, not parts and wholes. Locke defined a person as "a thinking intelligent being, that has reason and reflection, and can consider itself as itself, the same thinking thing, in different times and places."[3] Locke's view is taken as providing the "memory criterion" of identity.[4] When contemplating an imagined soul-swap between a cobbler and a prince, Locke allows that the body plays a role in the identity of the resultant *man*, but not in the identity of the resultant *person*.

Other philosophers have challenged the description of what occurs when a radical, life-altering change happens. They suggest that it is not memory or consciousness that carries identity with it; rather, memory along with the sameness of the body determines a person's identity in this view. Our beliefs about what makes a person the same over time are tested when extreme changes happen to a person's body-mind complex. Wilkes (1988) discusses in detail the case of multiple personalities of Miss Beauchamp and concludes, "Multiple personality patients present us with situations in which all the facts are in. . . . And here it appears that we have no clear consensus about what to say: the concept of a person fails to cope under this particular strain" (Wilkes 1988, 128). She shows that the ideas of personal identity either as "one body = one person" or as "one mind = one person" are both put under strain by the case. The psychiatrist treating the patient was able to empathize with the alternative personalities presented to him thus supporting the claim in favor of a plurality of persons rather than a singularity, but he was still tasked with identifying *the* real Miss Beauchamp, the one he must reach and help.[5]

Medical knowledge of complex brain conditions has also raised questions about identity. For instance, experiments on an epileptic patient with a bisected brain had exposed the possibility of two centers of consciousness in one body. In the experimental set up, the left hand literally did not know what the right hand was doing (Vesey 1977). While a normally cognitively unified person would be expected to behave in a coordinated fashion as one organism directed toward its goal, the brain-bisected epileptic patient

appeared to be behaving as two people in one body, often in conflict with
each other.

Locke's "memory criterion" of identity was challenged in the twentieth
century by Bernard Williams, who presented an alternative way of describing
what may happen in imagined cases. Consider, for example, if an emperor
wakes up with the memories of a peasant and the peasant wakes up with the
memories of the emperor after a magician's miraculously engineered swap.
Using Locke's memory criterion the person goes where the memory goes. In
Williams's alternative description, which holds that bodily identity is necessary for personal identity, the person stays where the body stays. Lockeans
will say that the peasant has woken in the emperor's body and the emperor
has woken in the peasant's body. But Williams questions the coherence of
the assumption that makes the story of the swap plausible, the assumption
that we are able to "distinguish a man's personality from his body." He argues
that the voice, facial features and comportment expressive of a personality
are bodily constrained:

> However much the emperor's past the sometime peasant now claimed to
> remember, the trick would not have succeeded if he could not satisfy the
> simpler requirement of being the same *sort* of person as the sometime em-
> peror. Could he do this, if he could not smile royally? Still less, could he
> be the same person, if he could not smile the characteristic smile of the
> emperor?[6]

It may be the case that our identity is based on our past as well as what
might be reasonable to hope for or fear in our future. As we grow, no less
magical than the results of a conjuror's tricks, our bodily changes may leave
one questioning whether one is the same person. For stability and reliability
it is tempting to fall back on Locke's conception of continuity of consciousness (one's self-knowledge) as making one the same person over the course of
one's life. Nonetheless, perspectives change, too, as one grows and develops
in a bodily way. By perspective I mean not ideas, beliefs and values, but instead a more basic "result of perception." Consider the ordinary experience
of meeting an older cousin after a very long time, someone not seen since
childhood. This cousin suddenly does not appear as big as remembered. The
world appears different from a height of 5 feet 3 inches than it does from a
height of 3 feet 5 inches. Likewise, objects a person had found unwieldy as a
child and was warned to avoid handling, such as a hammer, are easy to use as

a young adult. With a change in perspective on the world, new possibilities for action and identity arise.

1.3 Being-in-the-World and Body Schema

We have briefly noted that posing the problem of identity of persons as if it were a complex case of identity of a composite object—body plus memories—leads to problems in the application of the concept of identity. This is indicated by Wilkes's discussion of multiple personalities and by the thought-experiment of the peasant and emperor. In both cases it is difficult to decide who the "real" Miss Beauchamp or "real" emperor is. A rather more convincing account of the identity of human beings is presented in another Western tradition of philosophy, sometimes described as the "Continental" tradition mainly due to the geographical location (for example, France, Germany, Italy) of the philosophers who do philosophy in this way. Common questions about human identity are conceptualized in radically different ways in this tradition.

In the Continental tradition, a decisive turn is made in answering questions about the ontological status of human being, by which we mean questions about the status of *being* of homo sapiens. In this tradition, the identity of human beings pivots around bodily being, and bodily being is always enmeshed in the space of action broadly understood as including expression and communication. The human being is not only a sentient being but always an acting being. The clearest statement of the continental tradition of conceptualizing the body is by Merleau-Ponty. He writes, "The body is the vehicle of being in the world, and having a body is, for a living creature, to be intervolved in a definite environment, to identify oneself with certain projects and to be continually committed to them."[7] Merleau-Ponty posits being-in-the-world as a "pre-objective view." What this means is that first, our consciousness is not separable from our bodies and it is not already given, as it were, prior to the world of which it is a part. Instead, consciousness gets constituted through our engagement with the world. Second, when we step back from this immersion in the world to reflect on the relation between the body and the world, we may be unable to maintain our grip on the world. Habitual, everyday being-in-the-world is not an *act* of consciousness; rather, being-in-the-world is what can "affect the union of the 'psychic' and the 'physiological.'"[8]

A useful concept deployed to explain the body's being-in-the-world is that of "body schema" (not to be confused with body image). Body schema is my precognitive familiarity with my lived body. My body schema gives me the know-how of comportment in the world. For example, my body schema tells me how big a puddle I can jump, how heavy a suitcase I can lift, whether in a particular situation I can successfully suppress a surge of anger, or how reliably I can contain a burst of laughter. The "undivided possession" of the body is provided by the *body schema*, which is nonetheless *dynamic*, and means that "my body appears to me as an attitude directed towards certain existing or possible tasks."[9] When I lift up my foot to climb a step, my body is already attuned to exert itself with the necessary muscle contraction to complete the task. As I get older (or when I am ill) my ability to complete the same task unreflectively may be impeded. Over time, my body schema has to dynamically adapt itself to my new frailty. We can experience the adaptability of the body schema when we are ill or have an injury. With a twisted ankle, for instance, I have to recalibrate the exertion with which I normally climb steps, because my body schema is disturbed.

1.4 Kinds of Bodily Identity

Simone De Beauvoir, a central twentieth-century Continental feminist philosopher, writes that "to be present in the world implies strictly that there exists a body which is at once a material thing in the world and a point of view towards the world."[10] Human beings have a point of view on the world, which is their space of action. That is, a point of view is always from a location, always with limits, and within potentially shifting horizons. When the body is oriented toward a world of manipulable objects in a purposive way it has a comportment, a readiness to act (a motor intentionality). Alternatively, when the body is reduced to a mere object, its comportment is altered, its motor intentionality is inhibited.

Iris Marion Young juxtaposes Merleau-Ponty with Beauvoir, developing a picture of female body comportment. She shows that the possibilities for women are limited not by the type of body per se, but by the use to which the body is put.[11] From reported observations of how young girls use their bodies to throw a ball with how young boys use the full strength of their bodies, Young argues that girls are hampered by the lack of trust in the abilities of their bodies. Fear of failure also makes girls grow up with an "inhibited intentionality." They do not use the full force of their strength to project themselves in the world. They learn to be defensive out of fear of being hurt, because they are socialized into believing that they are fragile. She concludes: "Women often approach a physical engagement with things with timidity, uncertainty, and hesitancy. Typically, we lack an entire trust in our bodies to carry us to our aims."[12] What is typical is not true of all. With some help from others, people can devise ways of being-in-the-world that transcend the given.

In the film, we see that the open possibilities of self-realization, the flourishing of her being-in-the-world, are not limited by Aliya's blindness. Her body schema is adapted to capture the essence of subjects she chooses to photograph. It is in fact the regaining of sight that disorients her and distorts the familiar settings of her horizon to the extent that she is unable to practice her art. Moreover, as a blind woman, Aliya does not see the gaze that sees her. She is not consumed or inhibited by herself *being seen*, which is liberating in her case. In a different case, women who take up the hijab sometimes describe the power to see without being seen as liberating.[13] We should note that Aliya is from a privileged background, which might contribute to boosting her confidence in her professional expertise despite her perceived "limitation" of lack of vision. In materially impoverished social environments, blind girls live in fear of being attacked. Gendered horizons are modulated by class. Some identities readily available for rich girls are out of reach for the poor. Social and economic norms limit girls and women in different ways and depending upon their lived experience in specific locations, women negotiate their identities in different ways too.[14]

Philosopher Linda Alcoff (2006) carefully explains that a horizon "affects how one experiences the world and one's perceptions and interpretations. Horizons are open-ended, in constant motion, and aspects of our horizon are inevitably group related or shared among members of a social identity . . . we need to understand the situatedness of horizons as a material and embodied situatedness, and not simply mentally perspectival or ideological."[15] To analyze social identity, Alcoff argues, we must pay attention to the role of the body and of the body's "visible identity." Embodied situatedness is a useful idea to understand the identity choices of Aliya and Maitreya.

Our bodily identity is subject to all kinds of social normalization. Kathleen Lennon gives examples of such normalization: "Hair straightening, blue tinted contact lenses, surgical reconstruction of noses and lips, are practices in which the material shapes of our bodies are disciplined to correspond to a social ideal, reflecting the privileged position which certain kinds of, usually, white, always able, bodies occupy."[16] However, note that crafting one's body may also be rebellion against the given-ness of the so-called natural. Donna Haraway presciently challenged the "human vs. animal" and the "animal vs. machine" binaries three decades ago with her "manifesto for cyborgs." Aliya, as the blind photographer, uses a hand-held machine to call out the colors of objects that she cannot see, and her camera announces necessary information enabling her to capture "the essence of things." Her bodily being can be seen as a cyborg. The totality of her being includes the machines she relies on to practice her art, and her art is what makes her who she is.

1.5 Conclusion

A range of factors matter when addressing the puzzles of identity. We have to decide how to lead our lives: which paths to take, which decision to make, and how to live with our chosen identity. Or we must abandon the path hitherto taken in favor of a new identity. Our knowledge of our situation is bound up with our perception of the possibilities of action open to us.

Maitreya's perception changes when he is in the near-death situation. His preobjective beliefs, encapsulated in his being-in-the-world, are shaken when he slips into a delirium induced by his illness. He becomes unsure about what fate awaits him after death. At this crucial juncture, when asked by a devotee to answer if there is a soul, all he can utter is "don't know." Aliya's story shows us that one's way of being-in-the-world is necessarily immersed in and tied to one's activities. She acquires an outsider's view of herself as a blind photographer when she regains her vision, but then, she starts *thinking* about how she is doing photography instead of just doing it. Her previous habituated being as a blind photographer is disturbed. What restores balance is regaining her grip on herself, and finally, letting go even of the self-identity of a photographer. Navin's story shows that living with integrity, an important ingredient of personal identity as wholeness, has different meanings to different people. His story is a comment on the gulf between the middle-class do-gooder and poor man he wants to help when it comes to valuing bodily integrity. The best way to live with integrity is linked to available choices and to horizons within which these choices take shape.

The limitation of horizons is evident in the typical lives of girls and women socialized in patriarchal society to lack confidence in their lived body.

Philosophical discussions of personal identity in the analytical tradition, fuelled by imaginary cases of body/memory swaps tend not to pay attention to the very real constraints of embodiment in the world we inhabit. A corrective is offered by focus on the lived body developed in the Continental tradition, which feminist philosophers have productively deployed to throw light on the constitution of bodily identity.

Notes

1. Jains are followers of the religious creed of Lord Mahavira (500 BCE). They are against gratuitously causing suffering to animals. Among their other precepts is the idea of respecting the many-sidedness of truth.
2. A reference to Plato's allegory of the cave with ignorant prisoners taking illusion for reality is unmissable in this last scene when the protagonists learn the truth about the sole donor.
3. Locke distinguishes between the identity of substance, of man and of person. Person for him is a forensic term. "Wherever a man finds what he calls himself, there, I think, another may say is the same person. It is a forensic term, appropriating actions and their merit; and so belongs only to intelligent agents, capable of a law, and happiness, and misery. This personality extends itself beyond present existence to what is past, only by consciousness, whereby it becomes concerned and accountable; owns and imputes to itself past actions, just upon the same ground and for the same reason as it does the present" (Locke 1689).
4. See Vesey (1977) for summaries of various positions.
5. His views, however, "were to some extent determined by what he thought a young lady at the turn of the century *ought* to be like" (Wilkes 1988, 125). The upshot of considering such cases is that they illuminate the malleability of our concept of personal identity and show it to be an ethical, political, and cultural matter, not simply a matter of semantics or logic.
6. Williams (1973, 12).
7. Merleau-Ponty (2006 [1962], 94).
8. Ibid., 92.
9. Ibid., 115.
10. Beauvoir (1989 [1952], 39).
11. See "Throwing Like a Girl," originally published in 1980 and reprinted in Young (2005, 27–45).
12. Young (2005, 34).
13. See Dhanda (2008b).
14. Dhanda (2008a) shows how caste identity is negotiated when the ex-untouchable acquires the political self-identity of a Dalit (the crushed or broken).
15. Alcoff (2006, 102).
16. Lennon (2014 [2010]).

Bibliography

Alcoff, Linda. 2006. *Visible Identities: Race, Gender and the Self.* New York: Oxford University Press.

Beauvoir, Simone De. 1989 [1952]. *The Second Sex.* New York: Vintage.

Dhanda, Meena. 2008a. *The Negotiation of Personal Identity.* Saarbrüken: VDM Verlag.

Dhanda, Meena. 2008b. "What Does the Hatred/Fear of the Veil Hide?" *Ethnicity and Inequalities in Health and Social Care* 1, no. 2 (December): 53—57.

Gilbert, Paul, and Kathleen Lennon. 2005. *The World, the Flesh and the Subject.* Edinburgh: Edinburgh University Press.

Lennon, Kathleen. 2014 [2010]. "Feminist Perspectives on the Body." *Stanford Encyclopedia of Philosophy.* https://plato.stanford.edu/entries/feminist-body/.

Locke, John. 1689. *An Essay Concerning Human Understanding,* 2nd edition. Book II, chap. XXVII, "Of Ideas of Identity and Diversity." Project Gutenberg, https://www.uvm.edu/~lderosse/courses/intro/locke_essay.pdf.

Merleau-Ponty, Maurice. 2006 [1962]. *Phenomenology of Perception.* Translated by Colin Smith from original in French published in 1945. London: Routledge Classics.

Rorty, Amelie O., ed. 1976. *The Identities of Persons.* Berkeley: University of California Press.

Vesey, Godfrey. 1977. *Personal Identity.* Ithaca, NY: Cornell University Press.

Wilkes, Kathy. 1988. *Real Persons: Personal Identity without Thought Experiments.* Oxford: Oxford University Press.

Williams, Bernard. 1973. *Problems of the Self: Philosophical Papers 1956–1972.* Cambridge: Cambridge University Press.

Young, Iris. 2005. *On Female Body Experience: "Throwing Like a Girl" and Other Essays.* Oxford: Oxford University Press.

2

Autonomy

On Being True to Ourselves

Serene J. Khader

Figuring out who we are in light of messages to "be ourselves" or be "true" to ourselves can be a struggle. Consider the example of Starr, the central character in Angie Thomas' book, *The Hate U Give*. Starr lives in the mostly poor Black neighborhood of Garden Heights but attends an elite private school called Williamson Prep. She sees herself as having a different self in each world,[1] going so far as to give a separate name to her "school self." Her school self, " 'Williamson Starr,' doesn't use slang—if a rapper would say it, she doesn't say it, even if her white friends do. Slang makes them cool. It makes her 'hood.' Williamson Starr holds her tongue when people piss her off so nobody thinks she's the 'angry Black girl.' Williamson Starr is approachable. No stank-eye, no side-eyes, none of that. Williamson Starr is nonconfrontational. Williamson Starr doesn't give anyone a reason to call her ghetto. I can't stand myself for doing it but I do it anyway" (Thomas 2017, 71).

Consider also the words of Kiara,[2] the author of a post on beauty on *Femsplain* and *Teen Vogue*. "After years of consuming anxiety-inducing ads that alert me of my 'flaws' (my blackness, my shortness, etc.), I've begun to realize the alarming ways in which I, at times, view myself. I admit that, during one of my most vulnerable moments, I've asked Google, 'What is inherently ugly about being short?' I went deeper and deeper into this wide web, stumbling on blogs that offered various answers including: 'Clothes look best on a proportioned, lengthened body.' I looked down at my short torso and my somewhat bloated stomach and despised what I viewed as mistakes. . . . While I lurked online, I noticed what was being touted as the solution: an ad for leg-lengthening surgery. I could hear the male, authoritative advertising voice attempting to sell the surgery to me" (Femsplain 2015).

As Starr's and Kiara's stories help us see, we can act in ways with which we do not identify. The mere fact that a person acts does not yet tell us whether

Serene J. Khader, *Autonomy* In: *Philosophy for Girls*. Edited by: Melissa M. Shew and Kimberly K. Garchar, Oxford University Press (2020). © Oxford University Press. DOI: 10.1093/oso/9780190072919.003.0003.

the "real" her is doing the acting. Starr performs the role of Williamson Starr but says she hates herself for it. Kiara says that the call to hate her body comes from a "male, authoritative advertising voice." Yet their stories also suggest reasons not to dismiss the idea that behaviors and motivations with which we disidentify belong to us in some sense. Starr clearly becomes Williamson Starr because it is consistent with goals that are important to her. Even if Starr hates herself when she becomes Williamson Starr, her choice to represent herself as that person is strategic. She knows what she is doing, and she is doing it with a specific goal in mind: to be perceived in a certain way by her white, upper-class peers. She even writes in other parts of the book that her code-switching is so routine and integrated into her everyday behavior as to have become effortless, to seem as though it happens *to* her without her participation. For example, she writes, "My voice is changing already. It always happens when I'm around other people" (Thomas 2017, 95). Though Kiara does not seem to explicitly have the goal of complying with oppressive beauty standards, the male advertising voice seems deeply embedded within her to the extent that she looks at her own stomach as a "mistake" and believes at times that she is going to get an objective answer about what is "inherently ugly" about being short from asking Google.

Philosophers use the concept of personal autonomy to describe the ability to lead lives that are our own, lives that reflect reasons and values that genuinely belong to us. We can get clearer about what it means when we say beliefs, desires, and motivations are really our own by examining philosophers' thoughts on autonomy. It might seem that there is a straightforward answer to questions about autonomy, namely, that our autonomous views are the ones that have not been socially shaped. After all, much of what Starr and Kiara find stultifying are the demands of a society that tells them they count less because of their race and gender. Philosophical tools can help us see some deep problems with the argument that socially shaped preferences are nonautonomous. Philosophers believe that we should pay attention to what the *implications* of a claim are when deciding whether that claim is likely to be true. Implications are other claims that must be true if a claim is true. If a claim has false or absurd implications, philosophers usually think that is a reason to reject the claim. For example, consider the claim that all dogs have soft, furry ears. This claim has the implication that hairless dogs are not dogs. As a result, I should probably reject the claim that all dogs have soft, furry ears. We do not need to limit our use of this type of reasoning to discussing cute animals, though; we can apply it to concepts that give meaning to our lives.

Most philosophers reject the claim that autonomous values and motivations are characterized by not being socially shaped because of its strange implications. One disturbing implication is that *none* of our existing beliefs and desires are autonomous (see Meyers 1991; Christman 2004). All of us are subject to processes of social shaping that begin before birth. We are fed certain foods and not others, spoken to in certain languages, raised in certain religions and cultures, and we learn by mirroring caregivers who have their own values and habits. It might seem as though this is only true until a certain age, perhaps our teens, and then we become able to form desires that are not socially shaped. The teenage "self" that thinks it is choosing has already been shaped by forces beyond its control, however. It is no surprise that if a person grew up eating spicy food, she is more likely to choose to eat spicy food when she is older, or that if she grew up in a household of musicians, she is more likely to want to become a musician. It might seem as though if we just dig deep enough we will find a "true" self that has not been socially influenced, but the further into our histories we dig, the more layers of socialization we find. We always make decisions based on some preexisting set of wants and beliefs, and if we look far enough back in our own histories, we will find beliefs and wants that we did not instill on our own.

A second difficult implication of the view that our authentic values and motivations are those that are not socially influenced is that a person can never be autonomous if she does what those around her do or value. The view implies, for example, that a person cannot autonomously be a Muslim or a Christian if she lives in a society where that is the dominant religion, that she cannot autonomously love her parents if that is what they have raised her to do, or that she cannot autonomously dislike violence in a world where most people are raised to be kind to others. It nonetheless seems clear that people sometimes develop genuine values, motivations, and behaviors that are consistent with what the people around them value. In fact, we can even think of situations where the influence of other people enhances, rather than decreases, people's ability to find and live in accordance with their authentic selves. We have all experienced moments where our friends remind us who we really are, yet if our real selves were ones that were uninfluenced by others, such moments would be impossible. The reason that Starr does not identify with "Williamson Starr" is not just that Williamson Starr is what some group of people, the kids in her school, wants her to be. In fact, some-times other people's expressions of what they want her to be help Starr figure out and shape who she is. For example, Starr's friend Kenya calls her out for not speaking up for Khalil, her childhood friend who was killed by the police. When Kenya does so, she reminds Starr of her own values in a way that helps Starr decide to become an activist. Separating our authentic and inauthentic views in a manner that denies that others sometimes help us to become more autonomous is probably not one we should adopt. As philosopher Patricia Hill Collins argues, autonomy does not seem to have to be gained by separating the self from others (Collins 2000, 124).

To be clear, rejecting the claim that views must be unsocialized to be au-tonomous does not require us to believe the opposite, that socialized views are necessarily autonomous. Instead, it seems we should conclude that whether a view is socialized or not is not what determines its level of au-tonomy. Both Starr's and Kiara's struggles for autonomy come from a desire to reject *certain* socially inculcated views. Kiara's struggle in particular seems to be about realizing that some social norms, racist and sexist beauty expec-tations, are not ones she wants to be her own. Yes, socialization has caused them to permeate her self-conception, but she wants to shed them now. If we want to avoid the odd implications of the view that autonomous views cannot be socially shaped, we need a different explanation of why the sexist and racist beauty norms are not autonomously Kiara's.

Philosophers have proposed alternative views concerning what makes actions, motivations, and values really ours. "Autonomy" derives from a com-bination of the Greek words for *self* and *law*, literally meaning being a law for oneself. The nineteenth-century philosopher Immanuel Kant (Kant 2012), for example, argued that autonomous actions had to be motivated by reason alone. Since he viewed rationality as the distinctive and most valuable ca-pacity of human persons, he thought the acts that truly belonged to a person were the rational ones. Kant also thought that rational acts were those that cohered with the moral law, which required him to believe that actions had to be morally good in order to be autonomous. Many contemporary autonomy theorists agree with Kant that autonomy is about acting on reasons that a person takes as authoritative but disagree that doing so requires acting ac-cording to correct moral principles. In fact, contemporary philosophers have come up with a variety of ways of specifying what it could mean for a person to act on her own reasons. Philosophers call three of such views "coherentist," "reasons-responsiveness," and "socially constitutive." Each of these types of views can clarify the struggles faced by Starr and Kiara to identify and act on their authentic desires without relying on the idea that autonomy requires freedom from social influence.

2.1 Coherentist Conceptions of Autonomy

The word "coherentist" comes from the word "coherent," which means consistent or noncontradictory. Coherentist conceptions of autonomy hold that autonomy requires a type of harmony within the self (see Frankfurt 1988; Friedman 2006). The best-known coherentist views of autonomy take autonomous actions, motivations, and beliefs to be those that a person endorses—that is, that a person affirms or stands behind. Coherentist conceptions of autonomy offer a clear way of characterizing Kiara's participation in sexist and racist beauty norms as nonautonomous. It's not that Kiara never acts in ways motivated by such norms. After all, we know she spends time Googling leg-lengthening surgery. This action is not coherent with her deeper sense of self, though. Rather than *endorsing* her own beauty behaviors and internet search habits, Kiara *repudiates* them. For the coherentist, what makes Kiara's behaviors nonautonomous is not that they are encouraged by a society that influences Kiara. What makes them nonautonomous is how they diverge from the rest of her deeply held values.

Coherentist conceptions of autonomy offer no hard and fast rules about *what* a person can autonomously do or value, which raises interesting questions about whether they are helpful or unhelpful conceptions of autonomy. Coherentist conceptions allow that someone other than Kiara might autonomously value the ability to engage in leg-lengthening surgery. This other imagined person might deeply believe that beauty is one of the most important goals in a woman's life and that long legs are required for it. Some philosophers think this reason a sufficient one to reject coherentist accounts of autonomy (see Stoljar 2000). These critics of coherentism think that if a conception of autonomy implies that women's choices to participate in self-subordinating practices are truly theirs, that something is wrong with that conception of autonomy. Coherentist conceptions seem to go so far as to imply that a person can become more autonomous by teaching themselves to accept the teachings of an unjust society (Khader 2014). Think about Kiara as an example. If Kiara is already critical of sexist and racist beauty standards, she can become more autonomous in the coherentist sense by criticizing advertising, but she can also become more autonomous "I" in the coherentist sense by stopping criticizing the beauty norms and just deciding she is going to follow them. As long as her views are internally consistent with each other, the coherentist says they are candidates for being truly hers.

Coherentist conceptions can also weigh in on the topic of the autonomy of Starr's code-switching. The "real" Starr says she hates Williamson Starr, so it may seem that Williamson Starr cannot be a part of Starr's true self for a coherentist. Coherentism also offers another, more nuanced, way of looking at it, however. Starr's behavior does not *reveal* her true self, but her acting as Williamson Starr might still be thought of as coherent with the values of her true self. If Starr has the goal of succeeding in a world where Black women are readily excluded for displaying affinities with Black culture, her code-switching can be viewed as an exercise of coherentist autonomy. She acts like Williamson Starr to fulfill a goal that she endorses. Some coherentist accounts of autonomy are what philosophers call "hierarchical." Hierarchical accounts hold that our higher-order perspectives, the perspectives from which we evaluate or "look down" on our own actions, are the most real or authoritative for us. Hierarchical coherence theorists think that we become autonomous by making our behaviors, values, and motivations cohere with our highest-order perspectives on those beliefs, values, and motivations. Even if Starr does not like being Williamson Starr, she might be autonomous in the coherentist sense because she endorses doing it as a means to her higher-order goals.

2.2 Reasons-Responsiveness Conceptions of Autonomy

A second type of conception of autonomy that philosophers have developed is the reasons-responsiveness conception. Reasons-responsiveness conceptions of autonomy try to overcome some potential problems with coherentist ones. Recall that coherentist conceptions of autonomy say that actions, motivations, and values become truly ours by being consistent with other actions, motivations, and values we have. It might be, though, that a person's views are coherent but based on false views about the world. For example, imagine a person holds a completely coherent set of values and motivations based on the belief that she can fly. It seems strange to say that when this person hopes to fly but jumps off a chair and falls instead, that the act of falling expresses their true self. The person does not intend to fall, but the problem is not that her values and goals are incoherent; it is that she is out of touch with what it would take to act successfully on these values in the world. A person might also hold coherent views without asking whether she *wants* to hold those views. For example, imagine a person whose values all cohere with a certain religion but who cannot raise the question of whether she *wants* to adhere to that religion. We might question whether a person can meaningfully endorse a set of values that she cannot distance herself from, regardless of how coherent those values are.

To solve these problems, reasons-responsiveness conceptions of autonomy (see Wolf 1990; Fischer and Ravizza 1998) focus on the importance of being able to translate our motivations and values into action. They hold that actions that are truly ours must be based on an appreciation of the reasons relevant to our actions. The reasons-responsiveness conception of autonomy can help us make sense of why Starr hates her own tendency to become Williamson Starr and why the type of code-switching she engages in, even if it does serve some of her purposes, does not seem really to reflect her values. Over the course of the book, Starr starts becoming more and more open with her white friends about where she comes from and what her values are. At the same time, Starr does not stop code-switching entirely. As the book goes on, Starr gets better and better at detecting when code-switching is consistent with her goals and when it is not. At the beginning, she thinks that all her friends at Williamson will abandon her if she reveals where she is really from. She learns over time that this is true of some of her friends but not others. For example, one of her friends turns out to be more racist than Starr realized, but a couple others turn out to be more willing to learn about how racism structures Starr's life than Starr initially thought. Philosophically, Starr seems to code-switch less at the end because she has gotten more skilled at figuring out the facts about when code-switching is beneficial and when it is not. In other words, she has become better able to respond to the facts about the world that are relevant to determining whether her action is coherent with her goals. Reasons-responsiveness conceptions of autonomy offer explanations about how learning more about the world and how other people respond to her can help Starr live a life that is more authentically hers.

Another strain of reasons-responsiveness conceptions of autonomy says that we cannot truly be ourselves if we cannot stand back and evaluate the reasons behind our motivations and actions. We need to be able to ask ourselves whether we want to be who we are if there is to be some kind of value in being who we are at all (see Meyers 1991, 42–58). Some reasons-responsiveness theorists in this vein even reject or question coherentism. They suggest that it is more important for being our true selves to be able to engage in the process of self-definition than to arrive at a state of coherence. Reasons-responsiveness conceptions can help explain why Kiara does not seem to be living out her values even though there are reasons to believe she cares about sexist and racist beauty norms deep down, deep enough that she feels like she cannot stop judging herself according to them. Reasons-responsiveness conceptions would say that Kiara is not defined by her acceptance of racist and sexist beauty norms if her goals of self-definition aim at something else. She is not defined by any set of beliefs, actions, or motivations but instead is defined by her activity of trying to shape the person she is.

2.3 Socially Constitutive Conceptions of Autonomy

Socially constitutive conceptions of autonomy are a third type of philo-sophical conception of autonomy. They hold that actions, motivations, and values can only really belong to us if we formed them under the right social conditions. We can understand this idea more easily if we contrast it with the coherentist conception examined earlier. Coherentist conceptions, you might have noticed, assume that autonomy is in our heads. For coherentists, what we think and feel about our own values and actions and how those thoughts and feelings relate to one another determines whether those actions and values really belong to us. For socially constitutive theorists, the world outside of our heads matters to our autonomy. Part of what matters is whether the world outside us gives us opportunities to become who we really want to be. To see how this idea works, imagine another person with the exact same values, actions, and thoughts as Kiara, but who lives under different social conditions.

Kiara, as we know, lives in a world where social norms about beauty en-courage women and people of color to devalue themselves. Moreover, in our actual social world, women and people of color are penalized for not living up to these norms. The other person, let's call her Layla, is just as interested in leg-lengthening surgery and having straight hair. Like Kiara, she feels like the risks and time put into these projects are not worth the benefits, but Layla lives in a society where beauty is less socially emphasized, where women and people of color are not penalized significantly for failing to be meet beauty standards. A coherentist would say that Layla and Kiara are equally living lives of their own because their thoughts have the same level of internal coherence. The socially constitutive theorist would say otherwise. The socially constitutive theorist can say that Kiara is living less autonomously than Layla because the society she lives in has given her fewer opportunities to be herself. Kiara's sexist and racist society penalizes her for trying to be who she really wants to be, so her desires to accept oppressive beauty standards is less authentic.

One type of socially constitutive conception of autonomy, discussed by the philosopher Natalie Stoljar (Stoljar 2014), says that acts, motivations, and values can only be ours if we have "freedom to do otherwise." If our society is structured so that there is really only one set of values we can form, or one set of actions we can undertake, those actions and values are not autonomous. We might lack the freedom to do otherwise necessary for autonomy because of a lack of imaginative possibilities, or our society or family might have failed to expose us to a wide variety of ideas about what we could do and value. We might also lack freedom to do otherwise when our social world makes the options we really want unavailable to us. Starr's case is a good example. She lacks autonomy or freedom to do otherwise because the choice not to censor her Blackness is sometimes punished at Williamson and because not censoring her Blackness will cause her to lose certain educational opportunities. It is not that Starr cannot imagine *not* code-switching; the fact that she sometimes hates herself for doing it suggests that she can. She cannot really live in the way she imagines as desirable, however, because a racist society will punish her educationally and professionally if she tries.

It might seem like socially constitutive conceptions of autonomy are just another version of an idea we rejected earlier—that autonomous motivations, actions, and desires must not be socially influenced—but these conceptions do differ in an important way. Socially constitutive theorists, at least those who focus on the significance of people being "free to do otherwise," do not claim that we must be free from *all* social influences for our values, actions, and motivations to count as autonomous. For them, society must have not influenced us only in certain, specific ways. The certain forms of social influence incompatible with finding our true selves or living lives that are really our own are forms of influence that make alternative views and behaviors unimaginable or very costly. Think back to the example of the person who adopts the religion or the political party of her parents. There is a difference between a person being influenced by her parents and never being exposed to other religious or political views. There is also a difference between a person hearing her parents advocate for a certain religion or political view and being penalized for not adopting it. A teen whose parents disown her for changing her religion, for example, would lack freedom to do otherwise. Kiara's case can also help us distinguish being merely socially influenced from having freedom to do otherwise. The reason Kiara's ability to form her own beliefs about beauty is compromised for the socially constitutive theorist is not that she has seen ads for leg-lengthening surgery or hair-straightening on Instagram, but because alternative views about beauty are hard to access and because she will lose certain social benefits for failing to follow them. She might, for example, be viewed as less professionally qualified if she goes to a job interview with natural hair. Thus, the socially constitutive theorist says that whatever desires she has to engage in these practices may not really be hers.

2.4 Conclusion

How do we know which of our values and motivations are really ours, and how do we know when we are living lives guided by them? Different philosophical conceptions of autonomy offer distinct approaches to distinguishing lives that are genuinely our own from lives in which we are externally driven, alienated from ourselves, or just going through the motions. Coherentist conceptions of autonomy say that what makes actions, values, and motivations autonomous is how consistent they are with our other actions, values, and motivations. Reasons-responsiveness conceptions say that what matters is our ability to consider reasons relevant to deciding how to act or what we should value, such as facts about the world or reasons that the values and identities we form are worth adopting. Socially constitutive conceptions say that in order to be authentically our own selves, we must have had opportunities to believe and do otherwise than we actually do. These theories all offer criteria for identifying autonomous actions, values, and motivations without simplistically claiming that it is never authentic to act in ways that are socially influenced.

Philosophers disagree about what autonomy is. It might be tempting to conclude, then, that no answer is better than any other, that there's nothing here to study, because it is all just a matter of opinion. That is not how philosophers think about it though. Instead, if all the views seem equally good, it might be because we have not looked at them closely enough. Even plausible viewpoints can have hidden flaws. One advantage of debating them is that we can learn about implications that we did not initially see. Rather than assuming that disagreements reveal the impossibility of arriving at a good answer, philosophers see the fact that there are three or more plausible views about autonomy as evidence that it poses deep puzzles worth looking at more closely.

Furthermore, even if we never *solve* the puzzle, debating different theories of autonomy can help us approach our everyday experience with more wisdom and clarity. I began this chapter by pointing out that we all struggle with questions about what it means to "be ourselves." Having a better sense of what we might mean by this can help us shape our lives better. It might have helped Starr to avoid self-hatred for being Williamson Starr to know that her code-switching could count as autonomous for coherentists because of how it advances her other goals. It might have helped Kiara to understand that even though her discomfort with racist and sexist beauty standards caused her internal conflict, just raising the question of who one wants to be could be thought of by reasons-responsiveness theorists as an expression of autonomy. Similarly, knowing the details of philosophical theories can help us know which standards we are really holding ourselves to when we feel like we have succeeded and failed at being autonomous or authentic. When you think you need to do a better job being true to yourself, do you mean you need to create harmony within yourself, that you wish you lived in a society where you would not be penalized for trying to make different choices, or something else entirely? When you think you have succeeded in showing your true colors, is it because your actions are based on an accurate assessment about the facts of your situation, or because they are consistent with the rest of what you believe about yourself? This type of deeper self-understanding is offered by philosophical examinations of the concept of autonomy.

Notes

1. For a philosophical discussion of how racially oppressed people can develop multiple senses of self to navigate multiple worlds, see Dubois (1996).
2. The blog post is anonymous. I have given the author the name "Kiara" for reasons of style.

Bibliography

Christman, J. 2004. "Relational Autonomy, Liberal Individualism, and the Social Constitution of Selves." *Philosophical Studies* 117, no. 1: 143–164.

Collins, P. H. 2000. *Black Feminist Thought.* New York: Routledge.

Dubois, W. E. B. 1996. "Of Our Spiritual Strivings." *The Souls of Black Folk.* New York: Penguin.

Femsplain. 2015. "Who Is the Fairest One of All?" https://femsplain.com/who-is-the-fairest-one-of-all-1848e8b1a2f9.

Fischer, J., and M. Ravizza. 1998. *Responsibility and Control.* Cambridge: Cambridge University Press.

Frankfurt, H. 1988. "Freedom of the Will and the Concept of a Person." In *The Importance of What We Care About.* Cambridge: Cambridge University Press.

Friedman, M. 2006. *Autonomy, Gender, Politics.* Oxford: Clarendon Press.

Kant, I. 2012. *Groundwork of the Metaphysics of Morals.* Cambridge: Cambridge University Press.

Khader, S. J. (2014). "Empowerment Through Self-Subordination." In *Poverty, Agency, and Human Rights,* edited by D. Meyers, 223–248. New York, Oxford: Oxford University Press.

Meyers, D. (1991). *Self, Society, and Personal Choice.* New York, Columbia: Columbia University Press.

Stoljar, N. (2000). "Autonomy and the Feminist Intuition." In *Relational Autonomy: Feminist Perspectives on Autonomy, Agency, and the Social Self,* edited by C. M. a. N. Stoljar, 94–111. Oxford: Oxford University Press.

Stoljar, N. 2014. "Autonomy and Adaptive Preference Formation." In *Autonomy, Oppression, and Gender,* edited by A. Veltman and M. Piper, 227–254. New York: Oxford University Press.

Thomas, A. 2017. *The Hate U Give.* New York: Balzer and Bray.

Wolf, S. 1990. *Freedom Within Reason.* New York: Oxford University Press.

3

Pride

The Complexities of Virtue and Vice

Claudia Mills

An orphan, bullied and belittled by the relatives charged with her care, is sent off to boarding school, where she is bullied and belittled by the tyrannical headmaster. She then becomes a governess in the home of an overbearing man, who falls in love with her despite insuperable obstacles to their marriage. This scenario constitutes the plot of Charlotte Bronte's novel *Jane Eyre*. At Mr. Rochester's home, Jane is further bullied and belittled by his aristocratic house guests, the Dowager Lady Ingram and her daughters, Blanche and Mary, who both have faces "not only inflated and darkened but even furrowed with pride" (Bronte 1991, vol. 1, 221). In one scene, Blanche launches into an extended discussion about the inferiority of governesses, intending for governess Jane to overhear: "Mary and I have had, I should think, a dozen [governesses] at least in our day; half of them were detestable and the rest ridiculous . . . were they not, mama?" (vol. 1, 227); her mother responds that merely by looking at Jane, she can "see [in her] all the faults of her [lowly] class" (vol. 1, 227). Here we see the moral ugliness of pride as a vice.

Jane herself, however, frequently exhibits a fierce pride of her own. When her aunt, Mrs. Reed, tells her children that impoverished Jane is not fit to associate with them, Jane shouts back at her, "They are not fit to associate with me" (vol. 1, 29). Further, when Mr. Rochester, a proud man himself, insults Jane, she replies with an outburst:

> Do you think I am an automaton?—a machine without feelings? and can bear to have my morsel of bread snatched from my lips, and my drop of living water dashed from my cup? Do you think, because I am poor, obscure, plain, and little, I am soulless and heartless?—You think wrong!—I have as much soul as you—and full as much heart!. . . . I am not talking

Claudia Mills, *Pride* In: *Philosophy for Girls*. Edited by: Melissa M. Shew and Kimberly K. Garchar, Oxford University Press (2020). © Oxford University Press. DOI: 10.1093/oso/9780190072919.003.0004.

to you now through the medium of custom, conventionalities, nor even of mortal flesh: —it is my spirit that addresses your spirit; just as if both had passed through the grave, and we stood at God's feet, equal,—as we are! (vol. 2, 17–18)

When in despair she asks herself who in the world cares for her, she gives the proud reply: "*I care for myself.* The more solitary, the more friendless, the more unsustained I am, the more I will respect myself" (vol. 2, 102). Here we see the moral beauty of pride as a virtue.

Pride is philosophically puzzling because it seems at the same time to be a vice, as we see in the snobby Ingram sisters, and a virtue, as we see in Jane's spirited defense of herself. As philosopher Gabriele Taylor notes, pride "has often been praised as a virtue [but] also labelled the deadliest of the deadly sins. So it has been regarded as both a wholly desirable virtue and a thoroughly destructive vice" (Taylor 2006, 70). One of the most prominent modern philosophers who has written on the topic of virtues and vices, Philippa Foot, identifies virtues as "beneficial characteristics . . . that a human being needs to have" (Foot 2003, 107) both for her own sake and for the sake of others. She explains, "Human beings do not get on well without them" (106). Vices, by contrast, are traits of character that are harmful for human flourishing, as we know from Aristotle's treatment of them in ancient Greece. How can pride be both?

It seems clear from the *Jane Eyre* examples that there is virtuous pride ("good" pride) and vicious pride ("bad" pride): "bad" pride is identified with arrogance, vanity, and conceit; "good" pride is identified with self-respect and a sense of one's own dignity and worth. It is more difficult to explain what grounds this distinction, though. Perhaps the difference between pride as a virtue and pride as a vice is simply a matter of degree such that it is good to have pride in oneself, but not too much. Or maybe virtuous pride is based on a truthful and realistic assessment of one's positive attributes, while vicious pride is based on an exaggerated and distorted view of oneself. Perhaps the distinction between pride as virtue and pride as vice depends on the object of pride. Maybe the difference between the two turns on how pride is expressed to others. This chapter wrestles with these questions and raises problems with some of these proposed answers before offering tentative conclusions on what kind of pride is truly virtuous and valuable, and why.

3.1 The Objects of Pride

As noted earlier, a first attempt to answer the question about the requirements of virtuous pride might be that the difference between "good" pride and "bad" pride is simply a matter of degree: it is good to have pride in oneself, but only in the proper amount. On this view, if someone has too little pride, she's a meek, mousy doormat, but if someone has too much pride, she's "stuck on herself," "full of herself," "in love with herself," or a narcissist. This position does not seem quite right, though. Jane Eyre has enormous pride in herself, pride that enables her to stand up to all those who seek to diminish her, even the man to whom she has given her heart. It does not seem right to say that the difference between spirited Jane and nasty Blanche is that Blanche has *more* pride than Jane does.

A second possible answer might be that "good" pride is based on a truthful and realistic positive assessment of one's attributes, while "bad" pride is based on overly positive self-perception. In a related discussion, philosopher Julia Driver argues that *modesty*, which she deems a virtue, involves "an agent underestimating self-worth in some respect, to some limited degree," while self-deprecation, which she identifies as a vice, involves a degree of underestimation which "dramatically misses the mark" (Driver 1999, 827). If modesty and self-deprecation involve (mild and extreme) underestimation of self-worth, we might think that "bad" pride (arrogance) involves overestimation of self-worth, while "good" pride (self-respect) scores a bulls-eye for accurate self-perception. But as an analysis of pride, this does not seem quite right, either. Vain Blanche is clearly proud of her economic and social standing, and she is in fact wealthy and from a titled family. She is completely accurate in noting her own privileged social and economic position compared to that of Jane and others who serve in the houses of the rich and powerful. Her self-assessment in this regard appeals to indisputable fact. It is not based on a false overestimation of her situation.

Yes, we might say, but perhaps wealth and social position themselves are not how pride should be based. Maybe the difference between pride as a virtue and pride as a vice is that the former is pride in what is *truly* valuable, what *really* matters, whereas the latter is pride in what is not worth prizing. If pride is understood in this way, Blanche's vicious pride would indeed involve overestimation not of her wealth and rank, but of her self-worth. Pride in money and rank seems misplaced, for these entities are not worthy objects of pride. In contrast, we might say, pride in good character or genuine accomplishments is well directed. This distinction seems to point us in a more promising direction.

If this is the case, though, we now face the challenge of how to decide which assets and attributes are, and which are not, worthy of pride. We can all come up with our own favored lists and can offer challenges to lists put forward by others. For example, it is good to be proud of ourselves for doing right, for working hard to achieve our goals despite obstacles, for standing up for ourselves against insults from others, for trying to make the world a better place. It is wrong to be proud of ourselves for being born rich, or of a privileged social group, or for wearing designer labels, or for driving a fancy car. We must defend our reasoning behind these two lists, though. I have an intuitive sense that I have gotten something right in my suggested list, but it is harder to say what reasons support how I have done this sorting.

One reason might be that *I* should be proud only of what has the right kind of connection to *me*, what is connected deeply with my own *identity*. As philosopher Tara Smith writes, "Pride is a kind of attitude concerning the self" (Smith 1998, 74). I should not feel pride in what has little to do with who I am, what does not reflect who I am as a person. How does one decide the contours of an identity, though? Further, who determines what counts as truly a part of who I am? Surely I would have some right to answer these questions in my own way. Perhaps Blanche feels that being the daughter of Lady Ingram is an important part of who she is, or that her wealth has shaped her sense of herself in all kinds of ways. Why then should she not be proud of them?

It may be the case that she should not be proud of them because she cannot claim any responsibility for being wealthy or well-born. According to Smith, "Pride differs from joy in that the sources of pride are things for which the proud person is responsible or to which she bears some especially close association" (Smith 1998, 74). Blanche has not personally achieved her wealth or stature. Her station just happened to her. It was not brought about through her own agency or effort. But suppose that, instead of being proud of herself for being born rich and inheriting a fortune from her parents, she had worked hard to earn her money despite daunting circumstances and made considerable sacrifices to amass her wealth. Wealth acquired in this way seems more pride-worthy than being proud simply because of the accident of wealthy birth. Yet it still strikes me as shallow and superficial—sad, really— to be proud of achieving such an unimportant goal as mere wealth, the sheer amassing of money for its own sake. This point leads me to posit that there is not a clear-cut distinction between "good" pride and "bad" pride, but rather a spectrum of pride, with pride in some kinds of objects *better*, that is, more virtuous, than pride in some others, even if not the *best*.

I happen to think mere wealth in itself is not of much value, which is why I am denigrating wealth-based pride here. I also do not think that looks, a person's mere physical appearance, is inherently valuable. If I had a choice among being rich, beautiful, or smart, I would take being smart. It would be a topic for a different project to try to justify this value ranking, and maybe in the end this choice is just my own personal preference. In any case, I want to note that it nonetheless seems strange to be *proud* of being smart. Whether we attribute intelligence to nature (one's inborn genetic endowment) or nurture (one's early childhood environment and educational opportunities), either way intelligence does not seem like something we are *responsible* for ourselves. We don't *deserve* to be smart. Now, just as some people work extremely hard to amass wealth, others may work extremely hard to develop whatever cognitive assets came their way through nature or nurture: they studied hard, read widely, sought out every chance for learning. Many of us would judge that a person who "made something of herself" in this way has more reason to be proud than someone who just happened to have an extraordinary IQ or the resources to attend elite schools.

Nonetheless, it seems incontrovertible that some people are just better at *trying* than others. I am actually very good at trying, almost a specialist. I love to make lists and cross off the items on these lists one by one; I love to give myself deadlines and meet those deadlines; I gobble up books on time management, but this just seems to be a feature of my particular temperament and personality, perhaps enhanced by how I was raised. It is not clear that I should be proud of being good at trying any more than I should be proud of being smart. I am not really responsible in the right kind of way for either one. Thus, we need to be careful in how much we attribute to our own efforts, if even the ability to "make an effort" may be something for which we cannot claim credit. We need to think harder about what exactly we should feel proud about.

Still considering pride in the acquisition of wealth or education, perhaps I seek income or learning in order to make a positive difference in the world, say, to create my own philanthropic foundation for ending starvation and eradicating poverty. Dedication to a good cause seems a more worthy reason for pride than simply having a bunch of money or a resume filled with impressive degrees. For just this reason, it may be that I am really proud not of my wealth or intellectual attainments per se, but of the good I have accomplished with them for the benefit of somebody other than myself. On this understanding, pride is better directed to objects that have moral worth, those that are not just useful for achieving our own personal goals but which make the world a better place for all. Virtues, after all, are traits of character that benefit others as well as ourselves. Yet here, too, it may be a lucky accident of how my own character was formed or of my own position in the world that I seek nobler goals than mere self-advancement.

3.2 Relative Pride versus Absolute Pride

At this point I have advanced two tentative observations about proper versus improper objects of pride: 1) pride is more appropriate for what is genuinely worth having or achieving, especially for the morally good; and 2) pride is more appropriate for what we have accomplished through our own efforts than for what has merely come our way through luck or chance. I have also noted that it is hard to provide unassailable reasons for thinking that some things are more worth having than others. Further, the more I reflect on what is really a product of my own effort, the more I start to wonder whether anything is, given that I may not be able to claim credit even for the ability to "make an effort." Returning to *Jane Eyre*, both of these factors do seem to be absent in the case of Blanche's pride in herself, so both seem to play a role in our deciding when pride is and is not justified. Blanche seems to have pride only in her inherited wealth and position, rather than in what 1) is genuinely worth having or of any moral significance; or 2) was achieved through her own efforts, even if she was able to make these efforts only because of fortunate circumstances beyond her control, which might include having an excellent governess like Jane herself. We may indeed feel comfortable placing Blanche's pride toward the vicious end of the pride spectrum for this reason.

In contrast, Jane's pride in herself is grounded in . . . well, what *is* it grounded in? It is not that easy to say. She acknowledges that she is "poor, obscure, plain, and little" (Bronte 1991, vol. 2, 17). She does not point toward any distinguishing features of herself that are either genuinely valuable or morally significant *or* owed to her own determined efforts, the two features of desired objects that might ground or justify pride. Instead Jane's pride seems based not in what differentiates her from others, but in what she shares in common with them. Jane tells Mr. Rochester that despite her lowly status in comparison to him, she has just as much "soul" and just as much "heart" as he does. It is not completely clear what she means by "soul" and "heart," though. If she means compassion, she certainly has more "soul" and "heart" than Blanche does, but Jane seems more focused on asserting her *equality* with Rochester than any *superiority* to him. She says that if she "stood beside him at God's feet, she'd stand as his equal" (vol. 2, 18).

This reflection on the source of Jane's pride suggests a second, and very different, set of considerations for identifying the objects of bad pride versus the objects of good pride, of vicious pride versus virtuous pride. We can take pride in our *relative* or *comparative* position to others, in the ways we are better than they are: richer, smarter, prettier, stronger, kinder, more talented, more honest, more just. Let's call this "relative" pride. Relative pride is pride in the outcome of some kind of formal or informal competition, where there are winners and losers. Blanche is proud that she has "beaten" Jane in some unspoken competition for rank and privilege. Although we do not see this in the novel, Jane could also be proud that she has "beaten" Blanche in an unspoken competition for good character, not to mention just plain good manners. There is also, however, a different kind of pride in oneself that is not comparatively based at all. Let's call this "absolute" pride, which is pride in one's dignity merely as a human being, pride in oneself as simply *being* equal with everyone else. *This* kind of pride is what Jane asserts.

We must then consider whether relative pride is "bad" while absolute pride is "good." I do not want to make this kind of sweeping judgment. Nonetheless, asserting one's own fundamental worth, and insisting that one be treated with the respect owed to all members of the moral community, seems a form of pride whose value is difficult to deny. The project of trying to establish oneself as better than others, on the other hand, even if better in attributes that are clearly worth valuing, has certain problematic features. Indeed, the better the aspect in which one takes pride, the odder it is to take pride in one's superiority in this regard, vis-à-vis others. One of the most valuable traits to possess is a good moral character; better than the posses-sion of wealth or fame, beauty or skill, is possession of virtue. The possession of virtue can help a person achieve a specific kind of excellence in her life. Philosophers understand the achievement of moral goodness through dif-ferent virtues, with some arguing that pride plays a significant role in doing so. As Smith writes, "Pride, as a virtue, is . . . the commitment to achieve one's moral excellence" (Smith 1998, 76). Yet truly good people do not seem to spend a lot of time thinking about how good they are, or in fact in focusing on *themselves* at all. Certainly, good people do not seem to spend a lot of time assessing themselves comparatively and dwelling on their own superiority. "I'm morally better than you are!" is an exceedingly strange proclamation from the lips of someone who is morally good. It makes more sense as a defensive strategy. If my own virtue is impugned by someone else, I might make this statement as a retort. I hope I would not think in these terms, or speak in this way, otherwise.

Still, it seems natural, and morally sound, to take pride in some of our differential features such as in being good at an activity, where this does mean being better than someone else. It is satisfying to win an award for excellence in sports, acting, writing, or philosophy. It is less satisfying if everyone gets the same award, such as those "participation trophies" for youth sports, or bogus citations given out at elementary school weekly assemblies. I cherished the comment written on one college philosophy paper until I discovered that the professor had written the same comment on my friend's paper as well. If we are all special, then nobody is, and it seems we do crave being special, special in some way, not absolutely indistinguishable from all others. It may thus be going too far to denigrate relative pride in our differing abilities as invariably a form of bad pride. Nonetheless, if we pursue pride in simply being the "best," this enterprise is doomed to disappointment. "Best" is itself relative to a given comparison group, and the more we advance on any dimension of excellence, the more we are likely to place ourselves in a more sophisticated peer group, as high-school superstars discover when they head off to elite universities. Competition can be stimulating, but it can also breed envy and dissatisfaction. As Smith notes, the relative view of pride turns into a "game of me versus you"; it makes pride, in her view, "a menace" (Smith 1998, 80).

Absolute pride, on the other hand, fosters cooperation. We can all strive to be morally better, without one person's success occasioning another person's failure. The world turns out to be a better place when we take pride in features of ourselves that others can share, and take pride in themselves. In fact, vicious relative pride arguably shows a lack of absolute pride. Taylor argues that vanity is not an attitude "of a person who is secure in her self-esteem" (Taylor 2006, 72); "a self-esteem requiring constant reassurance [of one's superiority over others] can hardly be secure. It is a sham self-esteem" (74). Blanche might not need to flaunt her superiority over Jane if she had true respect for herself in the way that Jane does. Nonetheless, relative pride is not going to disappear, nor should it. Here problems seem to arise most centrally in how pride is *displayed*. Even if Blanche had taken pride in an object worthier than wealth or position, and one for which she could claim more responsibility, it would be morally despicable for her to gloat about it in the presence of someone less fortunate and to express outright contempt toward that person. Blanche is about as clear an example of morally flawed—nay, obnoxious—pride as we can find.

3.3 The Expression of Pride

With all of these ideas in mind, we might be able to get clear on the ways we can express pride in our comparative accomplishments, in contrast to those who might say we should not express pride in ourselves at all (does the world really need to hear every detail of how wonderful we think we are?). Not to share our pride in ourselves with others, or at least not to share those aspects of ourselves that occasion the pride, would be to withhold part of what makes us who we are, especially if, as I suggested earlier, we take the greatest pride in features most connected with our sense of our identity. Furthermore, others may themselves take pride in our accomplishments, either because they played a causal role in helping to bring about those accomplishments (e.g., as teachers and mentors), or simply because they are so close to us as family members or friends that our achievements are in some sense theirs as well. My younger son resented my expressions of pride in him for just this reason because it signaled a way in which I was appropriating his accomplishments and making them *mine*. If I did not feel that his good report card or stellar concert performance was in some sense *mine*, why should I say, "*I'm* so proud of you," rather than merely saying, "*You* should feel so proud of *yourself*"?

In the age of social media, we may also feel pressure to advertise our professional accomplishments as part of promoting our careers. We feel the need to "blow our own horn" for sheer professional survival, though self-promotion can easily become counterproductive if we trumpet our own accomplishments too frequently, with too many exclamation points. Sometimes, too, the rest of us may take delight in others' displays of pride and find touching their open and transparent delight in success. For example, I get teary-eyed watching athletes weeping at a victory, or performers beaming at a standing ovation.

In some of my earlier philosophical writing, I explored the ethics of "bragging, boasting, and crowing." There I concluded that while some expressions of pride are appropriate and welcome for the reasons I have cited, we bristle when others take up too much space in touting their own accomplishments; here the sheer quantity of expressed pride can be irritating. We appreciate it when expressions of pride in accomplishments are accompanied by an equally candid confession of disappointment in failures. I would now add that we also expect pride in our successes to be accompanied by an expression of gratitude to those who helped make those successes possible. This addition resonates with my observation about how much any accomplishment is owed to factors beyond our control, which often include how our very beings have been shaped by parents and teachers. Most important for my purposes here, we resent it when others seem overly concerned to demonstrate not merely pride in their own accomplishments but an implicit and unfavorable comparison to ours: "Many braggers at least implicitly take their good news to ground a favorable comparison to others, and in particular, to you" (Mills 2003, 11).

Even though relative pride is, of course, inescapably relative, we do not need to rub others' faces in the relativity of the comparison when expressing our pride. The more that my expressed pride is expressed pride in *superiority*, the more problematic it becomes, morally. The expression of pride then becomes a mechanism to enforce hierarchy. This is exactly what happens with Blanche's sneering at the lowly status of governesses in the hearing of the only available governess. Her evident agenda is to police class boundaries against possible encroachment from the less fortunate. In contrast, Jane's frequent expression of absolute pride—that is, pride in her own dignity and self-worth—challenges oppressive hierarchy. That said, as a child, Jane expresses disdain for those even poorer than she. Even to escape the cruelties of the Reed household, she is "not heroic enough to purchase liberty at the price of caste" (Bronte 1991, vol. 1, 25), herself guilty of this kind of hierarchy-protecting relative pride.

The power of absolute pride to challenge oppressive structures is a chief reason why those benefiting from such structures recommend humility, the opposite of pride, as the fitting virtue for the disadvantaged. The autocratic headmaster of Lowood School tells Jane's aunt that "Humility is . . . peculiarly appropriate to the pupils of Lowood . . . I have studied how best to mortify in them the worldly sentiments of pride" (Bronte 1991, vol. 1, 38), expressing pleasure in how his own daughter exclaimed over the "quiet and plain" attire of the Lowood girls, who marveled at her own dress "as if they had never seen a silk gown before" (38). Pride is to be "mortified," apparently, only in the lowly. We thus cheer for Jane when she persistently asserts her own worth in the face of others' persistent assaults upon it.

It is worth noting, as we draw toward a conclusion, that pride can be and often is group-based as well as individual. Smith calls this "social pride" (Smith 1998, 89). We can experience pride as members of a family, a faith, a fandom, a profession, a nation. Some of these affiliations are chosen, so that we can perhaps congratulate ourselves for our good sense in deciding to attend a certain educational institution, or pursue a certain profession, or abandon the faith of our childhood for a faith whose tenets and practices we find more satisfying. Other of these affiliations are mere accidents of birth: family, ethnicity, nationality. Group-based pride, however, does not seem different in these two scenarios. It is based less on a sense of responsibility for the affiliation than on the strength of the affiliation itself. Much group pride is simply a matter of loyalty toward fellow group members and empathetic solidarity with them. I feel this way myself if I meet anyone who grew up near where I did in central New Jersey. Group pride becomes problematic, though, when it is the pride of those who are empowered in relation to the disempowered, that is, when it is the pride that is manifested in racism and sexism. Blanche shows this problematic pride in her classism, for example, by sneering at Jane for her need to earn her bread through her own efforts. Group-based pride is problematic also when it becomes bellicose, as when it is expressed in warlike nationalism. Here absolute pride in common humanity is an important corrective to relative pride in the superiority of one group over others.

3.4 Conclusion

In conclusion, our moral assessment of whether pride is a virtue or vice varies according to a range of factors. Pride is more justified to the degree that we are proud about what has to do with our own identity, something for which we can take responsibility; "pride must be earned" (Smith 1998, 81). Pride is also more justified if it is directed toward what is more valuable, especially of great moral value, in its benefit for others. Relative pride in our own superiority to others has certain problematic features, whereas absolute pride, in the form of self-respect for our common worth as human beings, is worthy of celebration. Relative pride is most problematic when it is displayed in a way to reinforce oppressive hierarchies. We resent Blanche's snobby assertion of her wealth- and class-based pride in her superiority over lowly governess Jane. We also cheer for Jane's staunch defense of herself as anyone's equal, for her ability in the face of tyranny to assert her claim to respect from others, and most fundamentally, for her undaunted respect for herself.

Bibliography

Bronte, Charlotte. 1991. *Jane Eyre.* New York: Knopf/Everyman's Library.

Driver, Julia. 1999. "Modesty and Ignorance." *Ethics* 109, no. 4 (July): 827–834.

Foot, Philippa. 2003. "Virtues and Vices." In *Virtue Ethics*, edited by Stephen Darwall, 105–120. Oxford: Blackwell.

Mills, Claudia. 2003. "Bragging, Boasting, and Crowing: The Ethics of Sharing One's Glad Tidings with Others." *Philosophy & Public Policy Quarterly* 23, no. 4 (Fall): 7–12.

Smith, Tara. 1998. "The Practice of Pride." *Social Philosophy and Policy* 15, no. 1 (Winter): 71–90.

Taylor, Gabriele. 2006. *Deadly Vices.* Oxford: Clarendon Press.

4

Questions

The Heart of Philosophy

Melissa M. Shew

In Nicole Krauss's novel *The History of Love* (2005), Alma Singer is a fifteen-year-old girl who wants to fix her mother's grief and console her little brother in the wake of their father's untimely death. Her mother is sad all the time, and her brother worries that he will forget their father. In attempts to make sense of her own grief and also to figure out how to cheer her mother and help her brother belong, Alma tells her part of the novel through lists she makes. Some headings of her list entries expose her interior desires ("27: ONE THING I AM NEVER GOING TO DO WHEN I GROW UP"), and other headings indicate matters of fact ("32: FOR TWO MONTHS MY MOTHER HARDLY LEFT THE HOUSE"). She falls in love, tries, fails, regrets, and hopes, and questions, cataloguing her life through entries that put a microscope on different aspects of who she is and who she is becoming.

The novel comprises two initially distinct narratives. The second story follows Leo Gursky, an old man with a sense of humor and whose heartache and desperation echo in the hearts of all who have suffered, loved, lost, and grieved. Leo also questions, albeit sometimes in a nonrational way. For instance, when describing Leo's young and formative love of his life, Krauss writes, "Once upon a time there was a boy who loved a girl, and her laughter was a question he wanted to spend his whole life answering."[1] This line might elicit eyerolls but actually plays wryly and tenderly on a fairy tale trope against the backdrop of the Holocaust. It also raises the possibility that questions may arise from our experiences and encounters with others, even if these questions are not articulated in explicitly logical ways. In any event, the "girl" is Alma, though a different one. Alma Singer was named after Alma in *The History of Love*, which is a book based on Leo's great love for this actual woman (when he knew her, as a girl). After a passionate young love, Leo goes

Melissa M. Shew, *Questions* In: *Philosophy for Girls*. Edited by: Melissa M. Shew and Kimberly K. Garchar, Oxford University Press (2020). © Oxford University Press. DOI: 10.1093/oso/9780190072919.003.0005.

into hiding for years to avoid the genocide sweeping Poland. Young Leo and Alma only see each other once more.

As the author of this novel within the novel, Leo mythologizes Alma through different ages and kinds of love. He invents different "ages" in the history of love to praise love as a result of his pure experience with it. The Age of Silence names a time of gestures before language, for instance, and the Age of Glass concerns an era in which human fragility actualizes itself in glass skeletons.

As it happens, Alma's mother is translating this book, though neither of them knows of Leo, of course. In fact, they think the book is written by someone else entirely. Alma reads a chapter that her mother has translated, writing it in her lists. "33: *THE HISTORY OF LOVE*, CHAPTER 10." This chapter is the Age of Glass. Though this age ends wistfully, as love often does, she reads these words about the other Alma: "Her kiss was a question he wanted to spend his whole life answering."[2] A kiss, like laughter, can too be a question, as can be the question of how to solve a person's grief or console a despairing brother. In fact, nearly anything can become a real question if a person listens closely enough. We can even become questions to ourselves.

Near the end of her portion of the story after she has tried to match-make for her mother once again, Alma makes an entry in her catalogue, titled "12. I GAVE UP." She writes, "That was the end of my search to find someone that would make my mother happy again. I finally understood that no matter what I did, or who I found, I—he—none of us—would ever be able to win over the memories she had of Dad, memories that soothed her even while they made her sad, because she'd built a world out of them that she knew how to survive in, even if no one else could."[3] Alma initially sought information that would help solve her mother's problems, came to knowledge in terms of the limitations of what she could do to help, and realized something else entirely instead, mirroring the trajectory of coming to philosophical questions as described in this chapter. At the end of the novel, she finds herself on a park bench sitting next to Leo, connected not only through the name Alma but through a desire to seek meaning in a world where neither feels like they belong. As we shall see at the end of this chapter, this belonging together of the strange, of Alma in her precocious earnestness and Leo in his desire to live fully even at the end of a long and often painful life, invests the world with significance and vitality, signifying a philosophical comportment that gathers them, and potentially us, together.

4.1 The Nature of Philosophical Questions

Philosophical questions differ from other kinds of questions. Arising in times of boredom, despair, love, crisis, quiet contemplation, conversation with another, or in numerous other ways, philosophical questions tend to be the kinds of questions that stick with a person. This person may find, in fact, that these questions unsettle her and that easy answers elude her grasp. She may also discover that she keeps coming back to these questions, which endure for her in a way that other questions do not. She may note these questions in her literature, history, and science books; she may seek solutions to problems from various sources, from mathematical and physical to ideological and psychological; she may wonder about how the universe seems to fit together so seamlessly at times, but in other moments, presents itself as a chaotic, random mess. These juicy questions contrast with other kinds of questions that we ask in the world on a much more regular, daily basis. The differences between fleeting transactional questions and enduring philosophical questions can be seen through the nature of information juxtaposed against that of knowledge and wisdom.

We live in a world of answers. Consider: if you want to buy a piece of pie but see no sign denoting the cost, you ask the seller, who tells you that a slice costs $5.50. What you have gained is information through a transaction: you ask "how much," "what," or "where" questions, which simple answers from another person readily satisfies. Most questions we ask on a daily basis involve these efficient and useful questions, for they are questions designed to answer our immediate desires (for pie, say), satiate our passing curiosity about obscure trivia, or help us get what we want. These questions often require little to no reflection or critical engagement, though they are wholly useful and ought not be disparaged. Indeed, these questions are primarily directed toward use and amount to some of the most approved forms of questioning in our contemporary world: What's your major? Which classes do you need to take to complete your field of study? How much will your degree make for you when you graduate? Where will you get a job? How many internships have you had? And so on. Questions of these kinds seek information about a person's productivity and practical goals. When a person answers, the responses tend to be sorted into different filing cabinets in people's minds: "Economics major, then law school, then moving to a major city to work for a small firm . . . okay, that makes sense. It's a solid plan." They have received the information they have sought and have filed it away into digestible bits of data in their minds, like Alma does with her more factual categories in her lists. No continued questions are required in order to seek a response, and there is no further information to be gathered. The question is settled and you move on. Hence these questions are *transactional* because they rely on the input of certain kinds of data to resolve them and are complete when the requested information has been given to the asker.

In contrast, philosophical questions tend not to be useful or at least not entirely so, for they cannot be satisfied by pure information alone. Philosophical questions often seek wisdom and certainly entail knowledge. Both of these categories, wisdom and knowledge, differ in kind from information. Consider: if a student is measured for her smarts solely by way of regurgitating information for an exam, then that's a transactional approach to education. If a student is assessed according to her ability to apply her knowledge to solve different kinds of problems, then that solving can include but is not limited to information. If a student is encouraged to think critically about an issue or problem, then she moves nearer to the realm of philosophy. With information, a student may strike a right answer through chance, though that information may be easily forgotten. Schools are filled with students who cram as much relevant data in their minds as possible only to forget it immediately after taking a test, like following directions given by a GPS without understanding a map. Once the test is complete or the destination achieved, the information vanishes.

Thus, information can be a matter of acquisition, like memorizing Scrabble's two-letter words without knowing what they mean or being able to recite the correct formula on a physics exam by chance or through the use of a mnemonic device. In these cases, the information-holder may be successful in winning the game or earning a passing grade, so this information proves useful in the end. Also, transmission of this information to another person is obscured by the fact that the information-holder lacks knowledge of why and how the information works as it does. When asked, for example, what the two-letter words mean, the information-holder cannot explain because she does not know. Thus, one clear indicator that a person has knowledge and not mere information is that the person with knowledge is able, if even theoretically or hypothetically, to teach what she knows to another because she understands how and why something is as it is. In other words, the knowledgeable person is able to demonstrate and explain her knowledge to another. Lacking context for her content and reasoning within a field of knowledge, the information-holder may produce satisfactory responses and may even *appear* knowledgeable even if she is not.

It seems, then, that knowledge is a greater good to pursue due to its lasting power and ability to foster confidence and understanding in the knower. Moreover, since knowledge can be taught to another person, it is also potentially helpful (or harmful) both individually and socially. Additionally, knowledge can be applied to particular situations or circumstances, like when a person is asked to demonstrate her knowledge of math by solving new equations or by being able to generate well-crafted essays based on principles of sound writing. Knowledge, then, improves upon information because it is *of* a particular subject or topic and does not rely solely on specific data or examples alone. We may even take this idea one step further: knowledge is a greater good than information because it addresses possibilities arising in a certain field or subject-matter, for the knower can address new questions and problems in her field that an information-gatherer cannot do. The underlying reason for this difference lies in the fundamental skill that the knower develops, namely, that of *learning how to learn*. At its base, knowledge is about learning as much as information is about having, with the former indicating a dynamic activity open to future growth and the latter relying on facts and already-settled answers.

Now consider how a knower might respond to being asked one of the transactional questions about college or post-college life indicated earlier. Surely her response would diverge from the information-gatherer's answer, and the result may be a quizzical look on the inquirer's face due to the dynamic curiosity of the knower. When asked, for example, what someone studies in college, if she responds, "Well, I love an art history class I'm taking. Italian Renaissance art seems to foreshadow crises of spirituality and meaning that anticipates later epochs," or "In physics, we had an intense discussion about the potential eventual collapse of the universe," more than likely she will see a puzzled and possibly glazed look pass over the asker's eyes, for while she answered his question, the response may not compute. He had asked *what*; she had responded with *how* and *why*. She may realize that he was just being nice and that she has ripped the social fabric of polite conversation. Or he might engage her back as an equal knower, curious to learn from her what she knows. In this way, he may demonstrate *epistemological curiosity*—that is, curiosity about a topic or idea to be investigated.

4.2 Epistemological Curiosity

Without a doubt, philosophers are stamped by ongoing epistemological curiosity, which is a desire to learn about an object. By "object," I simply mean a topic, idea, or entity worth investigating or learning about. Epistemology is the field of philosophy that explicitly theorizes about knowledge, from what we can know to what knowledge itself is. Often, epistemological curiosity is displayed through dialogue with others, though it can also happen individually. After all, an individual is not monolithic, for even by ourselves, each of us is a dialogical creature, composed of questioning and answering beings "within" us, often in conversation with ourselves. This activity of questioning (because it is an activity) speaks to the core of who we are and might be as human beings.

For philosophers, this distinctive curiosity about what we can know and how we can know it persists far beyond transactional questions, leading from question to question in ever more complex and nuanced ways. For instance, issues of how to treat people fairly can lead to considerations about environmental and social topics, what is meant by equity, and even the nature of justice itself. These conversations can become esoteric and abstract, which is a point embraced by philosophers so long as the world itself is kept in view, and sometimes even when it's not. Knowing is thus intimately tied to thinking, though thinking goes between and beyond specific academic disciplines and is a characteristic that we all share as thinking beings. As twentieth-century German philosopher Hannah Arendt notes, "thinking's chief characteristic is that it interrupts all doing, all ordinary activities no matter what they happen to be."[4] She characterizes the moment that thought interrupts our daily activities as moving "into a different world," for, as she explains, "When I am thinking I move outside the world of appearances."[5] What it is to apprehend a concept is to grasp it with our reason or intellect, an activity that punctuates and can disrupt what we are doing at any given moment. When extended for a period of time, we may find ourselves disoriented when resuming our regular activities. According to her, the "paralysis of thought is twofold: It is inherent in the stop and think, the interruption of all other activities, and it may have a paralyzing effect when you come out of it, no longer sure of what had seemed to you beyond doubt while you were unthinkingly engaged in whatever you were doing. If your action consisted in applying general rules of conduct to particular cases as they arise in ordinary life, then you will find yourself paralyzed because no such rules can withstand the wind of thought."[6] For Arendt, this paralyzing effect can be crucial in our lives, even in warding off "evil deeds" that are far more commonplace and less cartoon-moustache-twirling than we might think. For instance, in noting the "extraordinary shallowness" of people who participated in carrying out Nazi orders, Arendt elsewhere speaks of a "banality" to evil in its ordinariness, reflected in extreme historical atrocities like the Holocaust but also evident in other parts of our world today. As Arendt provocatively states, a person enacting pernicious orders or employing rules mindlessly displays a "quite authentic inability to think."[7] She thus asks whether, at base, the activity of thinking itself, the "habit of examining and reflecting upon whatever happens to come to pass, regardless of specific content and quite independent of results,"[8] can ward off evildoing. In short, her answer is yes.

The reasons for an affirmative answer to this question connect to larger themes of this chapter. Though philosophers are often talented at debate due to their argumentative abilities, philosophers tend not to relish in *simply* "being right" or being merely persuasive. The point of a debate is to win; the point of philosophy is to be drawn nearer to the truth or truths of things. As noted in the first section, we often forget information if it has only been memorized and regurgitated, while knowledge requires that we cultivate other skills along with a general desire to learn. This knowledge requires memory. About memory in particular, it might be worth noting that the word we usually translate from ancient Greek as "truth" is *alethēia*, has as its root *lēthē*, meaning "forgetfulness" or "concealment." The *a-* at the beginning is an alpha privative, which makes the word the opposite, like using "un-" at the beginning of a word. In this view, truth thus is a matter of "unforgetting" or "unconcealment," indicating for our purposes a process of learning that cannot amount to finding or obtaining answers. It is instead a matter of seeing what can be seen, if we let ourselves be open to doing so. It is a matter of constant growth and discovery, of memory and learning. On this view, it might be that we can never even fully know ourselves, for we may not be static objects or beings in this way, a point addressed in the next section of this chapter.

Yet on the face of it, many people appear to lack epistemological curiosity, having been trained and educated out of it. Arendt puts the point bluntly: for many, the goal of asking questions is to have answers so that they don't have to think. Thinking goes beyond mere knowing because it is resultless, a persistent activity of our lives, and is available to everyone, despite a person's expertise in a given field. On this front, though it may sound strange, it would be possible to be knowledgeable while being "thoughtless," even. As Simone de Beauvoir notes, novelist Marcel Proust "observed with astonishment that a great doctor or a great professor often shows himself, outside of his specialty, to be lacking in sensitivity, intelligence, and humanity. The reason for this is that having abdicated his freedom, he has nothing else left but his techniques."[9] These techniques often maintain a person's ego at the detriment of others due to a lifetime of training and knowledge that makes a person a privileged knower but one lacking in humanity. We may think of those who are unapproachable after a class or outside their working hours, when they have to be "on." Their renown can fuel fragile egos, be entertaining, and help them and their friends climb to positions of power, but they do not a philosopher make. These people can lack the "living warmth" necessary to amount to anything more than a culmination of their techniques or ideologies, which can be seen in their dismissal of students who demonstrate their own epistemological curiosity. This dismissal happens when students are simply answered and are not encouraged in their own questions, as though an educator *were* the answers in the back of the textbook and nothing else.

Beyond a classroom, work, families, relationships, and more can deaden a person's epistemological curiosity as well. This deadening can happen also through discrimination, marginalization, and oppressive structures that dehumanize people. Moreover, though it may appear otherwise, ideology, debate, and techniques alone are not philosophical qualities; indeed, they are not even the proper consequence of our humanity as such because we are not, at base, transactional creatures intended to trade jabs and verbal barbs as though the point of life were to "win" in the first place.

This is not to say that philosophers do not have their own opinions, politically and otherwise. Of course they (we) do. This book is filled with philosophers who hold strong opinions, for instance, though we may note that these opinions rarely stay merely at the level of superficiality or opinion as such. Rather, as we know by now, philosophers delight in, and are often tormented by, the "hows" and "whys" of a host of issues we can and do deem philosophical. As philosophy ought to draw us closer to communion with each other, these "hows" and "whys" are available for all to enter into dialogue about, reflect on, and so on. If we do those things in a certain way, we are doing the "job," or, better, are living the *vocation*, of a philosopher.

I designate Beauvoir's ideas about living warmth as part of a required attitude and disposition that a philosopher needs to have in exploring her epistemological curiosity, insisting on dialogue with others and not mere intellectual exercises of debate. In truth, however, this living warmth is required of all of us. It can counter dehumanization, sterility, the ways we're anaesthetized by the world that should wake us up, and heighten our conscious awareness and critical thinking skills in order to face the very serious challenges in our world. Admittedly, the world does a pretty efficient job of training and instructing us away from our originary and inherent curiosity to the point where philosophers may even appear as foolish to others. Per the first section of this chapter and as surely has been the experience of most, if not all, of the contributors of this book, I can recall the hundreds of times people have asked, "Philosophy, huh? What are you going to *do* with that?" from people with scoffing tones in their voices, which is only partially their fault. "Live better" became my only response after a while. It was the only honest answer I could muster, for they had missed the point entirely.

Until this point, the pursuit of knowledge as a good in itself suggests the possibility that knowledge is self-contained, likely remaining at the level of neutrality and objectivity even though a living warmth is required for a true philosophical disposition. Certainly, knowledge of a certain kind can and does have these traits, as we understand from the first section and here, but what distinguishes a general desire for knowledge from philosophical questioning more broadly can perhaps be teased out by the kinds of qualities and examples detailed thus far. Our desire to know also often connects to a desire for meaning, which pushes us from a realm of scientific objectivity inhering in most disciplines to a broader, more existential scope of questioning. The heart of philosophy thus intimately indicates the existentially transformative power that those questions can have in our lives.

4.3 Questions as Existentially Transformative

To question is to create. To create is to bring something into being that wasn't there before. It is not the repetition of the same, a mimicry of the simulacrum of the factical world. Questioning opens a domain of human freedom that challenges the world anew and that ought to bring us into closer proximity with each other through the sheer creation, expression, and exploration of philosophical questions sincerely pursued. Thankfully, perhaps, none of us is self-sufficient but in need of much. We are incomplete "subjects-in-becoming"[10] or "subjects-in-process/on trial."[11] In this view, our ontological vocation, that is, our calling according to the kinds of beings that we are, for ontology is the study of being, is to become *more* human, to grow into the kinds of beings that we are. Were we to be born fully formed like Athena bursting forth from her father's head, this becoming would neither be necessary nor possible. We might be immortal, then, or maybe dead, and we certainly wouldn't have any questions.

The view of a person articulated here is one of being in constant search. Philosophers address this issue in different ways, though many make the same point about the ontological humility, or stronger, the ontological incompleteness, required to affirm our philosophical natures. This idea means that we are at our core dynamic beings, always in the process of becoming. Consider, for example, how a person might even be surprised by liking something unexpected, or consider how a person might fixate on achieving a goal at the expense of many other things she might like to do or be. In these and other instances, she may not quite be the person she thought she was. Iris Murdoch writes of the importance of pushing aside our "fat and relentless ego" that is the "enemy" of moral philosophy in particular and in trying to become a decent person generally.[12] Beauvoir amplifies this point by saying that every person "casts himself into the world by making himself a lack of being" and "thereby contributes to reinvesting [the world] with human signification. He discloses it."[13] This disclosing of being is a complicated idea because it is not purely negative, as might be suggested by the language of making oneself a "lack" of being. The point is not to erase oneself from existence but instead to throw oneself into the world in order to participate in the movement of freedom that is in itself lively and life-giving. In accord with prior comments about "living warmth," Beauvoir also reminds us that "what is called vitality, sensitivity, and intelligence are not ready-made qualities, but a way of casting oneself into the world and of disclosing being."[14] We might think of this point in terms of the constant effort required to maintain what we value. Consider, for example, how relationships break bad if people in them simply take them for granted, as something that will "always" be there. We might also think of education in actual classrooms and the rituals that accompany the meeting of students and educators day in and day out through a semester and year. It could very well happen that we will collectively cease to value these ways of making and creating meaning together, telling tales to younger generations about how—believe it or not!—people used to trudge to a classroom at the same time every day or nearly so. Relationships, like education, are not ready-made, and like everything else in our lives, only have value so long as we are committed to investing them with it.

Within this scope, philosophy may seem to be a fool's errand in a world that clearly devalues it. *Les jeux sont faits*, perhaps; the chips may already be down, and there might not be a choice but to play out our lives according to other people's answers and expectations for us. Nothing could be further from the truth, however. As psychoanalytically trained philosopher Julia Kristeva writes, "The speaking being is a believing being."[15] "There is no such thing as an adolescent without the need to believe,"[16] she writes, where believing means "I hold as true."[17] Tracing the philosophical etymology of belief, Kristeva notes that *credo* (belief) is derived from the Sanskrit *kredh-dh/srad-dha*, which means "to give one's heart, one's vital force, in the expectation of a reward" and designates an "act of confidence, implying restitution."[18] This foundation of belief is not to be mistaken for certainty, however, and instead it denotes a constant search and commitment to that search without surrender. As Kristeva writes elsewhere: "For the speaking being [,] life is a meaningful life; life is even the apogee of meaning. Hence if the meaning of life is lost, life can easily be lost: when meaning shatters, life no longer matters. In his doubtful moments the depressed person is a philosopher."[19] Though Kristeva in part jests in her last quip about the depressed person being a philosopher, she is also serious: the break between a person and her life denotes a crisis of meaning, which is a crisis of life itself. Often this schism happens when a person does what she thinks she is supposed to do only to realize that her heart, her "vital force," as Kristeva might say, wasn't in it. That is, she failed to believe, taking refuge instead in the expectations of others.

Arendt echoes this point by discussing the very act of thinking as interrupting our daily routines, addressing in a different way the need to pursue meaning and not just knowing. For her, a person "has an inclination and, unless pressed by more urgent needs of living, even a need . . . to think beyond the limitations of knowledge, to do more with [her] intellectual abilities, [her] brain power, than to use them as instruments for knowing and doing."[20] This inclination is a philosophical one that transcends a computer's ability to crunch data and achieve "results." In working by way of questions, then, philosophy is deeply connected to our humanness, indicating a surprising conclusion: philosophy indicates an ecstatic way of being in the world. To be ecstatic is to stand outside of, or away from, oneself or one's situation. From that vantage point, we can perhaps look more clearly at our lives, the world, the universe, and more. We will have the ontological humility and intellectual courage to punctuate a static world and work toward building one that will affirm this ecstatic attunement in us all.

It turns out, then, that we may not be the kinds of creatures we typically take ourselves to be. Like Alma, who thought at first that she could solve the puzzle of her mother's grief; like Charlotte in Sophia Coppola's film *Lost In Translation* (2003), who wanted to know her purpose and know there's "nothing wrong" with her; like Kambili in Chimamanda Adichie's novel *Purple Hibiscus*, who saw the hypocrisy of her father's actions and sought a different kind of spirituality and way of being despite her family's relatively high social status; like so many from literature, history, myth, and more, we too stretch ourselves out toward knowing in philosophical ways, buoyed by the curiosity that marks our humanity. In her 2019 commencement speech at Yale, Chimamanda Adichie reminds us to "never admire quietly" what we see in others, for "we do not always recognize what is beautiful in ourselves, in our spirits, until someone has pointed it out to us."[21] I understand her as saying that we are always otherwise, and much more, than we know ourselves to be. She then says that "paying attention is one of the most beautiful acts of kindness," a kind of eulogizing of the living, perhaps. We should pay attention to encourage others and ourselves in our own ways to pursue the questions that we have in our interior lives. Despite everything, and I mean *everything*, we are curious, thinkerly creatures, after all.

***

At the end of *The History of Love*, when Alma is sitting next to Leo and just before he dies, readers of the novel might recall an otherwise innocuous comment early in the story: "When I go, it will be my heart," he says in a one-off comment in the context of facing his mortality, as sometimes people do when they speculate about how it will end for them. His heart is both what grants him his ability to love and create through his words and actions as he does over the course of his long life; it is also what kills him in the end. It is that heart that all of us know all too well: the desire to stretch ourselves farther than we can see, to know more than what we are given or told, and to become who we are as the thoughtful, loving beings that we are or can be. That heart, which Alma also knows, is filled with questions. It is the heart of philosophy.

Notes

1. Krauss (2005, 11).
2. Ibid., 62.

3. Ibid., 181.
4. Arendt (1971, 423).
5. Ibid., 423.
6. Ibid., 434.
7. Ibid., 417.
8. Ibid., 418.
9. Beauvoir (1976, 5).
10. This term from Paulo Freire is used to explain our human nature as fundamentally incomplete and pervades his book (Freire 2000).
11. Kristeva uses this term widely and repeatedly in her books to designate our permanent state of being in process and never complete.
12. Murdoch (1997, 342).
13. Beauvoir (1976, 49).
14. Ibid., 41.
15. Kristeva (2009b, 1).
16. Ibid., 13.
17. Ibid., 3.
18. Ibid., 4.
19. Kristeva (2009a, 6).
20. Arendt (1971, 11).
21. Adiche (2019).

Bibliography

Adiche, Chimamanda. 2019. Yale Class Day Speaker. https://www.youtube.com/watch?v=e9JhU2fXet8.

Arendt, Hannah. 1971. "Thinking and Moral Considerations." *Social Research* 38, no. 3: (Autumn): 417–446.

Beauvoir, Simone de. 1976. *The Ethics of Ambiguity*. New York: Kensington Publishing.

Freire, Paulo. 2000. *Pedagogy of the Oppressed*. New York: Continuum Press.

Krauss, Nicole. 2005. *The History of Love*. New York: Norton.

Kristeva, Julia. 2009a. *Black Sun: Depression and Melancholia*. New York: Columbia University Press.

Kristeva, Julia. 2009b. *This Incredible Need To Believe*. New York: Columbia University Press.

Murdoch, Iris. 1997. *Existentialists and Mystics: Writings on Philosophy and Literature*. London: Chatto & Windus.

5

Self-Knowledge

The Importance of Reflection

Karen Stohr

Emma sat down to think and be miserable.[1]

Emma Woodhouse, the title character and heroine of Jane Austen's novel *Emma,* spends a considerable amount of time sitting down to think about herself and her actions, an activity that often does produce some miserable feelings. Of course she is not trying to make herself miserable; she is simply trying to know herself better. For Emma, reflection is a tool through which she improves her understanding of herself and the world in which she lives. In the novel, it is to Emma's credit that she is willing to engage in this kind of reflection and take an honest look at herself and her actions, despite the potential unpleasantness. Self-knowledge is worthwhile, even when the process of acquiring it makes us miserable. But what is it about self-knowledge that makes it so valuable? Why is it something we should aim to have? And what role does reflection play in acquiring knowledge of ourselves?

The idea that self-knowledge matters is an ancient one. The command to "know oneself" is reported to have been inscribed in stone at the Temple of Apollo at Delphi.[2] Many philosophical and religious traditions hold that self-knowledge is an essential step on the path to wisdom. The thought is that if we want to know anything at all, we have to start by knowing ourselves. This is because gaining wisdom often requires being willing to acknowledge and let go of the many pleasant illusions that we create around ourselves, our beliefs, and our actions. Reflection helps enable us to recognize those illusions and rid ourselves of them, making it possible for us to see ourselves and the world more clearly. But as we will see, the kind of reflection that produces self-knowledge isn't quite as simple as just sitting down to think.

Karen Stohr, *Self-Knowledge* In: *Philosophy for Girls.* Edited by: Melissa M. Shew and Kimberly K. Garchar, Oxford University Press (2020). © Oxford University Press. DOI: 10.1093/oso/9780190072919.003.0006.

5.1 Where Emma Goes Wrong

The source of Emma's misery is her realization that she has been utterly and totally wrong about something.[3] Like most of us, Emma hates being wrong. In this situation, however, her mistake is not just something that she finds embarrassing or frustrating. It is something that is about to cause a lot of pain to her closest friend, Harriet. Emma has been trying to set up Harriet with the parish vicar or priest, Mr. Elton.[4] Elton is good-looking, charming, reasonably rich, and most importantly, single. Socially speaking, Harriet is a step below Mr. Elton, something that mattered a great deal in that time and place. Emma knows this, but she conveniently ignores it because she enjoys the idea of making this match work. She thus convinces herself that Mr. Elton is so in love with Harriet that he won't mind marrying beneath him. (She also manages to convince Harriet that Mr. Elton is in love with her.) By framing all of Mr. Elton's behavior in terms that support her desired conclusion, Emma immerses them in a narrative in which Mr. Elton will soon propose to Harriet and they will all live happily ever after.

Alas, Emma's narrative is a false one. Mr. Elton is not in love with Harriet and he has no intention of proposing to her. Emma discovers this only when Mr. Elton proposes to *her* instead. As Emma has never been interested in him and certainly doesn't want to marry him, she is completely taken aback by his proposal. She has no idea how Mr. Elton ever came to the conclusion that she would be willing to marry him. Her shock, confusion, and distress lead her into reflection, which temporarily creates even more misery. Reflection forces her to recognize the illusory nature of the narrative she has created for herself and for Harriet. Since Emma prides herself on her good judgment, she is particularly upset by what she regards as her own failures to pick up on important pieces of information:

> How she could have been so deceived! He protested that that he had never thought seriously of Harriet—never! She looked back as well as she could; but it was all confusion. She had taken up the idea, she supposed, and made everything bend to it.[5]

Emma is correct about what went wrong. She had taken up the idea that Elton was in love with Harriet and, as she says, made everything bend to it. She does not realize this immediately; it takes some time before she can begin to appreciate her own involvement in the construction and maintenance of the false narrative. Emma comes to see that she had been so caught up in her own version of events that she failed to notice how various incidents and remarks could lend themselves to different interpretations. Behavior that she interpreted as Mr. Elton flirting with Harriet she can now see as Mr. Elton flirting with her instead. And she can also now see her own behavior, which she had meant him to think of as encouraging his relationship with Harriet, as reasonably construed as flirting with him in return.[6]

5.2 Two Types of Failure

In thinking about how Emma went wrong, it's useful to divide her mistakes into two categories—epistemic failures and moral failures. Broadly speaking, an epistemic failure is a failure relating to knowledge, belief, or judgment. A moral failure is a failure relating to a person's character or values, and the choices that she makes as a result of that character or on the basis of those values. Not all epistemic failures are moral failures. Sometimes we just make mistakes in our reasoning. For instance, I might miss a plane because I misjudged the amount of time it would take me to get to the airport. And not all moral failures are epistemic failures. I might become unreasonably angry at other drivers as I rush to the airport without making any reasoning errors or false judgments about them.

Often, however, epistemic and moral failures are intertwined. Suppose that I blame the other drivers for going too slowly and making me miss my plane. Here I am reasoning badly about the real cause of my lateness, which is the fact that I left for the airport too late. But my desire to put the blame on other drivers in the first place is a moral failure. This moral failure predisposes me to epistemic failures. I draw unwarranted conclusions about other drivers, but the reason I do this is that I am trying to take my problems out on other people rather than accepting responsibility for them myself. Moral failures can lead us into epistemic failures, making it difficult for us to make correct judgments. Moral failures can also make it difficult for us to recognize or admit our epistemic failures. Maybe later, after I have calmed down, I will acknowledge that my lateness was my own fault. Or maybe I will just keep blaming those other drivers because it's more convenient and pleasant than owning up to my mistakes. In that case, I will remain under the influence of that false belief. My ability to reason well about the world is affected by my moral character.

Emma's failures have both epistemic and moral dimensions. She believes that Mr. Elton plans to marry Harriet, a belief that proves to be false. Of course we are not always at fault for having false beliefs, but in Emma's case, she acquires her false beliefs through errors in her reasoning that she could and should have avoided. She assumes she knows a great deal more about Mr. Elton's desires and motivations than she does. She also takes for granted that she knows what is best for Harriet. With these foundational assumptions in place, she proceeds to "find" evidence that supports her desired conclusion that Mr. Elton is planning to propose to Harriet. As a result, her perceptions and her reasoning get distorted. Whatever Mr. Elton says or does appears to Emma as an expression of his admiration for Harriet. In fact, she is so solidly in the grip of the story she is telling herself that she seems unable to interpret his behavior in any other light.

But it is probably more accurate to say that she is *unwilling* to interpret it in any other light. Emma is a very intelligent and perceptive young woman. She is generally an excellent judge of character and she also has exceptionally good social skills. It's not as though she can't read a room, understand hidden meanings, or pick up on social cues. And indeed, Emma does notice some inconsistencies in her narrative about Mr. Elton's being in love with Harriet. But instead of using them to rethink her judgments, she dismisses them or explains them away. This helps make sense of why she was so caught off guard when he proposed to her instead. She never imagined this scenario unfolding. Still, it does seem like she should have been able to imagine it, even if she didn't.

We might describe Emma as engaged in what philosopher Tamar Gendler calls "imaginative resistance."[7] Imaginative resistance occurs when there is some kind of constraint on our ability to imagine an event or narrative, a constraint that can have a number of origins. Gendler argues that imaginative resistance is sometimes the result of our not wanting to take up a particular perspective on the world. In other words, I resist imagining what I don't want to imagine. Emma does not want to imagine any version of the narrative that does not end in Mr. Elton and Harriet's marriage. She becomes so attached to that narrative (in part because she is the one who constructed it) that she refuses to imagine alternative narratives, even when those alternative narratives fit the facts better.

Emma's excessive attachment to her own narratives produces epistemic failures, but its roots lie in a failing that has moral dimensions. Emma is too invested in being right. More specifically, she is too invested in being the person who is right. Everyone enjoys being right, of course, since being wrong is usually not much fun. But for Emma, being right is closely linked with her self-image. She thinks of herself as having excellent judgment and she takes pride in having special insights into other people and their behavior. Being wrong affects her sense of self, giving her a powerful motivation to avoid mistakes. This motivation will prove helpful to her in the end, but it does pose an obstacle to her capacities to understand the world and herself.

5.3 Fixing our Mistakes

Emma certainly has a great deal of self-confidence. That is not a bad thing, of course, and in her case self-confidence is justified. Most of the time, she does get things right. But the fact that Emma is usually right makes it harder for her to recognize and accept being wrong. This is exacerbated by the fact that she is almost always surrounded by people who defer to her. She spends most of her time immersed in a positive feedback loop in which her judgments are constantly affirmed. So it is not terribly surprising that Emma has trouble seeing her mistakes. The only person who ever challenges her judgment is her neighbor (and eventual love interest), George Knightley. Mr. Knightley has plenty of respect for Emma's intelligence, but he is not afraid to tell her when he thinks she is wrong. Sometimes Emma listens to him and sometimes she does not. Whether she listens to him depends on whether the subject is one on which she thinks she has more expertise than him. This is generally a reasonable standard to use when trying to decide whether to take seriously someone else's opinion. Of course we should pay attention to the perspectives of those who know more than we do and ignore people who are just spouting off their mouths. In Emma's case, however, it backfires because Emma is not always good at assessing her own level of expertise.

This is not an unusual problem. Indeed, according to research in psychology, it is quite common. The phenomenon known as the Dunning-Kruger effect suggests that we are often lousy judges of our own abilities.[8] Experiments have shown that people who aren't particularly good at a task tend to overestimate their performance with respect to it. They don't realize that they're performing badly, like someone doing karaoke who has no idea that they are singing wildly off-key. Nor are they likely to be persuaded by evidence to the contrary. Bad drivers will continue to think they are highly competent, bad singers will continue to think they are headed for Broadway.

What the Dunning-Kruger effect implies is that we should not be quick to assume that we are judging our own abilities correctly. If I am a good singer, I'm likely to believe that I'm a good singer. But if I'm a bad singer, I am also likely to believe that I'm a good singer. So how can I know whether I am really a good singer or whether I'm a bad singer with a whole lot of self-confidence?

Emma rarely doubts her own judgments about anything; she just assumes that her take on the world reflects how the world actually is. But it's worth asking whether her self-confidence is serving her well in this situation. After all, her misery after Mr. Elton proposes is due in part to her realization that in this case, her confident reliance on her own assessment of the situation was a huge mistake. Her assessment proved false and so that self-confidence was unwarranted. When she realizes this, she experiences something we might describe as a crisis of self-trust. The philosopher Trudy Govier describes self-trust as "the ability to rely on one's own critical reflection and judgment."[9] Self-trust means, quite literally, that you trust yourself to make correct judgments and good decisions.

Everyone struggles with self-trust in some way or another. We are all familiar with the experience of being unsure of ourselves and our assessments, wondering if we misunderstood something or whether what we're thinking about doing is worth the risks. For many people, self-doubt is a constant companion and not a helpful one. As Govier points out, self-trust is important for cultivating independence, self-respect, and autonomy. If we are always second guessing ourselves and our decisions, it can make it difficult to take ownership of our lives. When self-doubt is pervasive in our thinking, it will undermine self-trust and perhaps even our most basic sense of self. On the other hand, self-doubt also has an important role to play in creating and facilitating appropriate self-trust. Carefully applied, self-doubt can lead us to have more confidence in our judgments and our assessments. The challenge is to figure out when self-doubt is contributing to self-trust and when it is damaging it. What is the right amount of self-doubt?

5.4 Appropriate Self-Trust

The ancient Greek philosopher Aristotle famously claimed that every virtue is a mean between two extremes of vice.[10] One vice represents an excess whereas the other vice represents a deficiency. Although this claim sometimes gets distorted or given too much weight in discussions of Aristotle, there's a certain plausibility to it. Here's the basic idea. As Aristotle sees it, there is such a thing as the appropriate amount of anger to feel in a given situation. The virtuous person will get exactly as angry as the situation requires. She will be very angry when she sees people expressing racist ideas or behaving cruelly. And she will not be very angry when the person in front of her in the self-checkout line has twenty-one items in her cart when there is a twenty item limit. Getting really angry because you are delayed by a few seconds at the grocery store displays the vice of excess anger. On the other hand, *not* getting angry when you are insulted or when someone spouts racist vitriol in your presence shows the vice of deficient anger.

We can say something similar about self-doubt. There is such a thing as having too much self-doubt and also such a thing as having too little. Emma errs on the side of having too little self-doubt. She overestimates her own ability to judge what people are thinking and planning, as well as what would make their lives go well. Other people err on the side of doubting themselves too much, having too little confidence in their abilities and judgments. Now it may seem weird to call excessive self-doubt a vice. After all, the reasons why people don't trust their own judgment aren't necessarily their fault. All kinds of bad things can happen to a person (abuse, for instance, or gaslighting) that can make it difficult for her to develop or maintain self-trust.[11] This is certainly true. But let's set aside the question of whether any of us are to blame for our issues about self-doubt and focus instead on how we can identify and remedy whatever deficiencies or excesses we happen to have. (Keep in mind that it's possible to have both—too little self-doubt in some domains and too much self-doubt in other.)

Govier presents self-trust as a kind of virtue. On her picture, a person who has self-trust regards herself as "basically well intentioned and competent and as able to make reasonable judgments and decisions and carry out reasonable plans of actions."[12] Notice that when described this way, self-trust is inward-facing. By that I mean that it focuses on how we see ourselves and our capacities for judgment. The person with the virtue believes herself to be competent at making decisions and judgments and so she has confidence in those decisions and judgments. But as we've seen with Emma, it's possible to be totally confident and also be totally wrong. So if self-trust really is a virtue, there must be some way of figuring out just how much confidence we should have in making a particular decision or judgment. To put it more dramatically, there must be a way of navigating a safe path between the Scylla of unwarranted self-doubt and the Charybdis of overconfidence.[13]

The twentieth-century British philosopher Philippa Foot described virtues as corrective, in the sense that they either help us resist temptations to which we are prone or else make up for deficiencies in our natural motivations.[14] If I have the tendency to get unreasonably angry, then cultivating the virtue of appropriate anger would mean learning to control my temper. In a similar way, if I have a tendency to engage in too much self-doubt, then cultivating the virtue of self-trust would mean learning to recognize when I am engaged in self-undermining patterns of thought and when I should have more confidence in my own judgments. Emma's problem, of course, is one of overconfidence. So for her, cultivating the virtue of appropriate self-trust means reining in her natural tendency to think that she is right. This means improving her self-awareness and recognizing when she is likely to make mistakes. It also means being more accepting of the mistakes that she does make. It is lucky for Emma that she has the habit of engaging in self-reflection, because it is primarily through reflection that she develops that self-awareness and acceptance of her own fallibility.

Reflection is a tricky business. It can easily turn into unhelpful and unproductive rumination. It can also reinforce our errors, leading us into even greater certainty that our false beliefs are true. In order for reflection to be useful in cultivating a virtuous form of self-trust, we need to engage in it well, with the right attitude and the right aims. In particular, we have to learn how to wield self-doubt effectively. In order to do that, we have to know enough about ourselves to understand how we operate and where we are likely to go wrong.

Many of the factors that go into our behavior are below our conscious awareness and beyond our immediate control. Seemingly irrelevant facts about our situation, such as whether the smell of freshly baked bread is wafting through the air, can affect what choices we make. Although none of us like to think of ourselves as simply the products of our environments, it would be a mistake to overestimate our ability to recognize and control all our behavior. Human beings are psychologically complex creatures, which means that self-knowledge is hard to come by. Much of the time, we don't know why we do what we do. Moreover, it turns out that we are also good at coming up with explanations for our behavior after the fact. At least sometimes, we tend to look at what we've done and only *then* come up with reasons why we did it. And like Emma, most of us are also fairly good at rationalization and self-deception.

It's worth noting that there may actually be practical benefits to a little self-deception. Psychologist Shelley Taylor's pioneering research indicates that positive illusions about ourselves can improve our well-being.[15] It can certainly help motivate us to achieve goals that could seem impossible if we were being more realistic. After all, unless you believe you can do something, you probably won't even try. Taylor's research also indicates that optimism about the future and a sense of control can improve well-being, even in cases where the optimism isn't necessarily warranted and we have less control than we think. Perhaps self-knowledge isn't always such a good thing. Perhaps when it comes to knowing ourselves, ignorance is bliss.

Whether this is true depends on what we mean by bliss and what value we place on self-knowledge and self-trust. These are big questions, and I can only skim the surface here. It seems likely that positive illusions about our abilities and capacities may very well help sustain and maintain self-trust in certain circumstances, like when we're about to take the SAT. But in other cases those positive illusions can end up doing a lot of damage, as Emma learns. Illusions have a way of running up against the facts. The bubble around Emma's false narrative is eventually burst in ways she can't exactly ignore. True, not all false narratives are so easily punctured. People do manage to spend their entire lives deluding themselves about things. But in general, self-delusion is not a promising strategy for building self-trust. When Emma realizes how wrong she has been, her self-trust is shaken. She doubts her own capacities to understand the world. But she is able to take that experience and turn it into something that eventually enhances her self-trust. Once she gets past the initial shock and shame of having messed up so badly, she engages in reflection that helps her understand herself and her motivations better. She then uses her awareness of her mistakes as a tool for building confidence in her future judgments. The self-knowledge she acquires through reflection gives her a stronger basis for virtuous self-trust.

In order for reflection to produce greater self-knowledge, it has to be conducted in the right way and in the frame of mind. There is, as we know, a difference between reflecting on an argument I've had with a friend and rehashing it. In the former case, I am open to new insights about the causes of the argument and how it played out. In the latter case, I am mostly justifying myself and my anger without really resolving anything. Emma's reflections do include some self-justification. But she eventually moves from that phase into one where she is more open and honest with herself about what transpired and how her own failures contributed to it.

5.5 Reflection, Self-Knowledge, and Self-Trust

Thus far I have mostly been focusing Emma's character flaws, but she also has character strengths. One of her strengths is that she is courageous enough to undertake painful reflection in the first place. She sits down to think even when she knows it will make her miserable. We should not underestimate the importance of this. Many of us deal with our problems by deciding not to think about them. This can be a wise strategy, since overthinking and overanalyzing problems can increase anxiety without producing any clarity. But avoiding reflection on our mistakes because we are afraid of what we might see is likely to undermine self-trust in the end. It's hard to trust a person you don't know, and so unless you know yourself, your self-trust will be resting on a shaky foundation. In order to understand ourselves, we have to be able to expose our full selves to our own inner gaze. We must be willing to take a hard look in the mirror and face unpleasant truths about ourselves that we would rather ignore. In Emma's case, the hard truth that she has to face is that she does not know nearly as much about other people as she thinks she does and moreover, that she does not necessarily know what would make their lives go well. This means that she has to admit her own ignorance, something that most of us find quite painful.[16]

It can be even more painful to expose our full selves to the gaze of others. In one cringe-worthy scene toward the end of the novel, Emma behaves rather cruelly to her neighbor, Miss Bates. When Mr. Knightley calls her out on it, she is mortified and ashamed of herself. Like most people, Emma doesn't always react well to criticism in the moment, often getting defensive or dismissive. In this situation, however, she accepts his judgment as a fair assessment of her actions. She manages to avoid engaging in imaginative resistance to the idea that she has been cruel, even though she does not like to admit it. Taking up Knightley's perspective on herself is painful for Emma, but it also enables her to counter it by apologizing to Miss Bates and making amends. In this way, Emma's improved self-understanding empowers her.

This capacity to shift perspectives and see our situation from another point of view is a skill, one that requires cultivation.[17] Emma cultivates this skill over the course of the novel, primarily through her habit of reflection. Emma, of course, needs to correct her tendency to pay too little attention to what other people think. For many of us, the challenge in acquiring virtuous self-trust lies in learning to pay *less* attention to what other people think. We have to find a way to incorporate the perspectives of other people without letting those perspectives take over, swamping our own sense of who we are. It's easy to move too quickly from "this person thinks I am wrong" to "I am wrong," particularly if we are already inclined to doubt our own judgments. Reflection is useful in helping us figure out what to do with the opinions of other people. It puts us in a better position to assess the judgments that others are making about us and decide whether to take those judgments on board or reject them.

Reflection creates distance, something that we often need in order to be able to take in criticism and use it productively. In reflection, we can take a step back from our behavior and view it more openly and less defensively. Reflective distance makes it easier for us to assess the merits of what others have said, as well as their motivations for saying it. We are more able to tell the difference between an actual criticism and an offhand comment, or the difference between a snide remark and a helpful suggestion. Reflection helps us give proper weight to the judgment of people we trust and discount the judgment of people who don't know us or on whom we shouldn't depend. Reflection also helps us recognize and admit patterns in our own behavior that we might not otherwise see. What this means is that over time, the habit of reflection improves our ability to incorporate the perspectives of other people in our self-understanding effectively. We can combine their insights with our own in order to know ourselves better. And the better we know ourselves, the more we can trust ourselves.

5.6 Conclusion

Emma's path to self-knowledge is not always a smooth one, nor is it complete at the end of the novel. Like most of us, she has a long way to go before she truly knows herself. Perhaps she never will. But reflection enables her to see herself more clearly. She comes to recognize both the errors in her reasoning and the flaws in her character, as well as the relationship between them. This helps her cultivate the self-trust she needs to make good judgments and relate well to other people. In the end, her improved self-knowledge enables her to be more open to new possibilities and engage in better relationships. Sitting down to think does sometimes make Emma miserable, but the alternative would be worse. Even when it is painful to acquire, self-knowledge brings with it the kind of happiness that is worth having.[18]

Notes

1. Austen (1933, 134).
2. This temple was also the location of a famous oracle, where the high priestess of the temple (known as the Pythia) would make prophesies. If you are familiar with the Percy Jackson books, you may recall the character of Rachel, who served as an oracle. That is more or less how the oracle at Delphi was supposed to have worked.
3. Even if you have never read *Emma,* you may find that Emma resembles you or someone you know. And if you have seen the movie *Clueless,* you may notice parallels between Emma and Cher, the lead character played by Alicia Silverstone. *Clueless* is actually a deliberate and very clever adaptation of Austen's novel.
4. In referring to Emma by her first name and Mr. Elton by his full name, I am following Austen's own usage. She calls the characters what Emma would call them, which means that formal names are standardly used except among family and close friends around one's own age and social status. If the novel were written from Mr. Elton's perspective, Emma would be referred to as Miss Woodhouse.
5. Austen (1933, 134).
6. Emma had been warned about this by her sister's husband, who correctly read Mr. Elton's intentions and also feared that Emma was accidentally encouraging him. Alas, she paid no attention.
7. Gendler (2000).
8. Kruger and Dunning (1999).
9. Govier (1998, 91). In her discussion of self-trust, Govier draws on the work of psychologist Doris Brown.
10. Aristotle first discusses the mean in Book II, chapter 6 of his *Nicomachean Ethics* (1999).
11. This is a really serious and important issue, and I don't mean to minimize it. It is much more difficult for some people to cultivate self-trust than others, and the reasons for this are at least partly due to systemic oppression. If you want to read more on this, here are some ideas: Dotson (2011); Abramson (2014); Fricker (2007).
12. Govier (1998, 91).
13. Scylla and Charybdis are mythical hazards on opposite sides of a strait, described by Homer in the *Odyssey.* Scylla is a six-headed monster and Charybdis is a whirlpool. Odysseus and his crew had to get their ship through them without being caught by either.
14. Foot (2002, 8).
15. Taylor and Brown (1994).
16. Indeed, the citizens of Athens found it so painful to admit to their own ignorance that they executed Socrates for the crime of relentlessly pointing it out to them.
17. For more on the importance of being able to shift perspectives, see Tiberius (2005).
18. Kim Garchar and Melissa Shew provided helpful comments on this chapter. I am also grateful to my daughter, Julia Nonnenkamp, for her advice on it.

Bibliography

Abramson, Kate. 2014. "Turning Up the Lights on Gaslighting." *Philosophical Perspectives* 28, no. 1: 1–30.

Aristotle. 1999. *Nicomachean Ethics*. Indianapolis: Hackett.

Austen, Jane. 1933. *Emma. The Oxford Illustrated Jane Austen*. Edited by R. W. Chapman. Oxford: Oxford University Press.

Dotson, Kristie. 2011. "Tracking Epistemic Violence, Tracking Practices of Silencing." *Hypatia* 26, no. 2: 236–257.

Foot, Philippa. 2002. "Virtues and Vices." In *Virtues and Vices and Other Essays in Moral Philosophy*, 1–18. Oxford: Clarendon Press.

Fricker, Miranda. 2007. *Epistemic Injustice: Power and the Ethics of Knowing*. Oxford: Oxford University Press.

Gendler, Tamar Szabó. 2000. "The Puzzle of Imaginative Resistance." *Journal of Philosophy* 97, no. 2: 55–81.

Govier, Trudy. 1998. *Dilemmas of Trust*. Montreal: McGill-Queen's University Press.

Kruger, J., and D. Dunning. 1999. "Unskilled and Unaware of it: How Difficulties in Recognizing One's Own Incompetence Lead to Inflated Self-Assessments." *Journal of Personality and Social Psychology* 77, no. 6: 1121–1134.

Taylor, Shelley, and Jonathon Brown. 1994. "Positive Illusions and Well-Being Revisited: Separating Fact from Fiction." *Psychological Bulletin* 116, no. 1: 21–27.

Tiberius, Valerie. 2005. "Wisdom and Perspective." *Journal of Philosophy* 52, no. 4 (April): 163–182.

SECTION II
KNOWING

6

Logic

A Feminist Approach

Gillian Russell

When a child clings on to a highly desirable toy and claims that his companion "doesn't want to play with it" I have found that it is wise to be suspicious.

—*Delusions of Gender*, Cordelia Fine

I read *A Wizard of Earthsea* several times as a teenager. The cover of my battered paperback—which used to belong to a local library and had "30p" written on it in black crayon—showed the wizard, Ged, half-transformed into a sparrowhawk, wings spread, green leggings on his still-human lower half. Years later I rediscovered the author, Ursula Le Guin, and learned that my novel was only the first in her Earthsea Cycle. I also learned some political background: Ged was dark-skinned and Le Guin had clashed with publishers who preferred the cover art to depict him as white. The image from my childhood had been a sordid compromise: a sparrowhawk isn't white, but the cover avoids showing that—in his own form—the hero isn't white either. More politics: I read Le Guin's essay "Introducing Myself" (now my favorite of her writings) and the rest of the Earthsea series, only to learn that the fantasy world of my youth was rancid with magic-infused misogyny: "*Weak as a woman's magic, wicked as a woman's magic,* she had heard said a hundred times. And indeed she had seen that the witchery of such women as Moss or Ivy was often weak in sense and sometimes wicked in intent or through ignorance. Village witches, though they might know many spells and charms and some of the great songs, were never trained in the High Arts or the principles of magery. No woman was so trained.

Gillian Russell, *Logic* In: *Philosophy for Girls*. Edited by: Melissa M. Shew and Kimberly K. Garchar, Oxford University Press (2020). © Oxford University Press. DOI: 10.1093/oso/9780190072919.003.0007.

Wizardry was a man's work, a man's skill; magic was made by men. There had never been a woman mage." Gender and the way it combined with magic in Earthsea made me feel queasy, and part of it was that the facts were unclear. Were women truly unable to do magic? Could they do it if they were properly trained, say at the School on Roke? (I felt anxious just thinking about the possibility that this might not be so.) Perhaps the women of Earthsea can have a *different* magic "Healing befits a woman. It comes natural to her." But then, is that real magic? As powerful, and as good?

The central question of this chapter is: *Is there any such thing as feminist logic?* I don't mean the question the way an internet troll might: "Bro, do feminists even *use* logic?" Rather I mean: Is there a legitimate and distinctive subject matter—feminist logic?[1]

On the one hand, there is logic: the technical, mathematical part of philosophy that studies argument structure, and in particular the structural features that make an argument truth-preserving. On the other, there is feminism, the ethical and political movement for gender equality, according to which a person's status, power, and options in life shouldn't be determined by gender.[2] But sometimes people speak as if there is a special part of logic—feminist logic—the way there is a special part of, for example, chemistry, *organic* chemistry. And my question is: What would that even be?

One possible view of the matter is that feminism doesn't have much to offer logic much as one might think it doesn't have much to offer geometry, or aeronautics. The result would be that there is no subdiscipline of logic worthy of the name *feminist logic*. Some philosophers have taken other positions: Andrea Nye thinks that logic and feminism conflict, and that there is no feminist logic because logic is *anti*-feminist; Val Plumwood argues that feminist logic is logic of a particular kind—*relevance* logic; others still, such as Susan Stebbing, have seen feminism as just one among many *applications* of logic. It's against this background of debate and disagreement that I will ask (and answer) my question here.

I'll start in the next section by getting clearer about what logic is. Then I survey four different views about what feminist logic is. I argue that we should reject views 1, 2 and 3, and that the fourth is correct. Then in last section I suggest that feminist logic could be *more* than this and my conclusion outlines a more ambitious vision for the future.

6.1 Logic

The subject matter of logic is good and bad arguments. Here's an argument:

(1)

P1	If Hera is human, then Hera is mortal.
P2	Hera is not mortal.
C	Hera is not human.

We have an initial conditional sentence—*if* Hera is human *then* Hera is mortal—and then a second sentence which denies the "then" part—Hera is *not* mortal—and finally a conclusion that is drawn from the first two sentences—Hera is *not* human.

It's useful to have some terminology for talking about arguments. We'll call the sentences which provide support for the conclusion—in our example P1 and P2—and from which the conclusion is supposed to be drawn, the *premises*. In a conditional like P1, we call the sentence that comes after the "if" the *antecedent*, and the sentence that comes after the "then" the *consequent*. Here are two slightly different arguments:

(2)

If Xanthippe is a woman, then Xanthippe is immortal.
Xanthippe is not immortal.

Xanthippe is not a woman.

(3)

If Xanthippe is a woman, then Xanthippe is immortal.
Xanthppe is not a woman.

Xanthippe is not immortal.

Logicians study the features that make arguments good. If you study the arguments here, you'll probably conclude that (1) is pretty good, but that (2) and (3) exhibit different errors; each is good in one way, but bad in another. What are these ways?

Two key properties of arguments are *validity* and *soundness*. An argument is *valid* if the truth of the premises *guarantees the truth* of the conclusion. Take argument 1. Suppose that all the premises are true, that is, that if Hera is human then she is mortal, and that Hera is not mortal. Well then, of course, given both those things, Hera is not human. The truth of the conclusion *follows from* the truth of the premises—that is what we mean by *guaranteeing* the truth of the conclusion.[3]

Contrast that with (3). Even if the premises of (3) are true, the conclusion *could* be false, since Xanthippe could be an immortal man. Since there is a way for the premises to be true without the conclusion being true, the argument is *invalid*. We call a (possibly imaginary) situation in which the premises are true but the conclusion is not, a *counterexample* to the argument. Counterexamples show that the argument is not valid by showing that the truth of the premises doesn't guarantee the truth of the conclusion.

The flaw in argument (2) is different. (2) *is* valid: *if* the premises were both true, then the conclusion would have to be too. The problem—of course—is that one of 2's premises—P1—is not true. That doesn't mean that the argument is invalid. Instead, it means that the argument isn't *sound*. An argument is *sound* if and only if i) it is valid and ii) all the premises are true. Since (2) satisfies i) but not ii) it is valid but not sound.

Arguments (1) and (2)—the two valid arguments—both have the same overall form: P1 is a conditional, P2 negates the consequent, and the conclusion is the negation of the antecedent. When we say that an argument is *logically* valid, we are saying that its form is such that any argument with that form will be valid. (This is one of the reasons logic is often called "formal logic.") We can emphasize the form, rather than the content of specific parts, by replacing parts with letters, like this:

> If P, then Q.
> Not-Q.
> _____
> Not-P.

Whether or not an argument is valid often turns on some quite subtle questions about what the words in the argument mean and there are some difficult issues about the meaning of the English words "if" and "not." For clarity, logicians often work in an artificial language in which the meanings have been stipulated. The conditional is often expressed with this symbol: "→" and negation with this one "~" and we can use these symbols to give the form of our valid arguments (on the left in the following table). The invalid argument—(3)—has a different form (on the right):

$$P \rightarrow Q$$
$$\sim Q$$
$$\overline{}$$
$$\sim P$$

$$P \rightarrow Q$$
$$\sim P$$
$$\overline{}$$
$$\sim Q$$

We stipulate "meanings" for our symbols "$\rightarrow$" and "$\sim$" by explaining how the truth-value of an expression containing one depends on the truth-values of its parts. For example, if P is true, then $\sim P$ is false. And if P is false, then $\sim P$ is true. We can represent this in a *truth-table*:

P	$\sim P$
T	F
F	T

We will also stipulate a table of this kind for "$\rightarrow$." Since "$\rightarrow$" takes two sentences as components, this time we will need to stipulate its truth-value for *four* different possible situations: both components true, one true the other false, the reverse of that, and then both sentences false.

P	Q	$P \rightarrow Q$
T	T	T
T	F	F
F	T	T
F	F	T

We can also use a truth-table to give a proof that *any* argument of the form of (1) and (2) will be valid. In the following table the two columns on the left represent the different ways things could turn out, and the columns under the premises and conclusion represent the resulting truth-values of the three sentences in the argument:

		P1	P2	C
P	Q	$P \rightarrow Q$	~Q	~P
T	T	T	F	F
T	F	F	T	F
F	T	T	F	T
F	F	T	T	T

Note that on every row on which both the premises are true (that's just row 4, in this case) the conclusion is true too. So the argument form is valid.

We can use the same technique to show that the argument form used in (3) is not valid:

		P1	P2	C
P	Q	$P \rightarrow Q$	~P	~Q
T	T	T	F	F
T	F	F	F	T
F	T	T	T	F
F	F	T	T	T

This time there is a row, the third one, in which both premises are true but the conclusion is false. So the truth of the premises *doesn't* guarantee the truth of the conclusion and the truth table shows that this argument is not valid.

We can now state more succinctly what logic is: logic is the study of argument validity in virtue of form. Imagine all the arguments there are (infinitely many of them), laid out before you. The job of the logician is to divide them into two groups: the ones which have forms which make them valid and the ones which do not.

6.2 Four Views on Feminist Logic

Given that this is what logic is, let's return to our question: Is there any such thing as *feminist* logic? Here are four possible views.

6.2.1 View 1: There's No Such Thing as Feminist Logic (Version 1.0)

View 1 is that feminism and logic are each legitimate disciplines, but their subject matters don't overlap, and so there is no subject matter for feminist logic to be about. We might call this the *nonoverlapping magisteria* view; the name is a bit of a joke, borrowed from Stephen Jay Gould's name for his view of the relationship between religion and science, on which "the lack of conflict between science and religion arises from a lack of overlap between their respective domains of professional expertise" (Gould 2001, 739). The analogous position for feminism and logic is that they involve theorizing about different things—gender inequality and argument validity—and since these topics don't overlap, feminism and logic shouldn't overlap either—so there is no feminist logic.

For someone who holds this view, a call for "feminist logic" might seem like a regrettable kind of ethical encroachment—a tendency for our ethical commitments to encroach into areas where they don't help very much—such as science or logic.[4]

This first view is a tempting one, but an important thing to note is that the argument from nonoverlapping domains is not valid (meaning, of course, that even if the premise is true, the conclusion doesn't follow from that premise). Even in the most literal cases of nonoverlap—where we contrast, say, rural studies and urban studies—there can be fruitful work to be done at the intersection; a syllabus on urban studies could legitimately include a section on the reasons people move from rural to urban areas. In other cases the question of overlap is less clearcut. Do botany and geometry overlap? I'm not sure. It would depend on how we precisified "overlap." Still, the fact that two subjects could reasonably be said to be about different things—plants and space—doesn't show that there is no sense in studying them together. Plant geometry is a nontrivial and interesting subject.

6.2.2 View 2: There's No Such Thing as Feminist Logic (Version 2.0)

There is a different reason some people have rejected the idea of feminist logic. Some writers have argued that feminists should reject logic completely because they think logic *harms* the fight for gender equality—that is, logic is *anti*-feminist. Professor Andrea Nye argues that logic (and abstract and mathematical methods more generally) are tools that men developed to exclude women. Here's a representative quote:[5]

> Desperate, lonely, cut off from the human community which in many cases has ceased to exist, under the sentence of violent death, wracked by desires for intimacy that they do not know how to fulfill, at the same time tormented by the presence of women, men turn to logic. (Nye 1990, 175)

Nye declines, in keeping with her thesis, to give a valid argument for her view, since on her view the demand for such an argument is a fake test designed to exclude her voice. What her book does do is tell a kind of *just-so* story about the origins of logic, designed to cast doubt on its use as a tool to discover truth, and suggest that its real purpose is to exclude women.

To someone who teaches logic—someone like me—this is a troubling charge. The thought that I find most unsettling is this: wherever we have unjust hierarchical systems that elevate one group above another—white above black, men above women, in-group above out-group—there is a temptation for people from the lower group to curry favor with the powerful by furthering their agenda: subordinating the less powerful for them and helping them feel comfortable about it. If logic is a tool of gender oppression, then the teaching of it is actively *anti*-feminist. It's like being the character of Aunt Julia in *The Handmaid's Tale*—getting on in the patriarchal system by helping to implement and enforce an oppressive system. To the masters, you are an especially helpful person from the subordinate class: you make them feel better about themselves, never suggest their position is unearned, and take certain unsavory and morally compromising tasks out of their hands. To yourself, it might seem as if you are just succeeding as well as you can in the system you were born into.[6] But what are you to the women whom you help to keep in line? And what are you from the perspective of genuine justice, where we recognize that the entire hierarchy is unjust and unearned, and that status within it depends on irrelevant features, such as gender or race? You are actively promoting oppression with your attempt to "win" in the oppressive system. I hope you understand then, that I find Nye's accusation very worrying.

The worry depends though, on Nye's thesis that that logic is a tool for excluding women. Because suppose it isn't. Suppose rather that knowledge and understanding of logic is like knowledge or understanding of mechanics, arithmetic, bookkeeping, history, cooking, farming, or medicine: things that—at least in normal circumstances—are empowering to someone who possesses them. Just as the powerful will appreciate those who help them maintain their position, so they have sometimes suppressed the teaching of skills that might empower the subordinated. Many US slave states, for example, enacted anti-literacy laws, making it illegal to teach slaves to read and write. Teaching reading and writing was a subversive act which worked *against* the unjust hierarchy. Everything depends then, on whether logic is itself a tool for excluding women, or whether it only excluded women because it was a useful tool they weren't offered access to.

It is a bit difficult to know how to engage with Nye's work, given that she (presumably) doesn't want to hear that we haven't been given a logical argument for her view (she won't care) and doesn't want a logical argument for the negation of her view. Perhaps she might listen to a debunking explanation of the origin of her own view: a kind of just-so history of how it came about, that threatens its legitimacy.

My suspicion about Nye's view is that it has its source in *gender symbolism*, rather than in anything about the nature of logic or gender itself. Gender symbolism (here is Professor Elizabeth Anderson's definition) "occurs when we represent nonhuman or inanimate phenomena as "masculine" or "feminine" and model them after gender ideals or stereotypes" (Anderson 1995, 57). Gender symbolism is ubiquitous. To see what I mean, try coming up with a list of ten foods and drinks, or animals, or musical instruments, academic disciplines or hobbies or toys or colors. Suppose people were asked to divide the things on your list into two groups, headed "masculine" and "feminine"—could you predict how they would do it? How would rosé be categorized? Cheap beer? Cheap white wine? What about about a bottle of very, very expensive red wine? For some items we might feel unsure or need to guess, but when I do this I am stunned by how many nonhuman things are clearly associated with one gender or the other, even when the things have no gender of their own (drums vs. harps, rosé vs. bourbon) or even contrary to their own gender (as the joke on the internet goes: all dogs are boys, all cats are girls). Marketers and advertisers sometimes seem to want to exacerbate this situation, by gendering *everything* as a means for selling it. Thus we get masculine and feminine razors and cocktail kits and pink guns and dumbbells and jeeps and "mansize" tissues and toothpaste "for men."[7]

Academic disciplines and methods of inquiry are not immune from gender symbolism. Mathematics, physics, classics, and philosophy are all traditionally masculine, as are logic, rationality, and reason. Literature, women's studies, art history, and intuition can all be seen as feminine in this context, though the picture is complicated by the fact that the subdivisions tend to repeat themselves within disciplines, with some subdisciplines being considered more masculine and some feminine. So—within philosophy— logic, philosophy of science, and metaphysics are all gendered masculine, whereas ethics and value theory are feminine. And then again within ethics, metaethics is gendered masculine, and normative and applied ethics as feminine.

Here, then, is what I think explains some feminists' inclinations to disavow logic: logic has traditionally been gendered masculine. Feminists want to resist the elevation of all things masculine and the accompanying deprecation of all things feminine. One way to do this is to reject the over-valuation of the masculine and value feminine things. In this spirit, we criticize the masculine things, and praise the feminine. In this particular case the result is this: logic sucks, alternative approaches rule.

As I see it, that's plausibly the source of the view, but now there are two problems with it: the first is that logic doesn't suck. (Just as reading and writing don't suck, even if these *were* used to exclude the oppressed.) And the second is that logic isn't *really* gendered; that's just more gender symbolism at work. What I think we feminists ought to do is not reject logic but reject the premise that logic is masculine. That removes the need to devalue it on feminist grounds, and opens up the possibility of reclaiming it.

6.2.3 View 3: Feminism Should *Reform* Logic

Feminist logicians have, unsurprisingly, rejected Nye's view.[8] Val Plumwood (1939–2008) was an Australian logician who also went on to become famous for her work in eco-feminism.[9] She thinks that Nye's argument proves too much:

> The area of intellectual activity potentially destroyed by such a program to eliminate abstraction and anything which departs from "normal" language begins to look alarmingly large—not only mathematics . . . and large areas of science, but "computer programming, statistics, economic models . . ." [54, p.181] and no doubt a great deal more we might not want to lose. Such

total rejection of abstraction would involve a program highly restrictive of thought. (Plumwood 1993, 439)

In short: logic and other abstract disciplines are too valuable to cede to nonfeminists. Plumwood does not think that logic should be rejected, but instead that gender bias has led to our adopting a mistaken theory of validity—so-called classical logic—and that we ought to adopt a different theory—relevant logic—instead. Essentially, she thinks that gender bias has led to logicians drawing the line between valid and invalid arguments in the wrong place. She is particularly critical of classical negation, which is the negation expressed by the ~-symbol we looked at in section 6.1.[10]

The structure of negation given by classical propositional logic—the dominant formal logical theory of our time—in particular has been privileged and selected over rivals on account of features which also make it appropriate to describe it as a logic of domination, features giving an account of the other in dualistic terms which naturalise their subordination. (Plumwood 1993, 441)

So *why* is classical logic the logic of domination? A key idea in Plumwood's work is that of a *dualism*. Dualisms are hierarchical distinctions—pairs of expressions such that the things one expression applies to are supposed to be superior to the things the other applies to—which exhibit a list of ethically pernicious properties:

1. **backgrounding**—the inferior side is characterized as *inessential* (even if the other side needs it)
2. **hyperseparation**—the distinctions between the sides are exaggerated, borderline cases suppressed, and features of both sides are regarded as a matter of their essential natures, even when alternative explanations are available
3. **relational identity**—one side is defined *in terms* of the other
4. **instrumentalization**—the values of the superior side dominate; their interests are taken as ends in themselves. The inferior side is assessed in terms of virtues that make them useful to the superior side
5. **homogenization**—both sides, especially the inferior, are treated as "all the same"

Plumwood's examples of dualisms include *master/slave, man/nature, reason/emotion*, and *masculine/feminine*. A protestor might claim that each is a mere distinction, selecting two classes from among the things in the world—the masters and the slaves, or the colonizers and the colonizing—but I think that if you have any sensitivity to human social relations, you can come to see some of the features of dualisms in our cultural treatment of the *masculine/feminine* distinction.[11]

Take, for example, the way that middle and working class men have traditionally been expected to work outside the home for money, while women have been expected to do the work of housekeeping and childrearing. Men's work was regarded as "real" work, necessary to support the family, whilst housekeeping was regarded as less important and unpaid. The women tended to be regarded as dependent on the men. In truth, of course the men were also dependent on the women: you can't go outside the house to work unless you have someone to take care of your home and children. This is an example of *backgrounding*.

Or take homogenization: in the first panel of a famous XKCD cartoon entitled "How it works," an onlooker watches a male stick-figure do a calculation on a chalkboard and says "Wow, you suck at math." In the second panel, the onlooker watches a female stick-figure do a calculation on the chalkboard and this time says "Wow, girls suck at math."

Or instrumentalization: the twitter feed @Manwhohasitall takes sexist, media-style quotes and inverts the gender terms, often with ridiculous results, such as this example of (reversed) instrumentalization: "Men! Just a little reminder to smile today, because women like positive men" or "To all intelligent men. Don't be AFRAID of your intelligence! It's OK to be a man and be intelligent. Some women actually find it attractive."

Plumwood argues that the *masculine/feminine* distinction is a dualism. Her further argument against classical logic then turns on the claim that "classical logic is the closest approximation to the dualistic structure I have outlined" (Plumwood 1993, 454). She thinks that classical logic was embraced by those in power *because* it supports dualisms—and hence the subordination of women. The key premise in Plumwood's argument then, is that classical logic has these relationships to dualisms, and it seems to me that the main problem with her argument is that it is not clear that this key premise is true. Here, for example, is what she says about classical negation:

In classical logic, negation, (~ p), is interpreted as the universe without p, everything in the universe other than what p covers, as represented in the usual Venn diagram representing p as a figure surrounded by a square which represents the universe, with ~ p as the difference. . . . what is important for the issue we are considering here is that ~ p can then not be independently or positively identified, but is entirely dependent on p for its specification. Not-p has no independent role, but is introduced as merely alien to the primary notion p. (Plumwood 1993, 454)

Plumwood is explicit that she is talking about "propositional" logic (454), meaning that p is a sentence, and ~ p the negation of that sentence. Still, her talk of Venn diagrams suggests that she might also be thinking of P as a predicate (I'll use the capital letter to mark the difference) and of the set of things to which P applies. So if the box in Figure 6.1 represents all the numbers, then the circle represents the set of numbers which "are P" (perhaps "P" is the predicate "is an even number" and the complement of that set (relative to the box) the set of things which are "not-P" (the odd numbers).

Now if you squint at the diagram a bit, you might be able to imagine that the things in the castle of the P-circle are privileged and "superior" to the homogeneous "other," roaming around outside in the cold of ~ P. But the problem is that all this would be an imaginative addition—none of that dualistic baggage is there in the classical account of negation. As evidence, I offer a counterexample: if we use P to pick out the even numbers and ~ P to pick out the ones that are not even, we still have a mere distinction between two kinds of numbers—the distinction doesn't become a dualism just because we used classical negation. In fact (adding to the diagram and throwing our imaginations into a different gear), we might use Q to pick out the set of things that are wandering around the universe at liberty, and ~ Q for the things that are locked away in the set-jail with the

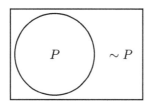

Figure 6.1 Classical negation
Source: author.

"*Ps*" and that too would be an addition compatible with what was already there. There is a *structural* feature in common between dualisms and mere distinctions, because dualisms are special kinds of distinctions—but not all $P/\sim P$ distinctions are dualisms. Dualisms add a hierarchy and the features in Plumwood's list. It doesn't follow that those features were *already* there in the $P/\sim P$ distinction.

There is something right though, in Plumwood's final point: "$\sim p$ can then not be independently or positively identified, but is entirely dependent on p for its specification. Not-p has no independent role, but is introduced as merely alien to the primary notion p" (454). The problem is that this claim is ambiguous between one that is right, but anodyne, and one that would be problematic if it were right, but which is clearly wrong—and the appeal of her point trades on this confusion. On one disambiguation she means that "$\sim P$" contains "P," so that we need the latter in order to express the former. This is true, but it is not distinctive of classical negation or logic. The same holds for any complex expression—including connectives in Plumwood's preferred relevant logic—since the meanings of complex expressions depend on the meanings of their parts. So if this is the reading she intended, it is true, but it won't give us an argument against classical and in favor of relevant logic. On the other disambiguation, Plumwood means that we can't define the class of things that "are $\sim P$" without starting with the class of things that "are P." But this isn't true. We could interpret another primitive predicate—Q—as having the extension of $\sim P$, and this would then give us a way to give the extension of P using Q: $\sim Q$. What we can do for one set we can do for the other, and hence, there is no hierarchy built into classical negation. $P/\sim P$ is a mere distinction, and so we have seen no sound argument that feminist logic should reject classical negation.

6.2.4 View 4: Feminist Logic Is Logic for Feminist Ends

The final view I will consider is that feminist logic is a useful tool in the struggle for gender equality; feminist logic is just ordinary logic, applied to feminist ends. One philosopher who exemplifies this view is Susan Stebbing (1885–1943). Stebbing was a logician and the first woman to hold a chair in philosophy in the United Kingdom. Her 1939 book, *Thinking to Some Purpose*, encourages the use of logic in politics and public life:

There is an urgent need to-day for the citizens of a democracy to think well. It is not enough to have freedom of the Press and parliamentary institutions. Our difficulties are due partly to our own stupidity, partly to the exploitation of that stupidity, and partly to our own prejudices and personal desires. (Stebbing 1939)

Stebbing doesn't use the word *feminism* explicitly, but her book contains two rebukes of eminent men regarding their treatment of women. The first is a response to the logician and philosopher, Bertrand Russell. Stebbing quotes from his book, *The Conquest of Happiness*:

If you are sitting in the Underground and a well-dressed women happens to walk along the car, watch the eyes of the other women. You will see that every one of them, with the possible exception of those who are even better dressed, will watch the woman with malevolent glances, and will be struggling to draw inferences derogatory to her. (Stebbing 1939, 100)

We might be struck by the speed and ease with which Russell singles out women to be the subjects of unflattering attitudes and preferences, as well as the conspicuous homogeneity he attributes to the gender (his remark bears comparison with the XKCD cartoon I mentioned in section 6.2.3). Stebbing questions both the truth of the premise that women on the Underground will watch the woman with malevolence ("So far as my experience goes, this does not seem to me to be true" (100)) and then she points out that the inferential move to the overly general (even with Russell's qualification) conclusion is not valid.

However that many be, it does not justify the inference that whenever you see a well-dressed woman enter a car on the Underground you will see *every* one of the less well-dressed women turn malevolent glances at her.[12]

Stebbing's second logic-based critique of anti-feminist rhetoric targets a passage concocted *by her* to exhibit standard fallacies in arguing against allowing women to vote.

The argument has been "made up" by me in much the way in which a patchwork quilt is made by concocting together various pieces brought together from different sources. . . . every argument that appears in this "speech" has been used by someone or other in the course of the prolonged controversy concerning Women's Suffrage. (Stebbing 1939, 156)

Here is a quote from the middle of the speech:

> Here Sir Frederick Smith put his finger on the true answer. Women have not the capacity of men. Women are women and men are men whatever be their class or rank or country. It is a shameful thing that women should attempt to usurp the powers and perform the duties entrusted by Nature to men and to men alone. Let them content themselves with the noble work some of them are performing so well of influencing their men to judge concerning the gravest political questions of the day. (Stebbing 1939, 156)

Stebbing notes three errors.

1. The second sentence makes a claim that is irrelevant to the question of whether women should vote, though it is probably especially effective because it is a tautology, and hence implies that the suffragists have denied an obvious truth: "The hearers are intended to get the impression that the speaker's opponents are contesting the indisputable fact that women are not men" (Stebbing 1939, 158).
2. The third sentence is a straightforward assertion of personal opinion, but we might add (though Stebbing does not) that even were it true it would have no bearing on the issue at hand unless we also claimed that *voting* was the natural power and duty of men alone. Without that, nothing follows logically about whether women should vote.
3. The final sentence is inconsistent with the first: it suggests that women are competent to make judgments on political matters (and then influence their men to vote wisely) while the first suggests that women shouldn't vote because they are not competent to make judgments on political matters.

I think Stebbing is right that logic can help critique and expose gender bias, but also that not every problem in these passages is a *logical* problem. Stebbing's targets employ a variety of rhetorical tools: in addition to "loud talk" there is the strategy of attributing too strong a view to an opponent and then simply joking about how ridiculous it is, as well as that of tacitly conveying (for example, through clearly presupposing) something that would be acknowledged as problematic were it said explicitly. Though logic is a useful weapon against some anti-feminist polemics, it is just a small part of what we need for an effective critique.

Still, here we do have an answer to our question: Is there any such thing as feminist logic? That answer is: yes: feminist logic is logic used for feminist ends, as a tool for exposing and confronting bias in arguments, and for formulating and defending arguments for gender equality.

6.3 What Feminist Logic Could Be

Can logic do better? On Stebbing's view, feminist logic would be applied logic and feminism one application among many. There would be conservative logic, and environmental logic, and even evil logic—logic for promoting evil ends! But for all we've said so far, these applications don't feed back to teach us anything new *about logic.*

But I think perhaps feminist logic could be more than this. Suppose we wanted to use logic to study social hierarchies, like the patriarchy, but including other dualisms and rankings of groups based on gender, race, class, age, ability, sexual orientation, and so on. We've already noted that classical logic does not incorporate such hierarchies through the very use of classical negation. But what if we were to try to add some hierarchical distinctions to classical logic *on purpose*, with the aim of better understanding and exposing them to scrutiny?

Looking at the history of logic, it seems well-suited to studying hierarchies. In mathematical logic we study the hierarchy of numbers, ranked by the < (less than) relation. A standard approach is to add some new primitive symbols, which may be treated as logical symbols (e.g., "=" and "∈") or—more usually with <—as non–logical symbols which are expected to have a certain interpretation. Another place hierarchies are found in logic is in Lewis's work on counterfactuals. Here we have sets of possible worlds which are ranked based on their similarity to the actual world. This has numerous applications, including giving truth-conditions for counterfactuals, identifying fallacies, and explaining the pragmatics of assertions. Unlike in the arithmetical case, Lewis doesn't proceed by adding a ranking expression to the formal language, but rather by adding ranking-structures to models and investigating the results—including the opportunities for adding expressions whose truth-conditions make use of the hierarchy.

Both the mathematical and counterfactual cases are in one sense *applications* of logic, but I think they can also with justice be regarded as work which contributes to our scientific understanding of logical consequence—and hence to logic itself. In one case we learn for example that the relation of first-order consequence on the language of arithmetic does not include every argument that takes axioms (of a certain sort) as premises and has an arithmetical truth as a conclusion. In the other we learn that arguments which might have been thought to be valid are not (e.g., Lewis's fallacies of strengthening, transitivity, and contraposition) and also that the new models can be used to give truth-conditions for interesting expressions.

Social hierarchies too, could be studied in logic. I gave *two* examples because I don't want to limit us to a particular approach here: we will have to see what works out. But preliminary attempts might start as analogues to either approach. One might—following Lewis—add to a first-order model a pair of nested sets—intuitively the smaller is the set of men and the difference between the smaller and the larger the set of women. And then we could look for hierarchy-sensitive expressions. Social hierarchies also have important interactions with permissibility and obligation (McGowan 2019) and with power, for example, with necessity and possibility. Given this, the interaction of a social hierarchy with modal and deontic logics looks especially interesting.

There is much work to be done here, and this suggestion presents feminist logic more as a subject matter for future study (perhaps your future?) than as a completed body of theory. But let me finish by noting that we now have an answer to the question with which I began: Is there any such thing as feminist logic? That answer is, yes. Feminist logic is both i) logic used to feminist ends and ii) that part of logic that studies (gender-based) social hierarchies and their influence on logical consequence.

Notes

1. This chapter was inspired by, and is modeled on, Elizabeth Anderson's paper "Feminist Epistemology" (Anderson 1995).
2. Question: Why call it "feminism" then, instead of "gender equality"? Answer: I *do* call it "gender equality," but it also gets called "feminism" because historically it's women who have been most obviously disadvantaged by sexism, so that in practice advocating for gender equality has often meant advocating for women. But it should

involve advocating for people of other genders—including men—where their gender has led to systematic, unjust disadvantage.

3. Sometimes you'll hear different terminology and it can help to know that the following are rough synonyms: the argument is *valid*, the premises *entail* the conclusion, the conclusion is a *consequence* of the premises, the conclusion *follows* from the premises.

4. It's not clear that such seemings are generally trustworthy—people who are being criticized on ethical grounds tend to feel as if this is ethics encroaching where it doesn't belong (business, war, private life and personal relationships, religion, finance, etc.). But it isn't clear they are right.

5. Nye also mentions other feminists who have rejected logic: "Logic, one current argument goes, is the creation of defensive male subjects who have lost touch with their lived experience and define all being in rigid oppositional categories modeled on a primal contrast between male and female. Or another: logic articulates oppressive thought structures that channel human behavior into restrictive gender roles. Or: logic celebrates the unity of a pathological masculine self-identity that cannot listen and recognizes only negation and not difference" (Nye 1990, 5).

6. As Anne Helen Peterson's memorable Buzzfeed article on Millennials put it, "We didn't try to fix the system, because that's not how we were raised. We tried to win it" (Petersen 2019).

7. There's a group called "Let Toys be Toys," which discourages separating toys into "boys" and "girls" toys and encourages simply letting toys be things for *children* to play with—whatever their gender—whether they are pink or blue, guns or dolls, trucks or tea sets. I'm inclined to think we might start a parallel group called "Let Things be Things," which would discourage separating *everything* into masculine and feminine and encourage, e.g., thinking of logic and literature as just things that *people* might chose to study, and sci-fi and romance, and action films and rom-coms and whiskey and rosé and guns and salad as things that *people* might choose (or choose not) to consume.

8. Plumwood (1993); Weiner (1994).

9. Fun fact 1: Plumwood was attacked by a crocodile in 1985 and wrote a striking article "Being Prey" about the experience.

10. Fun fact 2: Val Plumwood coauthored under her previous name "Routley" with her husband and fellow logician Richard Routley (née Sylvan), and the pair invented a special kind of semantic mechanism for relevant negation, which is sometimes called the *Routley Star* (Routley and Routley 1972)—though perhaps since it was a joint invention we should really call it the *Routley-Routley Star*.

11. To mark the contrast with mere distinctions, I will sometimes refer to dualisms as "pernicious dualisms." So, *odd number/even number* is a mere distinction, but *master/slave* is a pernicious dualism. *Odd number/even number*—and perhaps any distinction—has the potential to develop into a dualism. Perhaps if a teacher assigned each student a number and began to treat students differently depending on whether they were assigned odd or even numbers, the distinction could begin to acquire some of the baggage. The widespread prevalence of gender symbolism is something that might well contribute to the "dualification" of "mere" distinctions.

12. Stebbing generously suggests that Russell is employing "loud speaking" (hyperbole) as a rhetorical device and that he often does this in work intended for public consumption (Stebbing 1939, 100–101).

Bibliography

Anderson, Elizabeth. 1995. "Feminist Epistemology: An Interpretation and a Defence." *Hypatia* 10, no. 3 (August): 50–84.

Gould, Stephen Jay. 2001. "Nonoverlapping Magisteria." In *Intelligent Design Creationism and Its Critics*, edited by Robert T. Pennock, 737–749. Cambridge, MA: MIT Press.

McGowan, Mary Kate. 2019. *Just Words: On Speech and Hidden Harm*. Oxford: Oxford University Press.

Nye, Andrea. 1990. *Words of Power: A Feminist Reading of the History of Logic*. London: Routledge.

Petersen, Anne Helen. 2019. "How Millennials Became the Burnout Generation." *Buzzfeed*, January 5, https://www.buzzfeednews.com/article/annehelenpetersen/millennials-burnout-generation-debt-work.

Plumwood, Val. 1993. "The Politics of Reason: Towards a Feminist Logic." *Australasian Journal of Philosophy* 71, no. 4: 436–462.

Routley, Richard, and Val Routley. 1972. "Semantics for First Degree Entailment." *Nous* 6, no. 4: 335–359.

Stebbing, Susan. 1939. *Thinking to Some Purpose*. Harmondsworth: Penguin Books.

Weiner, Joan. 1994. "*Words of Power. A Feminist Reading of the History of Logic* by Andrea Nye (review)." *Journal of Symbolic Logic* 59, no. 2 (June): 678–681.

7

Doubt

Knowing and Skepticism

Julianne Chung

Ghost World, a 2001 film, follows Enid, a young woman who has just gradu-
ated from high school (or is close to doing so, as she must retake an art class
over the summer in order to *officially* graduate). Throughout the film, while
it is fairly clear that Enid feels far surer of what she doesn't want to be like
than what she does, it is equally clear that she isn't close to entirely sure about
even that. As with anyone in her position, much of Enid's life is fraught with
uncertainty, doubt, and anxiety.

Another important character in the film—at least for the purposes of our
explorations regarding doubt, knowing, and skepticism—is Norman. We
first meet him while he is seated on a bench onto which "NO SERVICE" has
been stenciled. Enid and her best friend Rebecca discuss him as they approach on foot:

REBECCA: Oh, look, there he is . . .
ENID: As always.
REBECCA: Waiting for the bus that never comes . . .
ENID: I wonder if he's just totally insane, or he really thinks the bus is
    coming . . .
REBECCA: Why don't you just ask him?
ENID LEANS OVER THE BENCH AND GREETS NORMAN:
ENID: Hi . . . what's your name?
NORMAN (LOOKS AT HIS WATCH-LESS WRIST, THEN DOWN THE STREET):
    Norman.
ENID: . . . are you waiting for a bus?
NORMAN: Yes.
ENID: I hate to tell you this but they cancelled this bus line two years ago.
    There are no more busses on this street.

Julianne Chung, *Doubt* In: *Philosophy for Girls*. Edited by: Melissa M. Shew and Kimberly K. Garchar, Oxford University
Press (2020). © Oxford University Press. DOI: 10.1093/oso/9780190072919.003.0008.

NORMAN: You don't know what you're talking about.

Another encounter with Norman comes later, while Enid is walking home alone and sits down next to him on the bench:

ENID: Hi.
NORMAN: Hello.
ENID: Do you remember me?
NORMAN: Sure. Sure.
ENID: You know, you're, like, the only person in this world that I can count on, because no matter what, I know you'll always be here.
NORMAN (KINDLY): Well, that's what you think. I'm leaving town.

Enid doesn't believe him. Thus, she's visibly surprised when what seems impossible to her happens: a bus pulls up in front of Norman's bench, stops to let him climb on, and drives away. She was wrong. She didn't know that a bus wouldn't come, or that Norman would always be there. Soon after that, we see Enid approaching the bench by herself, suitcase in hand. After some time, a bus arrives once again, picks her up, and drives her alone into the distance.

7.1 Uncertainty, Doubt, and Anxiety

Many of us can relate to Enid. Doubt is experienced by people of all ages, and often produces anxiety.[1] The precise sources and targets of anxiety often change over the course of a person's lifetime, but there's so much that's uncertain and unknown in life—and therefore so much to potentially worry about. Doubt can consequently make us uncomfortable and upset. As a result—as if that wasn't already bad enough—it can cause us to act in less than adept ways. (For instance, as I type this I'm reminded of many a past piano recital gone not quite according to plan.) We're thus often encouraged to "be sure of, and know ourselves," and to guarantee that "we know what we're doing, and why we're doing it." Self-confidence, self-knowledge, and decisiveness are frequently considered to be virtuous, and the lack thereof, vicious, as is explored in other chapters of this book. Indeed, in general ignorance and doubt are considered to be bad things, and knowledge and certainty, good things.

Might, however, doubt and uncertainty sometimes be good, rather than bad? Is it possible to wonder whether self-confidence, self-knowledge, and decisiveness are really as uniformly excellent as some people make them out to be? Are there times that we shouldn't be so sure of ourselves, or should be uncertain or otherwise skeptical about whether we know what we're doing and why, or whether we know the things that we think we do? What's more, should we perhaps even be skeptical in this way most, if not all, of the time?

We can take seriously the possibility that the answer to all of the questions raised here is: "Yes." This of course isn't to say that doubt should always be encouraged. It may rather be the case that it, like many other things in life, ought to be managed and developed to an optimal degree. Doubt, after all, plausibly indicates a vulnerability (to, e.g., not knowing, or to being wrong) that we'd do well to mitigate, or at least to cultivate.[2] We'll return to that possibility in what follows, too, if too briefly. There's so much that might be said about this topic—indeed, philosophers have been discussing it for thousands of years. What follows hence only starts to scratch the surface of these discussions, but it's my hope that it does so in a way that'll enable readers to dig deeper if they're interested in doing so.

Let's return to Enid. We might think that she not only *didn't*, but also *couldn't*, know that Norman wouldn't be leaving town, to say nothing of herself. To explain why, next I'll discuss what Enid thought she knew in connection with three interesting types of skeptical arguments discussed in the history of philosophy. I'll write in slightly more technical language than I've been so far, with the aim of showing how general these argument-types are: not only can they arguably be used to explain why Enid didn't, and couldn't, know that Norman wouldn't be leaving town, but they can also be used to induce (some measure of) doubt about (almost) any claim to know we could imagine.[3] Following that, I'll conclude by explaining how encouraging extensive—or perhaps even universal—doubt or skepticism might help us to live more flourishing lives.

7.2 Introducing Skeptical Arguments

One interesting feature of debates about whether knowing is possible is that they are not only enduring, but also widespread. Some of the most powerful skeptical arguments—including arguments from skeptical hypotheses, arguments from regress, and arguments from circularity—have been proposed, and attacked, by philosophers all over the world. Because of this, I'll explain how these arguments work in broad detail next, and in notes provide a small selection of readings concerning specific texts that discuss their history, too, for those who are interested in reading more about them.

7.2.1 Arguments from Skeptical Hypotheses

Skeptical arguments that follow the pattern discussed here are designed to call claims to know into question by raising specific *skeptical hypotheses*—incompatible with those claims—that supposedly can't be ruled out. They can be approximately characterized as having the following general form (where "S" designates someone who might be taken to know some claim, "p" designates some claim that we might take that someone to know, and "sk" designates a claim that is considered to be incompatible with knowing p and that supposedly can't be ruled out by S). One popular skeptical hypothesis in contemporary literature on such arguments is the possibility *that S is a brain-in-a-vat*, or, a bit more recently, *that S is living in a computer simulation* of some kind (say, along the lines of that depicted in the 1999 film *The Matrix*, directed by Lana and Lilly Wachowski). But there are many others: for starters, historically the possibilities that a person is dreaming or deceived by a powerful supernatural entity have also been widely discussed.[4]

Argument from Skeptical Hypothesis: General Form

1. (Suppose) S knows p.
2. If S knows p, then S is in a position to know sk isn't true.
3. S isn't in a position to know sk isn't true.
4. Therefore, it's not the case that S knows p (after all). (By *modus tollens*)

We can apply this general form of argument to the example involving Enid and Norman discussed from *Ghost World*:

1. (Suppose) Enid knows that Norman won't be leaving town.
2. If Enid knows that Norman won't be leaving town, then Enid is in a position to know that a bus won't come to pick up Norman.
3. Enid isn't in a position to know that a bus won't come to pick up Norman. (After all, one did.)
4. Therefore, it's not the case that Enid knows that Norman won't be leaving town (after all).

7.2.2 Arguments from Regress

Skeptical arguments that follow the pattern discussed here are designed to call claims to know into question by demonstrating that they rely on unverified assumptions that would have to be independently verified in order for claims to know to be true. This, however, threatens to result in what philosophers call an *infinite regress*, as there's no principled, nonarbitrary place to stop this process of verification. They can be approximately characterized as having the following general form (where, once again, "S" designates someone who might be taken to know some claim and "p" designates some claim that we might take that someone to know).[5]

Argument from Regress: General Form

1. (Suppose) S knows p.
2. In order for 1 to be true, S would need to verify all assumptions on which her knowing p relies. (In other words, one might think that knowing requires being able to completely "back up" one's claims, to ensure that no supporting claim is left itself unsupported.)
3. Any attempt to carry out the procedure outlined in 2 would itself rely on further assumptions that S would need to verify in order for 1 to be true. (And so on.)
4. There's no principled, nonarbitrary place to stop this process of verification.
5. Therefore, it's not the case that S knows p (after all).

We can again apply this general form of argument to the example involving Enid and Norman:

1. (Suppose) Enid knows that Norman won't be leaving town.
2. In order for 1 to be true, Enid would need to verify all assumptions on which her knowing that Norman won't be leaving town relies. (Examples include the assumption that a bus won't come to pick up Norman, that the "NO SERVICE" stenciling is accurate, etc.)
3. Any attempt to carry out the procedure outlined in 2 would itself rely on further assumptions that Enid would need to verify in order for 1 to be true. (And so on.)
4. There's no principled, nonarbitrary place to stop this process of verification.

5. Therefore, it's not the case that Enid knows that Norman won't be leaving town (after all).

7.2.3 Arguments from Circularity

Skeptical arguments that follow the pattern discussed here are designed to call claims to know into question by demonstrating that we can't substantiate them in what philosophers call a *nonviciously circular* fashion, as there's no independent way to verify them. Arguments from regress and arguments from circularity are often used together to mount skeptical attacks.[6] However, although arguments from regress and arguments from circularity often occur together, they can come apart. Consider the following example as in instance of this form of argument:[7]

1. All observed Fs are G (e.g.: All observed ravens are black.)
2. (Therefore) All Fs are G (e.g.: All ravens are black.)
3. Cases observed in the future will resemble cases observed in the past.
4. In order to be supported in moving from 1 to 2, one must already have support for 3.
5. The only way of getting support for 3 would be to infer it from claims like 1 and 2.
6. The move from 1 to 3 can't be supported in any other way.
7. As a result, there's no way to get support for 2 or 3, and thus, we can't know a claim by inferring it from previously observed cases.[8]

It has been noted, however, that it is rarely noticed that this form of skeptical argument generalizes, and can be used to undermine claims to know about the external world, other minds, and the past, among other things.[9] Also, we can once again apply this style of argument to the example involving Enid and Norman in order to explain why Enid didn't know that Norman wouldn't be leaving town using the same type of reasoning as mentioned earlier:

1. Every day that Enid has seen Norman waiting for the bus, no bus has come.
2. (Therefore) Norman won't be leaving town. (Since he never has.)
3. Since no bus has come for Norman, no bus will come for Norman.

But wait: in order to know 3, Enid would have to be supported in inferring 2 from 1. However, she couldn't be, unless she already knew 3. Hence, she couldn't know 2 or 3, and thus, she couldn't know that Norman wouldn't be leaving town—which he indeed did in the end. Thus, steps 4 through 7 from the example with which this section began could be added to this argument as well to again explain why Enid didn't (and couldn't) know that Norman wouldn't be leaving town.

7.3 Embracing Doubt and Uncertainty

Let's suppose that these types of arguments, suitably formulated, can indeed be used to induce (some measure of) doubt about (almost) any claim to know we could imagine. This raises the question: What might be the point of doing this? Shouldn't we be trying to eliminate—rather than produce—doubt, as intimated in the introduction to this chapter (at least in general, or most of the time)? Interestingly, many philosophers who propose skeptical arguments suggest that the answer is: "No." Rather, they propose skeptical arguments with the aim of helping people to live better lives via *encouraging* doubt. For instance, regarding skepticism in Greek philosophy, Katja Vogt writes:

> Socrates raises the challenge that it might be truly bad (for one's life, for the state of one's soul, and so on) to base one's actions on unexamined beliefs. For all one knows, these beliefs could be false, and without investigation, one does not even aim to rid oneself of false belief, which is admittedly a bad thing for one's soul. Only an examined life is worth living. Once we take this challenge seriously, as the ancient skeptics do, we embark on a kind of investigation that is seen as directly relevant to our lives. . . . Confidence in unexamined views seems misplaced. Others regularly disagree with us. With respect to even the most basic questions, such as whether there is movement, or whether there are good and bad things, we face conflicting views. In favor of each view, some arguments can be adduced, some practices invoked, some experiences cited. These conflicting arguments, practices and experiences need to be examined. But that just raises further views that are in conflict. As a consequence, suspension of judgment on every such question looks rationally mandatory. But it is also rational to persist in investigation. The skeptic is committed to a search for the truth,

on virtually all questions, even if this search repeatedly and predictably leads to suspension of judgment. (Vogt 2018)

Other philosophers have alleged that skeptical arguments can have yet another benefit: namely, that they can be used to produce a specific kind of peace of mind. To take one example, on Gisela Striker's interpretation, Sextus Empiricus—a Pyrrhonian skeptic—aims to help people to realize *ataraxia*, a state of tranquility that he's inclined to think might be manifested once one suspends judgment about all claims. According to Striker, the rough idea is that no one who believes that there are any real goods or evils, e.g., can ever be free from anxiety. This is because such beliefs will lead one to pursue intensely what one believes to be good, and to avoid what one believes to be bad. Moreover, should one by any chance obtain any of the supposed goods one desires, one's troubles will only renew, as one will now be anxious due to the fear of loss. By contrast, the Pyrrhonian skeptic—by means of, for instance, skeptical arguments—suspends belief about whether there are any real goods or evils, and hence (perhaps contrary to what one might have expected at first) stops worrying.[10] Likewise, the Buddhist philosopher Nāgārjuna aims to help people to realize *nirvana*, a state of unperturbed, unselfconscious desirelessness that he's inclined to think might be manifested once one stops being so concerned with proposing and defending theses or participating in activities connected with conceptual proliferation. Like his approximate contemporary, Sextus Empiricus, Nāgārjuna proposes a specific kind of peace of mind via suspending judgment.[11]

In a similar, but importantly different, vein, Zhuangzi—a Daoist philosopher—can be interpreted as aiming to help people to realize *wu-wei*, a state productive of spontaneous, fluid action that he's inclined to think might be manifested once one ceases to be so concerned with projecting one's own opinions about what is and what is not onto the world.[12] According to Edward Slingerland, "wu-wei" literally means "in the absence of/without doing exertion," and is often translated as "doing nothing" or "nonaction." On one way of understanding what wu-wei involves, it refers not to what is actually happening (or not) in the externally observable realm but rather to the state of mind of the doer. For a person who exemplifies wu-wei, proper conduct follows as instantly and spontaneously as the nose responds to a bad smell, and with the same sense of unconscious ease with which the body gives in to the seductive rhythm of a song. This isn't to say that actions that issue from wu-wei are automatic, completely unconscious, or purely physiological.

Individuals who exemplify wu-wei may still make choices and may even at times pause to weigh various options or consider the situations ahead. Such choices and deliberations, however, are themselves also performed with a sort of effortless ease. Unlike instinctual or merely habitual forms of thought and action, then, wu-wei calls for varying degrees of awareness on the part of agents, and allows for a considerable amount of flexibility in response.[13] For these sorts of reasons, translating wu-wei as "no-overdoing" or "no-forcing" may be preferable to aforementioned possibilities.

To better explain what wu-wei is meant to be, and what it's meant to be like, let's revisit one of my earlier examples. Consider the way that one thinks and acts when one gives a really good piano recital. Giving a really good piano recital is not purely physiological, completely unconscious, or auto-matic. It involves deliberation and choice. Indeed, there's a sense in which giving a really good piano recital is both *effortful* and *not easy*. However, there's another, different (and yet equally interesting) sense in which giving a really good piano recital is both *effortless* and *easy*. For, giving such a recital can be characterized as involving the same kind of unconscious ease with which, say, good dancers respond to a song: that is, when they do so in an absorbed, focused fashion, and when they aren't worried or nervous about, e.g., whether anyone is judging them, but just want to dance well for its own sake. This is true even in cases where dancing, or giving a recital, involves an array of conscious, deliberate, and even in a sense effortful activities as well—and even if they typically do so. Wu-wei, conceived as an ideal state, can thus be further characterized as involving a standing disposition (or set of dispositions) to act in a manner that exemplifies this sort of effortless ease all the time, even while engaged in conscious, deliberate, effortful activity. For the sense in which wu-wei action is effortless is that while exemplifying wu-wei, one's actions are in an important sense unforced—even if they in-volve intense mental and physical effort.

Wu-wei is thus characterized by spontaneity, flexibility, creativity, and playfulness, rather than excessively rigid reliance on self-serving plans, characterizations of prior experiences, and fixed preconceptions. It's about reflecting, responding, and adapting rather than projecting, disregarding, and imposing. Given this, one might see Zhuangzi's deployment of skeptical arguments as helpful rather than harmful insofar as such arguments can be productive of the open-mindedness as well as willingness and ability to take on fresh perspectives that wu-wei involves, without certainty, knowledge, or perhaps even belief. Thus, to more directly revisit the example of piano recitals "not gone according to plan" mentioned near the beginning of this chapter, a Zhuangist might suggest that I could've done better if I'd simply focused my attention on the task at hand in the face of uncertainty, rather than attempt to assuage or otherwise focus my attention on doubt about whether I'd do well. Perhaps the surest way to not play well, after all, is to worry about whether one will play well. We even have a variety of metaphors in the English language that are commonly employed in order to characterize what happens when one fails in this way that suggest a lack of fluidity or flexibility, such as "choke." (Chung forthcoming b).

We can thus see that a number of philosophers have framed skepticism as (more akin to) a *therapy*, rather than a *threat*. They take seriously the possibility that the best way to manage and develop doubt is to embrace it. And this possibility is something that we might take seriously, too, just as Enid does, when she decides—doubts and all—to bravely leave all she thought she knew behind to embark instead on a journey whose purpose and outcome were highly uncertain.

One of my favorite poems, and which I think nicely illustrates the possibility that there's very little, if anything, that we can know or be certain about (and that we might be better off embracing, rather than resisting, this thought) is "The Moment," by Margaret Atwood:

> The moment when, after many years
> of hard work and a long voyage
> you stand in the centre of your room,
> house, half-acre, square mile, island, country,
> knowing at last how you got there,
> and say, *I own this,*
> is the same moment when the trees unloose
> their soft arms from around you,
> the birds take back their language,
> the cliffs fissure and collapse,
> the air moves back from you like a wave
> and you can't breathe.
> *No,* they whisper. *You own nothing.*
> *You were a visitor, time after time*
> *climbing the hill, planting the flag, proclaiming.*
> *We never belonged to you.*
> *You never found us.*
> *It was always the other way round.*[14]

One thing that Atwood's poem speaks to is that—although we're often un-aware of them—there are so many undetected, undetectable, and uncontrol-lable forces that shape our lives, and on which we depend without realizing it. We can't force our will onto the world, nor can we have it belong to us. If anything, the situation is "the other way round": metaphorical as this may be, it's plausible that the world can only force its will onto us, and we can only be-long to it. Thus, the highly uncertain, externally determined (at least in part), and hence vulnerable and precarious nature of human life arguably makes it unsurprising that human beings tend to be creatures of doubt, and lead lives that tend to be marked by it.[15]

In light of considerations such as these, perhaps the only thing that we can be sure about is that there is and will always be room for doubt or uncertainty, at least as regards whether we can know things to be true, as some skeptical philosophers have claimed. Or, maybe, as others have suggested, we can't even be sure of that! Perhaps we can know things to be true in spite of skep-tical arguments, and can be sure or certain of it. Indeed many philosophers, historical to contemporary, have argued against skeptical arguments in a va-riety of ways. While this all might strike many as too dizzying or disorienting to think about, we might find it comforting to consider the possibility that the best thing about doubt—unsettling as it can be—is that it leaves so much open to possibility. If nothing is known, sure, or certain, then (as far as we can know) everything is possible. And this thought, though it can be bewil-dering, anxiety-inspiring, and even frightening, can also be calming or lib-erating (as some Pyrrhonians and Buddhists propose), or even freeing or exhilarating (as some Zhuangists suggest). Maybe we can't and shouldn't seek to eliminate doubt altogether, but rather can and should seek to embrace its presence (complete with all its benefits and drawbacks) in our lives—even if, as mentioned earlier, it may be the case that it, like many other things in life, ought to be managed and developed to an optimal degree. (And even if learning how to do this ends up being as much an art as it is a science.) In so doing, perhaps we too, like Enid, might travel—if metaphorically—(as yet) unknown distances to parts (as yet) unknown with reduced anxiety and even an increased sense of determination existing alongside doubt and un-certainty. After all, as skeptical arguments suggest, it's possible that none of us really know what we're doing, where we're going, or what to think more generally—at least not for sure. But isn't that possibly part of what can open us up to new possibilities, and help to make life such a wonderful, and won-drous, adventure?

Notes

1. For the purposes of this chapter, doubting can approximately be understood as a state of wondering, or calling into question (compare Vogt 2018).
2. For discussion of what might be termed "epistemic vulnerability," as well as why and how it might be fruitfully developed, rather than eliminated, see Gilson (2011).
3. I write "almost" because some claims may be indubitable (such as the claim that one exists)—although many who have discussed skeptical arguments in the history of philosophy have not been inclined to think so.
4. For discussion of the history of such arguments, see Raphals (1996), Weintraub (2006), Mercer (2017), and Chung (2017, 2018, and forthcoming a). Also, while these arguments will here be discussed in connection with what can be known, historically they have also been discussed in connection with what (if anything) should be believed; see Vogt (2018).
5. For discussion of the history of such arguments, see Kjellberg (1996), Mills (2016, 2018), and Chung (2017, 2018, and forthcoming a).
6. For example, as they are in what has been termed, "Agrippa's Trilemma." For more on this problem see Mills (2016). For more on Agrippa, see Vogt (2018).
7. For an explication of the general form of this argument, see Wright (2004).
8. For discussion of the history of such arguments, see Weintraub (1995), Wright (2004), Chung (2017, 2018, and forthcoming a), and Coliva (2015). For discussion of the history of skepticism as regards scientific method more broadly, see Keller (1997).
9. See Wright (2004).
10. Striker (1990, 180).
11. For discussion, see Garfield (1990, 2015) and Berger (2019).
12. This section draws heavily on Chung (forthcoming b).
13. Compare Slingerland (2003).
14. See Atwood (1995).
15. For discussion of the positive value of vulnerability in human life, see Gilson (2011 and 2013).

Bibliography

Annas, Julia. 1996. "Scepticism, Old and New." In *Rationality in Greek Thought*, edited by M. Frede and G. Striker, 239–254. Oxford: Oxford University Press.

Atwood, Margaret. 1995. "The Moment." In *Morning in the Burned House*, 109. Toronto: Houghton Mifflin.

Berger, Douglas. 2019. "Nāgārjuna (c. 150–c. 250)." In *The Internet Encyclopedia of Philosophy*, https://www.iep.utm.edu/.

Chung, Julianne. Forthcoming a. "Skeptical Arguments, Conceptual Metaphors, and Cross-Cultural Challenges." In *Ethno-Epistemology*, edited by J. Ganeri, C. Goddard, and M. Mizumoto. New York: Routledge.

Chung, Julianne. Forthcoming b. "Faith, Reason, and the Paradox of *Wu-wei*." In *Asian Philosophies and the Idea of Religion*, edited by Sonia Sikka and Ashwani Peetush. London: Routledge.

Chung, Julianne. 2018. "Is Zhuangzi a Fictionalist?" *Philosophers' Imprint* 18, no. 22: 1–23.

Chung, Julianne. 2017. "Taking Skepticism Seriously: How the *Zhuang-Zi* Can Inform Contemporary Epistemology." *Comparative Philosophy* 8, no. 2: 3–30.

Coliva, Annalisa. 2015. *Extended Rationality: A Hinge Epistemology*. London: Palgrave-Macmillan.

Frede, Dorothea. 1996. "How Sceptical Were the Academic Sceptics?" In *Scepticism in the History of Philosophy: A Pan-American Dialogue*, edited by R. H. Popkin, 1–26. Dordrecht: Kluwer Academic.

Garfield, Jay. 2015. *Engaging Buddhism*. Oxford: Oxford University Press.

Garfield, Jay. 1990. "Epoche and Śūnyatā: Skepticism East and West." *Philosophy East and West* 40, no. 3: 285–307.

Gilson, Erinn. 2013. *The Ethics of Vulnerability: A Feminist Analysis of Social Life and Practice*. New York: Routledge.

Gilson, Erinn. 2011. "Vulnerability, Ignorance, and Oppression." *Hypatia* 26, no. 2: 308–332.

Keller, Eve. 1997. "Producing Petty Gods: Margaret Cavendish's Critique of Experimental Science." *ELH* 64, no. 2: 447–471

Kjellberg, Paul. 1996. "Sextus Empiricus, Zhuangzi, and Xunzi on 'Why Be Skeptical?'" In *Essays on Skepticism, Relativism, and Ethics in the* Zhuangzi, edited by P. Kjellberg and P. J. Ivanhoe, 1–25. New York: SUNY Press.

Mercer, Christia. 2017. "Descartes' Debt to Teresa of Ávila, or Why We Should Work on Women in the History of Philosophy." *Philosophical Studies* 174, no. 10: 2539–2555.

Mills, Ethan. 2018. *Three Pillars of Skepticism in Classical India: Nāgārjuna, Jayarāśi, and Śrī Harṣa*. Lanham, MD: Lexington Books.

Mills, Ethan. 2016. "Nāgārjuna's Pañcakoṭi, Agrippa's Trilemma, and the Uses of Skepticism." *Comparative Philosophy* 7, no. 2: 44–66.

Raphals, Lisa. 1996. "Skeptical Strategies in the *Zhuangzi* and the *Theaetetus*." In *Essays on Skepticism, Relativism, and Ethics in the Zhuangzi*, edited by P. Kjellberg and P. J. Ivanhoe, 26–49. New York: SUNY Press.

Slingerland, Edward. 2003. *Effortless Action: Wu-Wei as Conceptual Metaphor and Spiritual Ideal in Early China*. New York: Oxford University Press.

Striker, Gisela. 1990. "Ataraxia: Happiness as Tranquility." *The Monist* 73, no. 1: 97–110.

Vogt, Katja. 2018. "Ancient Skepticism." In *The Stanford Encyclopedia of Philosophy* (Fall Edition), edited by Edward N. Zalta, https://plato.stanford.edu/archives/fall2018/entries/skepticism-ancient/.

Weintraub, Ruth. 2006. "What Descartes' Demon Can Do and His Dream Cannot." *Theoria* 72, no. 4: 319–335.

Weintraub, Ruth. 1995. "What Was Hume's Contribution to the Problem of Induction?" *Philosophical Quarterly* 45, no. 181: 460–470.

Wright, Crispin. 2004. "Warrant for Nothing (and Foundations for Free)?" *Aristotelian Society Supplementary* 78, no. 1: 167–212.

8

Science

Unmasking Objectivity

Subrena E. Smith

It was the eighteenth century and Europe was abuzz with Enlightenment reforms. The power of the Bible and the Pope to dictate knowledge was waning. People could investigate the world and figure out the answers to their questions. European intellectual life at this historical moment was bursting with what was called the "experimental method"—using experience to understand the world, rather than relying only on theory or the authorities of the past. Bologna, an ancient and populous city in the north of Italy, had lost its former glory as a hub for intellectual life in Europe, and there was a deliberate effort being made by the Pope and city patriarchs to reestablish it as a premier center for the life of the mind. A key part of this effort was the creation of the Institute of Sciences, which was built on and devoted to both the empirical sciences and the fine arts.

A woman named Anna Morandi was an important figure in the scientific rebirth of Bologna. Morandi was a world-class anatomist. Her achievements as an anatomist were extraordinary in themselves, but they were all the rarer because she was a woman working in a field that was almost completely dominated by men. As Rebecca Messbarger remarked in her stunning biography of Morandi, she "looked where others, most especially other women, rarely dared. She entered that most virile of the 'new' sciences, keeping company with the dead, handling cadavers and 'fresh parts' carted to her home from the city mortuary" (Messbarger 2010, 18).

Women were uncommon in the sciences. But Morandi not only moved toward science, she moved toward the science that was most unwomanly: the science of dead bodies, which involved cutting them apart after they had become stiff from rigor mortis, and had begun to putrefy, while breathing in their stench. Morandi was unquestionably a scientist. But she was not regarded as one during her lifetime. I will use her as a case study to explore

Subrena E. Smith, *Science* In: *Philosophy for Girls*. Edited by: Melissa M. Shew and Kimberly K. Garchar, Oxford University Press (2020). © Oxford University Press. DOI: 10.1093/oso/9780190072919.003.0009.

some aspects of the relation between science and the social world in which it is situated.

8.1 Who Was Anna Morandi?

Not much is known about Morandi's life prior to her meeting and marrying the artist Giovanni Manzolini. Manzolini was an established artist who served as chief assistant for the anatomy museum ordered by Pope Benedict. But there was discord between him and the director of the museum, and he resigned. He and Morandi then opened an anatomy school and studio in their home, where they instructed students in anatomical dissections and where they created highly realistic wax models of parts of the body for use in anatomical instruction. They dissected hundreds of cadavers, and Morandi took copious notes about the body's structures and their functions, some of which describe her own discoveries. At the age of thirty-nine her partnership with Manzolini ended when he died. Morandi continued running the school on her own, teaching wax-molding and dissections, and developing new ways for doing both.

In the spirit of the new science that was becoming the norm in Bologna, Morandi pioneered a new, systematic approach to anatomy. Not satisfied with merely dissecting cadavers and observing anatomical structures, she used her observations to interrogate existing anatomical and physiological theories, and offered alternatives to the existing accounts. It is important to understand that Morandi was doing much more than skillful dissections and making realistic wax models of parts of the human body. She was also discovering new facts about the human body and using her observations to assess the theories that had been proposed by other anatomists.

When Manzolini was alive, it was convenient for their contemporaries to characterize her work as an adjunct of and in relation to that of her spouse. It was convenient because as a woman in that time and place Morandi was expected to be a helpmate to her spouse rather a scientific innovator in her own right. But after Manzolini's death, it was obvious that she was a highly accomplished anatomist. On account of Morandi's accomplishments, her fame spread throughout Europe, and her celebrity affected how she was received in her home city. As Messenbarger points out:

> She received invitations from throughout Europe to relocate her practice and singular collection. It was precisely this outside notice . . . that

prompted Bologna's cultural patriarchs to recognize her work formally with a small annual stipend and a university appointment in anatomical exposition. Pope Benedict intervened with the Senate in these matters in Morandi's behalf, thereby keeping her home in Bologna. (Messbarger, 2010, 12)

Morandi's scientific stature is not widely known. One obvious explanation for this is that she did not fit with the common understanding of the "natural" standing of women that was prevalent both in her day and for centuries later. She was an affront to these assumptions about women and their roles, for she was a woman who flourished in a masculine science. This is surely a component of the explanation. But it is not the full story.

8.2 Morandi in Context

We must understand the cultural context of eighteenth-century Bologna, in which the science of anatomy and the art of anatomical wax-molding were forged, to appreciate Morandi's path to becoming the foremost anatomist in Europe. Earlier I said that Bologna was on its intellectual knees and keen to recapture its former glory. City leaders were desperate for it to once again be renowned as "The Mother of Learning." The creation of the Institute of Sciences was a direct response to this problem. The Institute was outfitted with the most scholarly professors, state-of-the-art laboratories, and the method of instruction was a mixture of "experiment, classification, and exposition" (Messbarger 2010, 5), which was a change from the traditional, primarily theoretical way of instructing. The Institute's mission was to unify the sciences and to tie the sciences more closely to the arts—a daring move that disrupted their traditional separation.

Anna Morandi's work exemplified the foundational principles of the Institute—the idea that gaining knowledge of the world requires one to engage with it through experimentation and classification and then to explain one's findings. She was a keen observer, a virtuoso in the precise techniques of dissection, and an artist who produced incredibly lifelike wax models of the interior of the human body. But her work went further than this, because she did not merely observe and represent the body, but also sought to explain it. She developed a systematic understanding of the body's structures, inferred the functions of discrete components, and articulated a holistic understanding of the relationships between seemingly discrete components of the human organism.

A central concern of the critics of her day was how to classify Morandi's work. Was it art or was it science? The question arose, in part, because although artistic work was informed by the sciences, and vice versa, there was an ongoing dispute about the aesthetic versus educational function of anatomical wax molding. Morandi's work straddled this divide. She created wax models in the image of the real body: in structure, form, color, and so on, so as to give the impression that the wax models were parts of living bodies. She could not succeed at this without having a systematic, detailed, and accurate knowledge of the intricacies of the human body. Her realistic portrayals of bodily organs demonstrated that she had amassed expert biological knowledge. So, Morandi was not simply an artist. She was a scientist, too: a scientist-artist. There seems to have been no question in the minds of the distinguished scientists who celebrated her accomplishments, that her work was a significant contribution to medical science. And yet despite the widespread recognition of the importance of her work, Anna Morandi the *person* was not granted a place among the scientists of her day. Although the scientific significance of her work was undeniable, she was not given the recognition as a *scientist* that her achievements warranted. Instead, she was considered by her critics as a gifted amateur—a talented craftswoman rather than a true scientific investigator.

What are we to make of the obscuring of Anna Morandi in light of the facts of her work and life? To answer this question, we need to make explicit some aspects of the nature of science.

We are usually confident that we know more or less what science is, and that we know what counts as science and what does not. Chemistry is clearly a science. Painting clearly is not. We usually agree that science involves certain kinds of activities, such as observing, experimenting, testing, and retesting, and that science is also theoretical, involving the exercise of thought, making connections between observable things and things that are not observable in ordinary ways. We usually recognize that to be a scientist a person has to have certain special skills and knowledge. But there are other aspects of science that although important, are given less emphasis.

It seems right to say that whether Morandi was a scientist should depend on whether her work was scientific. According to her peers, her work was of the highest scientific quality. However, they did not acknowledge her as a scientist. They seemingly drew a distinction between *being* a scientist and producing scientific work. It might seem strange that the scientific establishment of her time operated with such a distinction. But from the viewpoint of her peers, there were reasons for not including her in the "brotherhood" of anatomists. Examining the lens through which Morandi was viewed throws light not just on her fate, or the fate of women in the sciences more generally, but also on important aspects of science itself—in particular, the nature of scientific objectivity.

8.3 Philosophy of Science

Asking why Morandi was not accorded the status of a scientist is not asking a scientific question. It is asking a question *about* the practice of science and the institution of science. The question could be approached from several different viewpoints. It might be taken as a historical question or a sociological question. But if we address it as a question about the nature of science, it is a philosophical question or, more accurately, a question in the domain of the philosophy of science.

A familiar understanding of philosophy is that it deals with the big questions that are important to life such as human well-being, God's existence, justice, and morality. Such questions are thought to be abstract; they do not pertain to the particulars of practical living. In contrast, science is seen as concrete; it finds answers that we can see, touch, and benefit from. This is of course a limited understanding of science, but this is the perspective that is familiar to many.

The philosophy of science stands at the intersection of science and philosophy. Philosophers of science take science and do philosophy with it. Philosophy of science is called a "meta-discipline." In doing philosophy of science, a philosopher is usually not doing science but is instead bringing philosophical tools, understandings, and conceptual distinctions to bear on science: its practice, its methods, its aims, its forms of reasoning, and its claims about the fundamental structure of nature. Philosophers of science think about the nature and reach of scientific knowledge, the results of scientific inquiry, and methods used to get those results in any particular science (Godfrey-Smith 2003; Barker and Kitcher 2013).

We take science to give a general understanding of nature, but a general understanding of some aspect of nature is always based on a limited number of observations that scientists believe justify their general conclusions. These conclusions are also meant to tell us about cases that have not been observed. The relationship between observed cases and those yet to be observed is key for scientific knowledge. So, scientific knowledge is general knowledge, rather than knowledge of particular things as such. Take the case of medicine: medical science is concerned with how human kidneys *in general* work. Scientists use this general knowledge to understand the workings of individual kidneys.

This way of thinking might seem puzzling. Science is based on observation, but scientists cannot observe every human kidney. They must of necessity draw general conclusions about kidneys from limited sets of observations. This procedure is central to how science works, and it seems reasonable. But philosophers of science have long been concerned with how it can be justified (Salmon 2017). For instance, medical scientists say that tuberculosis is caused by a microorganism called *Mycobacterium tuberculosis*. They say this about *all* cases of tuberculosis—every case of tuberculosis that there has ever been and that will ever be—not just the ones that have been observed to have been caused by this bacterium. But why should we think that as-yet-unobserved cases will follow the same pattern as the cases that have been observed in the past? For philosophers, unless we can find some reason to justify drawing general conclusions from observed cases, it is not clear that we can claim to *know* that tuberculosis is always caused this way. One way to think about these issues is that in order for scientists to produce general knowledge, they have to assume that future observations will resemble past ones, while remaining open to the possibility that they may be wrong that the pattern will continue to hold. This exemplifies the scientific attitude: remaining open to correction in the face of evidence.

Although scientific knowledge is never certain, scientific practices are our most reliable means of generating knowledge. It is because science has special cognitive authority that it is important to be able to distinguish between those practices, theories, and bodies of knowledge that count as science and those that do not. In some cases, it is just obvious what distinguishes science from nonscience. Sports are not science (though they might involve science) because athletic activities do not aim to generate knowledge of any kind. And in a general sense, art is not science. But as the case of Morandi shows the boundary between the two is sometimes not sharp. She and Manzolini were both trained as artists, and their wax moldings of human anatomy are unquestionably works of art, while also being scientific representations of the human body. This fuzzy boundary made it possible for Morandi's critics to acknowledge her scientific achievements while characterizing her as an artisan rather than a scientist. The distinction between science and art can be put this way. Science aims at revealing how things really are, in the most general sense, but it need not be the goal of art to reveal the world as it really is. Artistic work can, but does not have to, aim at representing the world as it really is. But science must have that as its aim. Additionally, science is concerned with establishing very general truths, while the artist is free to focus on the particular.

In practice, it is rarely difficult to distinguish science from art. It is more difficult, and more philosophically informative, to address the problem of how to distinguish between real science and what philosophers call *pseudoscience*. The term "pseudoscience" refers to counterfeit science. It consists of activities, theories, and claims that are presented as science, and have the superficial characteristics associated with science, but which are not really science. Astrology is a classic example of a pseudoscience in the philosophy of science literature (Popper 2002). Astrology certainly looks scientific. It involves the use of astronomical tables and calculations to work out the positions of the heavenly bodies, and—similar to scientists—astrologers make predictions and give explanations on the basis of what they consider to be astrological "laws." But they are not doing science. Why is it that astrology is not science? The answer cannot be that astrology is false, because very many truly scientific claims turn out to be false. The answer must have something to do with the procedures that astrologers use to generate what they consider to be astrological knowledge. Astrology is not science because the methods that astrologers use are not scientific methods.

Philosophers of science do not all agree about *exactly* what it is that separates science from pseudoscience. There is however general agreement that the answer involves the methods that scientists use to establish knowledge. A scientific picture of nature needs to aim at accuracy. To achieve this, scientists need to be able to evaluate whether and to what extent their picture of nature is accurate, so that they can correct errors and move their picture toward how the world really is. For this reason, scientists have had to develop careful methods for evaluating their claims by looking for evidence for and against them. These evaluative methods are called *testing procedures*. To count as a test, a procedure needs to be clear, repeatable, and must involve rules for how evidence is used and interpreted. But pseudoscientific activities like astrology do not take testing seriously, and may be too poorly structured to make testing even possible. Because astrologers do not subject their claims to rigorous tests, there is no reason to think that astrology (and other pseudoscientific practices) provide us with an accurate picture of reality.

Here is a way to describe what it is that makes science special and sets it apart from other activities that aim at generating knowledge. Science uses methods that are likely to produce objective knowledge. It is important to be as clear as possible about what this means. Objective knowledge is knowledge of the world as it really is, regardless of what we believe or do not believe about it. We can say that objective knowledge is knowledge of objective— that is, mind-independent—reality. Knowledge that is not distorted by certain biases. Some biases can undermine scientific objectivity by influencing how scientists collect and interpret data. The rules governing scientific practice are supposed to protect objectivity from distorting biases.

Biases are thought to be problematic because they may embody certain kinds of values. To value something is to desire it, to prefer it, and to want it to be the case. Values can distort scientific objectivity when wanting something to be the case interferes with recognizing what, objectively, is the case. If a scientist wants her theory to be true, but the evidence counts against it, she might be inclined to discount that evidence. Her desire that the theory be true might lead her to ignore or minimize evidence that the theory is false.

The fact that certain biases can distort objectivity can lead to the incorrect conclusion that values have no place in science—that science should be value-free. The assumption is that the intrusion of values into scientific work is at best irrelevant and at worst destroys scientific objectivity. But scientific objectivity when understood in this sense—the sense of being free from bias—is problematic, because values *inevitably* play a significant role in science. Science is never practiced in a social vacuum. Science is a product of embodied beings living in a social world. And even if it were desirable to do so, scientists could not set all of their values aside. I say "even if it were desirable" because setting aside all values is *not* scientifically desirable. Scientific knowledge about any region of the world is the outcome of asking questions and setting out in a systematic, organized, and cooperative way to find answers to those questions. Science is practiced by teams or researchers interacting with other teams of researchers. So, scientific practices would be *impossible* in the absence of social values such as cooperation, interpersonal harmony and openness to dialogue. Furthermore, science is embedded in social institutions and is influenced by funding and other institutional priorities and constraints. Decisions about scientific research emerge from negotiations between both scientists and nonscientific stakeholders concerning which questions to pursue, which projects get priority over others, which human communities might be affected by the outcomes, how these might affect nonhuman organisms and environments, and so forth. In the sort of economic system that we have, potential profitability has a large impact on what sorts of research receive funding (for example, by pharmaceutical companies), and government contracts may prioritize research with military applications. All of these elements are integral to science because science is practiced by social beings.

Early in the twentieth century, when philosophy of science was just emerging, the social aspects of science were not very much in focus. Philosophers of science tended implicitly to see science as a set of practices that are isolated from the wider social world, and they devoted most of their attention to epistemological issues (issues concerning knowledge) that are internal to science itself. More recently, philosophers have become increasingly concerned with the social dimensions of science (Kitcher 1993). Helen Longino is a philosopher of science whose work focuses on how social values enter into and play a role in how scientists make sense of the world (Longino 1990), and she argues that the fact that social values enter into science is compatible with its generating objective knowledge. Longino theorizes that social values play a vital role in the production of objective, scientific knowledge. According to her, objectivity is "a characteristic of a community's practice of science rather than of an individual's" (Longino 1990, 74). This is because science itself is a cooperative, community-based activity.

It is clear that there is no possibility of value-free scientific theorizing and practice. Whether or not scientific research is objective has to do with the quality of interactions amongst members of scientific communities. These interactions are always imbedded in particular social contexts, and their research questions are always formulated in relation to those contexts. Objectivity emerges from the social systems in which the research is conducted. Science proceeds when research communities observe, classify, and make judgments about a part of the world. It also proceeds when people involved in discovery and theorizing engage with each other about the ideas and values that play a role in their research—ideas and values that are background assumptions that structure their research programs. These are *background* assumptions because they are often not made explicit, but cooperative social engagement can bring some of them out into the open so that they can be examined and, if necessary, challenged. Scientists can help each other to see which assumptions direct and shape how they understand the part of the world under consideration, and what effects these have on their work. The trick is to ensure that values arising from social contexts do not go unexamined, but are instead examined in relation to the aims of science.

Longino addresses values in science is two ways. One way has to do with the values that come from the goals of science itself. To engage in scientific work requires one to embrace certain *scientific values*, such as curiosity, respect for truth, precision, and intellectual humility. The other way that she considers has to do with the impact of the values of the broader society that scientists belong to. These can shape scientific research, for example, by influencing scientists to think that certain questions are more important to ask than others, to treat certain sources of data as more important than others, or to ignore scientific questions that concern marginalized groups. These can be contrary to the values of science.

A good example concerns the use of male mice in biomedical research. The overwhelming majority of mice used in laboratory studies are male (around 80% of drug studies use only male mice). The preference for male mice is driven by the view that female mice are more variable than male mice because of hormonal fluctuations in their estrus cycle. However, the result of this is that many such studies do not reveal the differential effects of drugs on males and females, leading to treatments that are not appropriate for human females. For example, the sedative Ambien was tested only on male mice before being given to human subjects, on the assumption that it works the same way for both males and females. However, it was later discovered that the drug stays in women's bodies much longer than it stays in men's bodies. Twenty-one years after Ambien was introduced, the FDA developed new dosage guidelines for women. The failure to consider female-specific effects may explain why far more women than men report adverse reactions to medication. The US government now requires all biomedical research to use both male and female mice, unless there are compelling reasons not to do so (Locke 2014).

In addition to the spheres of influence emphasized by Longino, social values can also influence science by determining the standing of individuals within scientific communities. Beliefs about class, gender, race, and disability can make a difference to which people are included and which people are excluded, who gets access to resources and who does not, who is recognized and who is ignored. There is an interplay between the ways that values affect scientific research and outcomes—the factors that Longino describes—and the ways that they affect the positions of individuals within scientific communities. Again, in the case of laboratory mice, the gender imbalance of biomedical researchers in favor of men may have influenced the preference for using male mice in clinical trials and experimentation. Scientific communities that exclude or discriminate against women may do science differently than those that include women on an equal footing, because they will not have access to women's perspectives and priorities. Consequently, objectivity may be compromised (Fox Keller 1996; Lloyd 2006).

Gender-based and class-based discrimination among the Bolognese scientific elites certainly had an impact on the obscuring of Anna Morandi. By the lights of the methods of the day for doing science, and by the lights of her peers' evaluation of her anatomical work, Morandi's work counted as science. What is curious is that she was not given recognition *as a scientist*. The scientists of her day were blinkered by unexamined social biases and values that were contrary to the values that are intrinsic to science.

8.4 Conclusion

In theory, the skills and knowledge that are needed to function as a scientist are the only ones that count, and anyone who possesses them can have access to the scientific community. The assumption is that science is a meritocracy, and that members of the scientific community are, collectively, an impartial judge of expertise. As the case of Morandi shows us, a person can function as a scientist without being given the full recognition that is due to them on the basis of the merits of their work. The career of talented scientists may be limited by taken-for-granted assumptions about the kinds of people that are suited for practicing science at the highest levels.

Objectivity is not a value-free realm. Instead, it is achieved by fostering those social values that contribute to the growth of science and discarding those that impede it. To do this, scientists must attend to social values and recognize that they are an essential part of science. They need to track how values insert themselves into the social structure of science and determine who is included, excluded, recognized, or marginalized, as well as how they impact on the specifics of research. It is only by attending to social values that science can hope to achieve the kind of objectivity that beings like us can have. And recognizing values as intrinsic to scientific objectivity leads naturally to ethical and political commitments that are often seen as completely separate from science, or even antagonistic to scientific objectivity.

Social justice and egalitarianism *promote* scientific objectivity because they create conditions that allow more people to fully participate in science, and a greater variety of viewpoints to inform scientific work.

The case of Anna Morandi illustrates that the social features of life are entangled with science. It was not lost on her that because of the kind of person she was—a female person from a humble background—she was not given her due by the gatekeepers of the scientific realm. She obliquely communicated this in her wax self-portrait. In it, she stands dressed as an upper-class lady, with a string of pearls around her neck and a human brain peering through its opened skull on the table before her, her hands poised to perform the delicate operation of dissecting it. In presenting the world with that image of herself, Morandi laid claim to the respect accorded to women of wealth, and by picturing herself dissecting that most intricate of organs she communicates a message to us, down through the centuries, that she was a woman with a brain.

Bibliography

Barker, G., and Kitcher, P. 2013. *Philosophy of Science: A New Introduction.* Oxford: Oxford University Press.

Fox Keller, E. 1996. *Reflections on Gender and Science.* New Haven, CT: Yale University Press.

Godfrey-Smith, P. 2003. *Theory and Reality: An Introduction to the Philosophy of Science.* Chicago: University of Chicago Press.

Harding, S. 2015. *Objectivity and Diversity: Another Logic of Scientific Research.* Chicago: University of Chicago Press.

Kitcher, P. 1993. *The Advancement of Science.* Oxford: Oxford University Press.

Lloyd, E. A. 2006. *The Case of the Female Orgasm: Bias in the Science of Evolution.* Cambridge, MA: Harvard University Press.

Locke, S. 2014. "US Government to Require Affirmative Action for Female Lab Mice." https://www.vox.com/2014/5/14/5717516/government-says-researchers-must-use-male-and-female-animals-and-cells.

Longino, H. E. 1990. *Science as Social Knowledge: Values and Objectivity in Scientific Inquiry.* Princeton, NJ: Princeton University Press.

Messbarger, R. 2010. *The Lady Anatomist: The Life and Work of Anna Morandi Manzolini.* Chicago: University of Chicago Press.

Popper, K. 2002. *Conjectures and Refutations: The Growth of Scientific Knowledge.* New York: Routledge.

Salmon, W. C. 2017. *Foundations of Scientific Inference.* Pittsburgh: University of Pittsburgh Press.

9

Technology

Experience and Mediated Realities

Robin L. Zebrowski

It was a dark and stormy night. Every horror story seems to begin this way, and this one is no exception. In 1816 Geneva, it really was a dark and stormy night in a giant villa on the Swiss countryside. A teenaged girl, the daughter of an early proto-feminist philosopher she never knew, was charged, by agreement with her friends, with writing a ghost story. Her mother, Mary Wollstonecraft, had once argued that young girls should be educated the way young boys were because girls are full and complete human beings and not merely eventual companions for their future husbands. *Philosophy for Girls* might very well be a continuation of Wollstonecraft's project, but it's the younger Mary whose story holds our interest now. On that dark and stormy night, Mary Shelley begin writing the novel that would eventually be titled *Frankenstein; or, The Modern Prometheus*. The story itself is now as cliché as the dark and stormy night that produced it, but Shelley's worries endure. The questions regarding lines between natural and artificial worlds and the hubris involved in the human need to muck about with technologies that hadn't been thoughtfully considered in advance are quite alive, even now. Especially now.

9.1 The Nature of Technology

The technology that Shelley chose as the focus of her story was the creation of life, of a mind, artificially in a lab. Two hundred years later, we can't open a single media interface (TV, Twitter, Facebook, proprietary news apps, newspapers, etc.) that isn't reporting on some aspect of artificial intelligence (AI), that is, the creation of a mind, artificially in a lab. The nature of technology is unclear, though there is a field of philosophy dedicated to studying

Robin L. Zebrowski, *Technology* In: *Philosophy for Girls*. Edited by: Melissa M. Shew and Kimberly K. Garchar, Oxford University Press (2020). © Oxford University Press. DOI: 10.1093/oso/9780190072919.003.0010.

it. Defining the scope of technology turns out to be a nontrivial part of the philosophizing about it. The computer on which I write is a technology, of course, but so is the fluorescent light humming annoyingly above me and the heavily scribbled volume of *Frankenstein* that sits beside me. Indeed, books are deceptive technologies because even if we can be convinced to re-member that the physical artifact is a technology, it often takes much more convincing to recognize that the language itself, contained in that book, is also a technology.

Much of the work in the philosophy of technology involves new and emer-ging technologies. We may spend our day considering what kinds of things must be true of human minds to make it possible to create a mind in a ma-chine, or we may think about the various ways virtual reality and robot tech-nologies are already affecting social institutions like education. A person might even be tempted to forget that fire and agriculture and shoes are tech-nologies and therefore also subject to the same kinds of examination and cri-tique. Thus, the nature of technology is, like all aspects of philosophy, up for debate. Nonetheless, I have yet to encounter a better definition than the one offered by science fiction writer Ursula LeGuin: "Technology is the active human interface with the material world." She reminds us that "technology is how a society copes with physical reality: how people get and keep and cook food, how they clothe themselves, what their power sources are (animal? human? water? wind? electricity? other?) what they build with and what they build, their medicine, and so on and on."[1] In other words, technology is not just what's happening in Silicon Valley or on our computers, but it is present in nearly every aspect of our lives. As such, technology makes visible much of what is invisible to us and is already part of the work we need to do.

Frankenstein was a horror story not because there was a monster on the loose (in fact, reading Shelley's *Frankenstein* you can find very little of the pop culture idea of the monster at all) but because an untested technological innovation was used secretly by a man in pursuit of his own selfish goals. Even worse, when the creature proved to have agency of his own, the creator refused to accept responsibility for the kind of thing he'd unleashed onto an unsuspecting society. Anyone who looks to the history of the invention of the telephone, or watches the founder of Facebook testify before the US Congress and UK's Parliament, should recognize this theme as it re-emerges again and again with every new communication technology. The social questions about responsible use of these new technologies are like Mary Shelley's worst nightmares, emerging over and over in real time.[2]

9.2 Technology and Boundaries

Almost every aspect of technological innovation and deployment is a valid and necessary point of philosophical examination and critique. There are few questions more deeply philosophical than asking what it means to be distinctly human in a way that separates us from other animals and other things in the world. We might take it as an obvious point that our bodies are part of who we are and that the technologies we interact with in the world are not, at least not literally. For example, I don't think intuitively of my phone as a part of who I am in the way I do think that my brain or my deeply held beliefs are part of who I am. If we poke around the edges, however, challenges to this intuition arise. Neuroscience tells us that when we use some kinds of tools, our bodies quickly take them up and represent them to our brains as though they were a part of our physical bodies themselves.[3] This absorption is true of a blind person and her cane and of the writer and her pen or keyboard. Many of our tools become a part of who we are to varying degrees, but perhaps a person doesn't want to allow for these external devices to count as a part of her body. What about implanted devices, then? Pacemakers or implants designed to stimulate various organs from the inside, or perhaps an artificial heart: Do these devices count as part of me? If not, I might think of the caffeine I am ingesting. At some point, there's no clear line between me and the molecules of caffeine, so surely, at least pharmaceuticals can be said to be a part of me. Likewise, many people speak of antidepressants as though they return the user to their true selves when the medicine is in their bodies. What it means to be the kinds of creatures we are and what counts as part of my body or my "self" are not settled matters of science or philosophy; these remain open questions, with different technologies pushing our intuitions in disparate directions.

The debate isn't just about how to circumscribe a human body, either. Some theorists have argued that it is actually human nature to be malleable in this way. According to them, we are the kinds of creatures who have always been deeply entwined with our technologies such that this engagement is the proper way to think of human nature.[4] They think that it is our nature to be able to engage with tools on a deeply symbiotic level. We simply are tool-using creatures and, as such, have evolved to adapt to those changing tools. Whether we should fear this way of losing ourselves in the world or embrace it hinges on yet more assumptions about what and where we are, however. There are doctors who use telerobotics to perform delicate surgeries from hundreds of miles away. Either the tools performing the operation are a kind of extension of the doctor's hands, or they aren't. If they aren't, it's unclear where we should place blame when a doctor makes an error and her patient suffers. We must decide whether the doctor's tool is a mere tool in a causal relationship between the doctor and her patient or whether it's more accurate to describe it as literally a part of the body and mind of the doctor. There are legal and social reasons to think of these tools as part of ourselves as much as philosophical and metaphysical reasons to do so. If a person relies on a prosthetic limb, for example, she seems to exist in the same relation to it that someone else may have with a biological limb. A stolen prosthetic, then, may have deeper legal and moral implications than stolen property.

If a human being is the kind of creature whose mind or self could be said to "leak" into the world because of her flexible boundaries with technologies, however, we might fear that this oozing threatens to dissolve the very sense of a self or our actual selves. If we fear it does, that's partly because of our deeply held conceptions of the nature of being human. For example, Western cultures tend to construct a sense of self that rests on some deep, unchanging core. Whatever it is, it's what makes five-year-old you and today's version of you both still something rightfully referred to as "you" despite radical changes to your body, mind, beliefs, interests, and so on through time. If we challenge that conception, though, and if we tell you that deep down, the kind of creature you are is one that *must* blend or already be blended with various kinds of technological artifacts or tools, then imagining yourself cut off, an individual with strictly bounded edges or a deep unchanging core, is to imagine you as a stunted, incomplete thing.[5] The stakes here are very high. If you approach the world as a being who is fundamentally isolated from other people and the environment, you're likely to end up with various kinds of rugged individualism. Instead, thinking of yourself as necessarily coupled with various parts of the environment (including, potentially, other people) offers a wildly different way of being. Imagine what the world looks like when approached from these different ways of being: from environmentalism to architectural design of public spaces, considering tools and people differently results in an entirely different kind of world.

Others wonder if we've mistaken the entire framework of how to talk about minds, a mistake that would carry over into our understanding of our technologies. As Louise Barrett describes it: "If we think of cognition as an active process, and 'mind' as something animals do rather than something they 'have,' then questions about whether 'minds' are things inside the head, or things that can exist outside them, don't really make much sense."[6] Just deciding what counts as legitimately a part of a person's body turns out to be a debate that takes place at the overlap between metaphysics and philosophy of technology. For these questions, there are no easy or obviously correct answers.

9.3 Where We Are

Theorist Sandy Stone tells a great story in one of her essays about how she fell in love with Stephen Hawking's prosthesis.[7] Hawking was a brilliant physicist who had ALS, a condition that made it nearly impossible for him to move more than his fingers or even to speak. As a result, he had an assistive device, including an artificial speech system and keyboard, with which he could interface in order to continue to give talks and communicate more generally. During one of his talks, Stone was initially unable to get a seat inside the auditorium and so sat in the overflow room, using a screen to watch the talk, which was happening in the next room. She eventually snuck into the room to see Hawking in person. As she reports: "And a thing happens in my head. Exactly where, I say to myself, *is* Hawking? Am I any closer to him now than I was outside? In an important sense, Hawking doesn't stop being Hawking at the edge of his visible body. There is the obvious physical Hawking, vividly outlined by the way our social conditioning teaches us to see a person as a person. But a serious part of Hawking extends to the box in his lap . . . Where does he stop? Where are his edges?" (Stone 1995, 395).

In this way, philosophical questions about technology overlap with discourses around and about disabilities. Stone's questions arose when she was confronted with Hawking's assistive devices. Her questions overlap with disability studies, which offer distinct perspectives into the philosophy of technology because of the unique role that assistive devices play in the everyday lives of their users. To this end, we might also look to the arguments of Sara Hendren, who has convincingly claimed that *all* technology is assistive.[8] If we consider what we use technologies for, we're likely to agree with her. For instance, my word processing software, combined with my laptop and its handy keyboard, are all enabling me to do a kind of fast writing and rapid revision that a pen and paper don't really allow for, though pen and paper are useful in other ways. Similarly, literature from disabled theorists and theorists of disability richly translates societal failures that may be invisible to many people because the not-yet-disabled or the not-that-way-disabled interface with the world in a different way.[9] For example, Rose Eveleth points out that in a rush to create newer, bigger, flashier technologies like exoskeletons, societies tend to entirely overlook social changes and changes to infrastructure that would benefit the would-be users of exoskeletons.[10] It turns out that there are serious physical limits on who can use exoskeletons as they currently exist due to issues like height and weight restrictions as well as bone density constraints and the need for the user to be able to use their arms. As a result of these challenges, we should inevitably be asking ethical and metaphysical questions about constructing landscapes that are more accessible to different kinds of bodies.

In her classic essay on the notion of a cyborg, Donna Haraway encouraged us to embrace the ways that we are both literally and figuratively blended with our machinery and environments in daily life.[11] She asked us to cast off our notions of essentialism and revel in the new world where everything is part one thing and part another. There is no pure essence of "woman" or "animal." Instead, there are many ways of being many things. This liberating view suggested that we would be free when we saw that we already are part machine. If the system of machines and programs we are embedded in is unhealthy or exploitative, however, such liberation might not follow. Unfortunately, there are many examples of technology companies building systems and devices in ways that reveal they may not be considering their users, the social implications of their technologies, or the infrastructure involved. In some cases, this can be a source of incredible social and personal damage. We'll come back to this soon.

9.4 Artificial Intelligence (AI)

An eighteen-year-old Mary Shelley is still lurking. Largely a catalog of ways that human beings can be terrible in the face of our own agency, greed, and uncontrollable creations, her book is also about the very nature of those creations. In AI, these same two issues are always in tension. Philosophers and psychologists have been arguing about the nature of the mind for as long as we've been able to ask the question. For instance, if we want to build an artificial mind, our minds must be the kinds of things that can be replicated in a particular kind of substance, like a computer. Some theorists believe the mind is the kind of thing a computer could do, be, or create. Even if a person rejects the deeply held religious beliefs of so many who think that the mind is not identical to the brain and can survive the death of the body to persist into an afterlife, she still may not accept that thinking is the same thing as computation.[12] I may find it unlikely that we can simply run some code on a computer and have it be the same sort of thing as what I'm doing when I think about a sunset, for example. The entire project of strong AI/AGI (Artificial General Intelligence), however, rests on the idea that minds and computers are the same kinds of things on a deep level.[13]

The underlying structure of the society that allowed Victor Frankenstein to pursue his scientific project and the ways the creature and Victor reacted and interacted in the face of those structures are, in many ways, the best way to think about many of the projects in the philosophy of technology.[14] One of the first philosophical topics raised and explored after reading *Frankenstein* tends to be about the ethics of it all. Readers seek ethical parameters and frameworks for a host of topics from the creation of the creature in the first place to how the creature is treated after coming into existence, who should be held accountable for real or perceived ethical transgressions, and more. These topics persist about the more mundane kinds of AI, such as AI that is not a mind and doesn't aspire to be one but instead consists of clever algorithms designed to perform most of the automated functions of daily life. Whereas between roughly 1950 and the early 2000s, most uses of the term "AI" were referring to the mad science project of creating a genuine mind, most now refer to the widespread use of algorithms that have been deployed in nearly every aspect of life around much of the world. Regrettably, most of that deployment has been driven by profit and naïveté rather than thoughtfully considered attempts to improve the well-being of people or the planet.

9.5 Algorithms

Some algorithms perpetuate, reinforce, reinvent, and enshrine ways to be racist, misogynistic, transphobic, and more, further marginalizing groups of people through our technologies. These harmful attitudes embedded in some algorithms are staggering, and we are only beginning to talk about ways to undo the damage already done. While the examples may change, the broad problems and questions about automation and its relation to human existence remain similar. Indeed, the now-iconic image of the robot Maria, from the film *Metropolis* (1927) and based on the book by Thea Von Harbou,[15] reminds us of the ways that bodies are thought of and used in a capitalist society facing increasing automation and income inequality. In this story, the human becomes machine, and the machine becomes human. A hundred years later, philosophers still worry about this same issue. We have so much fiction that explores these questions with the flavor and texture that only fiction can offer, but philosophy explores the very same worries, carving them up with different tools.[16]

Unlike philosophical concerns raised about automation during the industrial revolutions, philosophers now attend to automation happening via algorithms. Invisible proprietary code, often inscrutable to its own programmers, is built with large data sets spoiled either by intentional omission or ignorance in the training data, all coming together to affect our daily lives in ways that render us powerless.[17] Consider something fairly straightforward, like a company hiring employees. Like nearly all large tech firms in the early twenty-first century, Amazon realized there was a gender disparity among their employees. Amazon then built a tool to help scan resumes in order to identify candidates that would be a good fit for the company.[18] They used an algorithm to do so with the well-intentioned belief that it would cut down on unconscious discrimination on the part of a human hiring staff, who would be more likely to keep hiring men. In Amazon's case it was eventually discovered that the training set used was so heavily male that the program began to rank female candidates as less desirable; after all, they were clearly not what the company was looking for, or there would be more of them working there already. The algorithm began to downgrade résumés that used the word "women's" in any club, class, volunteer work, and so on that the candidate had engaged in. The system taught itself to value women less, based on the examples it was given to learn from. Amazon eventually scrapped the project after Reuters broke the story.[19]

We can also consider algorithms used for predictive policing. Predictive policing is an attempt by law enforcement to determine in advance what crime patterns might look like on a social or individual level in order to make decisions about sentencing and recidivism or the use of community resources. This topic is especially difficult because of recent and not-so-recent high-profile shootings of often unarmed black men in the United States by police officers. Imagine if every black man who came up for sentencing in a courtroom was given a harsher sentence than a white man for having committed the same crime because a judge ran profiles of each person through an algorithm that said the black man was more likely to recommit to a life of crime and less likely to reform. Imagine further that the algorithm being used was proprietary, having been sold to the courts by a private company that refused to allow the code to be examined so that their competitors couldn't access their work. In these cases, the defendant's attorney and the judge also can't tell the defendant why he receives the sentence he does. The United States certainly doesn't have a legal system set up for appeals under such circumstances, although this very scenario has happened.[20]

Imagine now if a corrupt police force consistently used abusive and illegal practices in their work, targeting minorities in stop-and-frisk or blatantly arresting people without cause. If they were to build an algorithmic tool that took into account how often someone had been arrested and included that data in their predictions about the likelihood that person would commit future crimes, the "dirty data" in the training set, which includes false arrests and police harassment, would have a snowball effect, causing even more injustice to be visited onto these individuals.[21]

Philosophers have a role in asking what it means to say something is "objective" and therefore trustworthy in relation to these technologies, and in asking if the potential good these technologies could do outweighs the life-altering harm to those unjustly targeted by the system. Philosophers consider whether it's even possible for algorithms like the two mentioned earlier to ever be objective, untainted by human influence or interpretation. If such objectivity isn't possible, a host of ethical issues follow regarding how to convince people to treat others justly through ethical algorithms.[22] Philosophy has a lot of work to do right now because these algorithms have tentacles that reach far beyond the places where the programs are written or the data is gathered.

When a person Googles labels related to her identity, like "black girl" or "queer" or "asexual," the search engine does not produce neutral results but suggests what may be associated with those identities. (For a fun time, Google "why are philosophers" and just let Google predict what you might be interested in about philosophers. We don't drink that much, and we aren't that depressed or arrogant. But if you don't know much about philosophers, Google is happy to give you some ideas.) This is now a well-studied phenomenon, but we still don't know what kinds of effects it has on various aspects of our social lives.[23] A search engine's suggestions can reinforce harmful stereotypes and offer new stereotypes that the person might not have considered. The social sciences matter here for doing the empirical work of understanding the ways these biases make their way into various social and technological systems, but the ethics of using said systems, and the role of that technology in our understanding of and quest for truth, are questions philosophers must and do take up in order to formulate the right questions. Socrates asked about the nature of truth and justice, and today we may still not have definitive answers, but we can point out things that are clearly unjust and damaging as our tools and societies continue to evolve and change around us.

Clearly, we need to examine philosophically current algorithmic technologies, but even more than that, we need philosophy to have teeth in these debates. Philosophers can already provide reasons for what's wrong with using facial recognition technology (broadly), particularly when it misidentifies black women at an enormously higher rate than white men.[24] What we need is someone to listen to philosophers when we talk about the ethics of technology (should all facial recognition technology be banned?),[25] about the metaphysics of technology (is strong AI even possible?),[26] about the epistemology of technology (can a computer program ever be "objective"?), about the relationship between humans and technology (am I always already part machine?), and about the nature of truth as it relates to communication technologies (what is "fake news," and how can we recognize nuanced truth in a world where deep fakes and Twitter propaganda challenge our usual checks and balances regarding what's true and actual?). Where do I stop, and where does my computer begin?

9.6 Conclusion

The subtitle of *Frankenstein* is "The Modern Prometheus." In Greek myth, Prometheus was most popularly understood to have stolen fire from the gods to give it to humankind. But other stories of Prometheus include the idea that he created humankind out of clay. If Victor Frankenstein is the Prometheus figure, there are interesting ways to understand what Mary Shelley was trying to warn us of in the book. Victor tells us about his childhood obsession with alchemy and how the excitement of electricity is the first thing that draws him away from the doomed pseudoscience.[27] Constantly, though, Victor reminds us that he had no early formal schooling, that his family were not scientific, and that if he had been more formally educated and learned scientific principles, he would not have been led so far astray. His father dismisses a book of alchemy as "sad trash," and Victor recounts that if his father had explained what was wrong with alchemy instead of dismissing it, "it is even possible, that the train of my ideas would never have received the fatal impulse that led to my ruin." The lack of engagement with the claims, the lack of evidence and argument with the ideas, and the push toward a science wherein he was not sufficiently grounded in the principles came together to produce a person who created an intelligent creature. And when he couldn't understand or control that creature, he cast it out into the greater world, causing deaths and societal harms he couldn't have imagined.

We are all surrounded by Victor Frankensteins right now, creating technologies without a grounding them in philosophical ideas and principles. We are watching technological creations gain strength and cause harm even as we can see they misunderstand the world in which they've been set loose. Mary Shelley's story is a premonition of the many ways that humans create and disavow powerful technologies, leaving others to clean up the messes and grapple with the fallout. Today it is algorithms, AI, technologies of climate change, and more, and tomorrow it will be something new. The story remains the same unless we commit to not making Victor's mistake. We must do hard the work of philosophy to save the world.

Notes

1. Le Guin (2004).
2. See also Midgley, particularly her chapters "Biotechnology and the Yuk Factor" (145–153) and "The Supernatural Engineer" (162–172) (2004).
3. Cardinali et al. (2009).
4. Clark (2003).
5. Hayles (1999); Barrett (2011).
6. Barrett (2011, 199).
7. Stone (1995).
8. Hendren (2014).
9. There are so many interesting arguments at the overlap of philosophy and disability studies. See, for example, Heflin and Johnson (2018); Thompson (1997).
10. Eveleth (2019).
11. Haraway (1991, 149–181).
12. For more on this, see the debates around the nature of AI and functionalism. A good starter anthology of classic texts is Boden (1990). There is significant recent work in this area.

13. Ibid. For interesting discussions about how we attribute intelligence to things versus how we understand those things to be by nature, see Dennett (1997), and the rich literature that follows, particularly Kukla (2018).
14. Systems, including social systems, are themselves a technology.
15. Von Harbou (1927; first English translation of 1925 book).
16. No recommendations could keep up with this genre, but movies with these themes include *Ex Machina*; *Robbie*; *Her*; and books like Ashby (2012).
17. Eubanks (2018); Noble (2013); Noble (2018).
18. Dastin (2018).
19. Read about this and so many more discriminatory systems from AI Now's white paper by West et al. (2019).
20. Hao (2019).
21. Richardson et al. (forthcoming).
22. There is an important point to be made here. If something like facial recognition technology is inherently immoral, we cannot simply talk about ensuring it doesn't discriminate against members of one demographic. Ensuring an unethical system doesn't discriminate continues to leave us with an unethical system. See, for an incredible meta-commentary on technologies criticism, Keyes et al. (2019).
23. Noble (2018).
24. Buolamwini and Gebru (2018).
25. For a robust discussion of approaching complex technological issues with human flourishing and virtue centered, see Vallor (2016).
26. Zebrowski (2010).
27. Shelley (1831).

Bibliography

Ashby, Madeline. 2012. *vN: The First Machine Dynasty*. Nottingham: Angry Robot.
Barrett, Louise. 2011. *Beyond the Brain: How Body and Environment Shape Human and Animal Minds*. Princeton, NJ: Princeton University Press.
Boden, Margaret A. (ed.) 1990. *The Philosophy of Artificial Intelligence*. Oxford: Oxford University Press.
Buolamwini, Joy, and Timnit Gebru, 2018. "Gender Shades: Intersectional Accuracy Disparities in Commercial Gender Classification." *Proceedings of Machine Learning Research* 81: 1–15.
Cardinali, Lucia, Francesca Frassinetti, Claudio Brozzoli, Christian Urquizar, Alice C. Roy, and Allessandro Farnè 2009. "Tool Use Induces Morphological Updating of the Body Schema." *Current Biology* 19, no. 12: R478–479.
Clark, Andy. 2003. *Natural Born Cyborgs: Minds, Technologies, and the Future of Human Intelligence*. New York: Oxford University Press.
Dastin, Jeffery. 2018. "Amazon Scraps Secret AI Recruiting Tool That Showed Bias Against Women." *Reuters*, October 9. https://www.reuters.com/article/us-amazon-com-jobs-automation-insight/amazon-scraps-secret-ai-recruiting-tool-that-showed-bias-against-women-idUSKCN1MK08G.

Dennett, Daniel. 1997. "True Believers: The Intentional Strategy and Why It Works." In *Mind Design II: Philosophy, Psychology, and Artificial Intelligence*, ed. John Haugeland, 57–80. Cambridge, MA: MIT Press.

Eubanks, Virginia. 2018. *Automating Inequality: How High-Tech Tools Profile, Police, and Punish the Poor*. New York: St. Martin's Press.

Eveleth, Rose. 2019. "The Exoskeleton's Hidden Burden." *The Atlantic*, April 25. https://www.theatlantic.com/technology/archive/2015/08/exoskeletons-disability-assistive-technology/400667/.

Haraway, Donna. 1991. "A Cyborg Manifesto: Science, Technology, and Socialist-Feminism in the Late Twentieth Century." In *Simians, Cyborgs, and Women: The Reinvention of Nature*, 149–181. New York: Routledge.

Hao, Karen. 2019. "AI is Sending People to Jail—And Getting It Wrong." *MIT Technology Review*, January 21. https://www.technologyreview.com/s/612775/algorithms-criminal-justice-ai/.

Hayles, Katherine N. 1999. *How We Became Posthuman: Virtual Bodies in Cybernetics, Literature, and Informatics*. Chicago: University of Chicago Press.

Heflin, Ashley Shew, and Keith Johnson. 2018. "Companion Animals as Technologies in Biomedical Research." *Perspectives on Science* 23, no. 3: 400–417.

Hendren, Sara. 2014. "All Technology is Assistive." *Wired*, October 16. https://www.wired.com/2014/10/all-technology-is-assistive/.

Keyes, Os, Jevan Hutson, and Meredith Durbin. 2019. "A Mulching Proposal: Analyzing and Improving an Algorithmic System for Turning the Elderly into High-Nutrient Slurry." CHI Conference on Human Factors in Computing Systems 2019, May, Glasgow, Scotland. https://dl.acm.org/doi/10.1145/3290607.3310433.

Kukla, Rebecca. 2018. "Embodied Stances: Realism Without Literalism." In *The Philosophy of Daniel Dennett*, ed. Bryce Huebner, 3–31. Oxford: Oxford University Press.

Le Guin, Ursula. 2004. "A Rant About Technology." Accessed April 25. http://www.ursulakleguin.com/Note-Technology.html.

Midgley, Mary. 2004. *The Myths We Live By*. New York: Routledge.

Noble, Safiya Umoja. 2018. *Algorithms of Oppression: How Search Engines Reinforce Racism*. New York: New York University Press.

Noble, Safiya Umoja. 2013. "Google Search: Hyper-visibility as a Means of Rendering Black Women and Girls Invisible." *InVisible Culture: An Electronic Journal for Visible Culture*, no. 19. http://ivc.lib.rochester.edu/google-search-hyper-visibility-as-a-means-of-rendering-black-women-and-girls-invisible/.

Richardson, Rashida, Jason Schulz, and Kate Crawford. Forthcoming. "Dirty Data, Bad Predictions: How Civil Rights Violations Impact Police Data, Predictive Policing Systems, and Justice." *NYU Law Review Online*.

Shelley, Mary W. *Frankenstein, or: The Modern Prometheus*. London: Henry Colburn and Richard Bentley, 1831. https://www.gutenberg.org/files/42324/42324-h/42324-h.htm.

Stone, Sandy. 1995. "Split Subjects Not Atoms: or, How I Fell In Love With My Prosthesis." In *The Cyborg Handbook*, ed. Chris Hables Gray, 393–406. New York: Routledge.

Thompson, Rosemarie Garland. 1997. *Extraordinary Bodies: Figuring Physical Disability in American Culture and Literature*. New York: Columbia University Press.

Vallor, Shannon. 2016. *Technology and the Virtues: A Philosophical Guide to a Future Worth Wanting*. Oxford: Oxford University Press.

Von Harbou, Thea. 1927. *Metropolis*. London: Readers Library Publishing Company.

West, Sarah Myers, Meredith Whittaker, and Kate Crawford. Year. "Discriminating Systems: Gender, Race, and Power in AI." AI Now Institute, April. https:// ainowinstitute.org/discriminatingsystems.html.

Zebrowski, Robin. 2010. "In Dialogue With the World: Merleau-Ponty, Rodney Brooks, and Embodied Artificial Intelligence." *Journal of Consciousness Studies* 17, nos. 7–8: 156–172.

10

Art

Seeing, Thinking, Making

Patricia M. Locke

Two painters, with very different styles, show how the artist comes to know and express what she knows. The painters I have in mind are Berthe Morisot (1841–1895) and Agnes Martin (1912–2004). Morisot, a French Impressionist, painted images of her daughter Julie and other family members, as well as outdoor scenes. Her works in oil, watercolors, and pastels were small, best seen in small-scale rooms like those in many of her pictures. Morisot helped bring about a revolutionary change in painting, since she was primarily interested in light and color rather than making a good copy of the things she saw.

Agnes Martin's mature style was very different: large 152.4 × 152.4 cm (6 × 6 ft) abstract oil paintings, often with grids or stripes in pastel colors. Most of the time her stripes are horizontal, to keep viewers from "falling in" to the painting when absorbed in looking. The titles of her late, luminous paintings are curious: often sweet or affectionate titles, like "Baby Love" or "Happiness." The titles make you ask, how are pale pink and baby blue stripes happiness? How do they call to us, when thin paint and even thinner pencil lines mark the canvas? I think it has something to do with the way natural light interacts with the surface. Instead of showing us light falling on objects, like Morisot does, her canvas *is* the object light falls on. You get to be the witness of this perceptual event happening when a cloud passes over the sun, and the painting shakes just a little in its excitement. You get to experience happiness!

Gertrude Stein, a pioneering literary figure and art collector, once said: "Artists do not experiment. Experiment is what scientists do; they initiate an operation of unknown factors to be instructed by its results. An artist puts down what she knows and at every moment it is what she knows at that moment." I think Gertrude Stein meant that the artist expresses what she

Patricia M. Locke, *Art* In: *Philosophy for Girls*. Edited by: Melissa M. Shew and Kimberly K. Garchar, Oxford University Press (2020). © Oxford University Press. DOI: 10.1093/oso/9780190072919.003.0011.

knows right now, gathered from perceiving, imagining, remembering, and handling materials in skillful ways. She has direct contact with her subject matter and helps us come to understand reality as well. Philosophers of art try to articulate *how* and *why* artists make what they make, and what effects their works have on us. By doing this, we come to know more about perception, and often raise questions that bear on our understanding of what it means to be human. Art making may help us wrestle with questions about how we are connected to others and the natural world, but the work of art *is* its own meaning, and does not primarily point to goals beyond itself. By looking closely at and comparing Morisot's and Martin's paintings, we can draw out the meaning of the experience of art. My big questions are: How is art a way of knowing? What do we know through our making and appreciation of art works?

10.1 Berthe Morisot

Morisot lived in nineteenth-century Paris, among artist friends and relatives. As an artist, she was respected by her peers: Renoir, Manet, Degas, and Cassatt, to name a few. Yet as a woman, she wasn't welcome in places where men socialized or found subjects for their work, like backstage in the theatre or in late-night cafés. Under those constraints, she painted her family reading, playing music, or getting dressed for a party. Sometimes she hired models, but the compositions primarily explore the intimate world of modern women. Interestingly, her work often shows girls and women alone. It makes me wonder: What are they thinking about? This question haunts the lovely pictures and keeps them from being too sentimental or too pretty.

In *The Human Condition*, the philosopher Hannah Arendt carefully distinguishes between labor, which is necessarily repetitious (like doing dishes), and work, which like art making and philosophical thinking, can be creative and unique. Labor does the activities we need to live, but its results disappear when we eat the food or wear the clothes. We end up having to repeat chores over and over, with effort that often goes unnoticed. Berthe Morisot translated the invisible tasks of housekeeping into permanent images. She painted women cooking, ironing, and doing laundry. *Woman Hanging Out the Wash*, for instance, shows the value of a woman's labor, with lovely arm gestures framed by rather abstract sheets in a garden setting.[1] As an upper-middle-class married woman, Berthe Morisot didn't have to sell her paintings to earn a living. Her subjects were often people like herself, yet she was mindful of servants and their toil. She was both restricted in the scope of her subject matter by being a woman and privileged by a secure financial situation. This support made it possible for her to be in the avant-garde of painting in her era: she successfully showed her work in all the Impressionist exhibitions from 1875 to 1886, except during the year her daughter was born.

In the 1860s and beyond, Morisot painted outside, *en plein air*, using the newly popular tubes full of oil paint. Despite her restrictive clothing and social customs, she found herself outdoors at her easel, trying new methods in watercolors as well. She gradually worked toward painting people in outdoor settings, with the effects of natural light. Morisot is known especially for her brushwork, which is light and airy. The French call this "*effleurer*," to touch the canvas as lightly as a *fleur*/flower petal. This sometimes looks soft, and sometimes scratchy, in ways that catch the light. Her light and feathery touch expresses the changing light reflected off of different surfaces. Absorbed in the problem of transitory effects, Morisot gave us lasting images.

When we look at her work slowly, we can think about a fleeting moment or particular place. Paradoxically, a painting like *Cottage Interior* takes the everyday incident of a young girl playing with her doll and makes that act have wider meaning (see Figure 10.1).[2]

Playing, like labor, leaves no trace. But like making art, playing with a toy can be creative and imaginative. When we look at this painting, we can imagine a whole morning unfolding. Even though Morisot leaves out many details, we can see a broad table with the breakfast dishes still on it, and a wicker chair, pushed back as if the girl just stood up. Julie stands in the middle, as her body and white dress divide the composition into four sections. Below her hemline are the table to the left and the chair to the right. The skirt hem connects visually to the window frame in a horizontal direction, while her standing body is partly framed by the window in a vertical direction. All is orderly structure, made with strokes of color rather than relying on lines. When I look at the window frames, for instance, I see that they are not outlined. Instead, my eye has to imagine connecting passages of different colors to "make" the long rectangles of a picture window with a view of a garden and harbor. The frames practically melt into the bay, creating an opening to a far horizon.

Each of the four sections offer something to the eye: a seascape out the window, a still life on the table, a shadowy upholstered chair where perhaps her father recently sat, dark against sheer white drapery. Color unites these

Figure 10.1 Berthe Morisot, *Cottage Interior*, 1886
Oil on canvas, 50 × 60 cm (19 11/16 × 23 5/8 in)
Museum of Ixelles, Brussels. Gift of Fritz Toussaint.

quadrants, since the overall impression of a wide range of blues tending to-ward white is offset by complementary touches of glowing oranges, yellows, and pinks seen in the wicker chair, the bread on the table, Julie's hair, and the wall next to her blonde-headed doll. There is energy and vividness in the brush marks, and a formal spaciousness supported by Morisot's handling of color. The whole feels infused with light, from the snowy tablecloth and dishes, to the highlights caught by her dress. I might even describe the top left corner as empty, while the top right is full—full of details and short strokes. The bottom right is half empty, just a floor contrasting with the wicker chair. This means the bottom left is—you guessed it—half full, with tablecloth and dishes. The image as a whole is flatter than objects usually appear. I have the sensation of everything being much closer, while the elongated disk of the table and the chair seat are seen from different points of view. As my eyes move around, my felt body grows and shrinks, like Alice in Wonderland.

I can shift between two places; I can juxtapose thoughts and find surprising connections.

I go on at length to show how complex, organized, and harmonious the painting is, as are strong philosophical arguments. I can know something about how color works from observing this painting, how light falls on objects and is represented by color. As a viewer, I am invited to join Morisot to see all these relationships that reveal how my imagination contributes to my understanding. My memories of morning light help me recognize what is going on in this time and place. And my love of stories makes me want to ask the girl: What are you and your doll talking about? What are you thinking, as you intently look at her, while your mother, the artist, intently looks at you?

Cindy Kang, an art historian, says that Julie is absorbed in her own world, and is neither really outside (though framed by the window), nor inside interacting with us. Instead, she is like an artist at work, "developing her own subjective interiority."[3] This means exploring her inner life, just like a philosopher at work! The immediate source of work of art is, in Hannah Arendt's view, "the human capacity for thought."[4] It is exciting that a sensuous and relatively permanent art object is evidence of thinking that sustains a human world. Morisot's representational style does not try to match a photograph, but to draw our attention to aspects of the world that we don't usually notice. We have a chance to enter into her space and vision, to watch as the world circles around a private conversation between girl and doll, or girl and her own developing self.

Solitude is necessary for thinking, as an individual person steps away from engagement with others. Gertrude Stein and Hannah Arendt would agree that thinking, whether the first stages of art or philosophy, is an *un*scientific activity. Unlike problem solving cognition, thinking does not have a specific goal at first. Unlike logical deductive reasoning, a certain amount of free play accompanies its ongoing activity. Thinking needs neither data to analyze nor abstract rules to derive its conclusions. Thinking can be described as an inner dialogue with oneself, a highly active state that does not follow fixed steps. Rather, different byways are explored and playful connections are made. Thinking does not care about time or external results in its seeking, yet its contents are transformed by memory into thought, "crystalized" in art as a material object. In this painting, we see Julie thinking out loud with her doll. Even though we can't hear what she is saying, the touch of white paint on her ear makes me know she is a good listener too.

Cottage Interior is a visible part of an ongoing human world, a thing of beauty. Ironically, Arendt notes that "remembrance and the gift of recollection, from which all desire for imperishability springs, need tangible things to remind them, lest they perish themselves."[5] The permanence of art works can crystalize thinking in its transitory, continuous activity. Thinking is a mental activity found in most human beings, even if few of us have the clarity of mind and the precision of hand that Berthe Morisot did. She painted the light falling on a tablecloth, for example, with brush strokes that also call out light. This makes us aware not only of the subject matter of the image, but how humans see and understand the world. Art works maintain themselves as long-lasting evidence of thinking, as tangible representations of brief moments. They are memorable.

10.2 Agnes Martin

Agnes Martin was an artist first in New York and later in rural New Mexico.[6] Born in Canada in 1912, she lived into the twenty-first century. Martin called herself an Abstract Expressionist, which meant to her that she gave up representational space (which shows, for instance, the distances between chairs and a table). Instead, she painted her emotions in an infinite space without figures in it. Like Morisot, she was interested in light, color, and expressivity. Yet her canvases look entirely different.

One odd thing about Martin's work is that it is hard to photograph. The interesting variations of a work made by hand are almost invisible unless you are looking at the real thing. Her brush strokes are smooth—almost the opposite of Morisot's—and her colors are quiet. Agnes Martin's painting retains an aura, in part because of its resistance to reproduction. It resists as well the impulse of the mass market to shock, to speed, to the hypervirtuality of social media. It is fully present for the viewer who takes time to let her eyes adjust, her breathing slow down, and her thoughts come to rest, open to the plain abstract painting. Under these conditions, we can ask: How does it *feel* to see? Can we see with Agnes Martin's paintings what *seeing* means to us even when there is no subject matter reflected on the canvas?

I would like to think about what "abstract" and "expression" mean relative to these questions of how and what we know through art. Martin agrees with Arendt that we need independent solitude to make things. Martin had a wider freedom from social expectations than Berthe Morisot, but much of her adventure was in the mind. Abstraction, for a philosopher, can lead to general statements. We let particular details fall away, and then we can say something that is applicable to many situations. For example, take a syllogism, a deductive argument in a general form: 1) All human beings are mortal. 2) Agnes Martin is a human being. 3) Therefore, Agnes Martin is mortal. If we know the definitions of "human being" and "mortal," and the first two statements are true, we know that the conclusion will follow in an orderly, general way. I can substitute my own name (but not my cat Webster) for "Agnes Martin" and the syllogism will still make sense. We are pointing simultaneously to a true feature of being human, mortality, and to a valid argument structure.

How is this like Martin's painting? She set herself very simple guidelines and held to them for many years. These rules maximized the abstract general nature of her work, but opened up a surprising casket of treasures. She never grew tired of her basic forms, which included the same format (6 × 6 ft canvas), same materials (acrylic paint and pencils), and similar techniques (ruled lines over neutral primer, horizontal stripes or grids determined by the frame).[7] These were the general parameters, as she abstracted (or should I say "subtracted"?) from figures. She once remarked: "If you are alone, you focus in on everything. The sky and the wind and everything, all nature . . . The best moments of my life were when I was alone. They were the most enlightening, and therefore the happiest."[8] What was enlightening to her were insights about the general structures of reality. Transient clouds and winds occurred in a predictable context. She worked with the tension between change and stability, with mathematical calculations for the sizes of her stripes and grids. This gave a genuine clarity to her paintings.

Agnes Martin maintained the same style of applying paint and thin pencil lines by hand, from 1960 until her death in 2004. How was it, I wonder, that she was able to renew her painting within such strict form, while the art world "moved on" beyond the fashion for Abstract Expressionism. The word "beautiful," which suits Morisot's paintings, seems no longer of use in twenty-first-century art, and the word "abstract" is outmoded. Martin's work is not Morisot-like abstraction from a photographic copy of the visible world; rather, it turns toward the inner life to rigorously express the sensations that accompany joy, beauty, and serenity. Her ambitious goal was to make formal perfection and expressive emotions visible through beauty.

Her real breakthrough in the expression of beauty comes from thinking of the picture plane itself as a neutral field. She asked herself: How can I show in a nonobjective way feelings that are wordless, and furthermore, do not appear to sight? She took a cue from Euclidean geometry. The point, the line, and the plane stem from an a priori source.[9] If displayed as marks on canvas, points/dots in rows give a sense of the indefinite expansion of the plane. Martin's grids begin by carefully connecting dots by hand with pencil over thin layers of translucent color. Thus, there is a tension between the symmetry of a mathematical grid and the irregularities coming from the materials and the human gesture. She said:

> When I draw horizontals you see this big plane and you have certain feelings like you are expanding over the plane. Anything can be painted without representation . . . I like the horizontal line better than every other line. It's not related to anything in this world like landscape or anything, it goes out. When you look at the painting you go in, over the horizontal line. But they are not about the horizontal line, the painting is about meaning.[10]

The horizontal bands of thin washes of color stand as a barrier and as a horizon. From a distance her late paintings almost appear to be walls with just a trace of articulation, as in *Contentment* (1999), for example.[11] When we stand at mid-distance from the work, the subtle blues and white color interactions show themselves. The washes in her later works tended to be pale colored acrylics lightly applied to a bright white gessoed ground. Unlike Morisot, Martin made brush strokes that minimize expression. She relied on the texture of the primed canvas to create shadows in the thin paint and to disrupt the pencil lines that border the stripes. When we get closer, the pencil line's sensitivity to the weave of the canvas and light's physical journey across its expanse cause us to feel changed in scale. I feel smaller and pulled irresistibly toward the painting! She anticipated our desire to climb over the lines and dive into the painting. In this way, we could be immersed in the delicate feelings evoked by her soft palette.

This physical approach to the painting from long to short distance to immediate merging with it is felt by critics and attracts a steady stream of admirers and collectors. However, it also attracts vandals. Martin's work has had a high incidence of vandalism, by angry people that write on or mark her work to fill in the intolerable emptiness.[12] She did not repair her work, as she thought that accident is a part of its history. She signed her work on the back, and lived a quiet, private life. Thus, the hostility her paintings drew out is, I think, a sign of a conflict in some viewers: either they cannot recognize the feeling of contentment in the subtle field, or they are frustrated by recognizing the great distance between contentment and themselves. The art work's resistance to conventional ways of thinking about things is *felt* by these vandals. Martin felt contentment; unfortunately, they felt anger and deprivation. The paint's interaction with ambient light causes the art works to become dynamic. Martin hoped each light-giving canvas would act as a "portal" in the space of a gallery, causing a gap in the external world. Not everyone feels imaginatively free enough to enter it.

In one lecture, Agnes Martin emphasized the prepersonal aspect of her art: "There is happiness that we feel without any material stimulation. We may wake up in the morning feeling happy for no reason. Abstract or nonobjective feelings are a very important part of our lives. Personal emotions and sentimentality are anti-art."[13] By slow and careful looking at these repetitious stripes or grid patterns that offer a map to inner responses, we can become more aware of our interior life. The physical sensations and emotions we feel are ones we have in common with other human beings. "What do I really feel in this moment? What do I really think?" are good questions to begin a process of sorting out our tangled mental life, and of realizing what we share. Some of the nonobjective feelings Martin sought to convey include: the "descending feeling" you have when you see geese flying in for a landing; the infant's response to love; the sensation of playing without reserve; wheat fields. Martin lists "the wind in the grass, how happy the grass looks. And the shining waves following each other. The blue sky is a different kind of happiness. And the night is a different kind."[14] You see where this is heading, and why it would be so difficult to paint the innocence of trees in a nonsentimental way.

She was not trying to paint her personal feelings about specific events in her life as a woman. Martin's self-imposed restrictions in color, composition, and format enhanced her creative powers to express general structures. Her goal to paint beauty as a presentation of innocence and happiness was everrenewing. She helps viewers experience their own subtle feelings of the visible world and its interwoven structure.

From her life experience, Martin concluded: "We make art as something that we have to do not knowing how it will work out. When it is finished, we have to see if it is effective. Even if we obey inspiration, we cannot expect all the work to be successful. An artist is a person who can recognize failure."[15] Each artist has standards of success and failure, whether the work can express what and how she knows what she does in this moment. These standards are not just preference, or taste, but based on what is true now and for the future.

10.3 What About Us?

Let's return to the original questions: How is art a way of knowing? What do we know through our making and appreciation of art works?

These are two examples of one variety of visual arts. I could have chosen examples from music or sculpture as well. But this comparison between Berthe Morisot and Agnes Martin shows thinking minds at work, holding open a space to clarify what it means to be human, to perceive the world, and to have an interior life. The worldly experience of the art work sets up viewers' rhythm of attention, solidarity, and retreat that mirrors that of the artist. We notice our feelings and thoughts as well as the marks on the canvas, we realize that the artist is a thinker, like us, who realizes something about being human and shares it with us. We can use our new insights to retreat into solitude ourselves, to be creative and think our own thoughts. Whether in visual arts or writing, they can be the springboard for new connections with the world. By world, Hannah Arendt refers to the ground for human action, a shared place of perception, language use, and meaning. The world is inhabited by other members of our species: thinkers, makers, and perceivers alike. It has stability because of art, and it can change because of our responses to art.

As a parallel to philosophical contemplation of ideas, the experience of beholding art is at first a holding open of time. The aesthetically organized given world places me within a continuum of past making and present meaning. For example, even though the content of Berthe Morisot's paintings is far from the everyday life I lead, her expressive use of color brings forth responses from me. The wonder that prompted philosophical thinking in Socrates is present in the wonderful artwork. At the same time, when I behold the artwork, I become aware of my perceptual capacities. The pleasure that accompanies belonging in the world can also accompany me in retreat to my own internal dialogue. I claim, perhaps more than Arendt would, that perceiving a work of art is an alignment with others' perceiving, and a place of my own experience. Unlike nature, the work of art is in conversation with others of its kind over time.

If we open onto a common world, structured in part by our human productions of art works, buildings and languages, rituals and music, we have confirmation that others have thought before us, and left real evidence of their mindful creations. Thinking opens onto a world of long-lasting made things as evidence of others. We have solidarity with other people even when we turn to solitude for our own thinking. Arendt's careful distinguishing of work from labor on the one hand, and thinking from cognition on the other, allows us to see the vivid significance of works of art like those of Morisot and Martin. They draw out our own capacity for thoughtfulness. Art offers ways of knowing that make thinking and wordless feelings visible to us. While we look at practices of art making, or our own practices of paying attention, the artwork stands as unique in helping to make meaning in a human world.

Notes

1. Berthe Morisot, *Woman Hanging Laundry* (*La Blanchisseuse*), 1881. Oil on canvas, 46 × 67 cm (18 1/8 × 26 3/8 in); Ny Carlsberg Glyptotek (2018), Catalogue. 4. Look online for color images of works mentioned in this chapter.
2. Berthe Morisot, *Cottage Interior* (*Intérieur de cottage*), 1886. Oil on canvas, 50 × 60 cm (19 11/16 × 23 5/ in). Museum of Ixelles, Brussels, Gift of Fritz Toussaint, FT 104. CMR 201. https://www.wikiart.org/en/berthe-morisot/cottage-interior-also-known-as-interior-at-jersey
3. Kang (2018).
4. Arendt (1998, 168).
5. Ibid., 170.
6. In 2015, the Tate Modern held a major Agnes Martin retrospective. See videos as well as still images of her work on their website at https://www.tate.org.uk/context-comment/video/agnes-martin-road-trip.
7. In her later years, Martin made a concession to the difficulty of handling the canvasses that were taller than she was, by changing to a 5 × 5 foot format. Either way, the paintings fill the viewer's whole field of vision.
8. Martin (2003). This film is a documentary shot from 1998 through 2002, and is 37 minutes long.
9. *A priori* means prior to (before), or outside of experience. A pure thought in mathematics doesn't need an example in the world. Could an artistic thought be derived in this way?
10. Martin (2003).
11. Agnes Martin, *Contentment* (from *Innocent Love* series), 1999. Acrylic and graphite on canvas. 152.4 × 152.4 cm (6 × 6 ft). Lannan Foundation; long-term loan to Dia Art Foundation, https://www.diaart.org/program/exhibitions-projects/agnes-martin-collection-display.
12. Chave (1992).

13. Martin (1998, 154).
14. Ibid.
15. Ibid., 154–155.

Bibliography

Arendt, Hannah. 1998. *The Human Condition*. 2nd ed. Chicago: University of Chicago Press.

Chave, Anna C. 1992. "Agnes Martin: Humility, the Beautiful Daughter . . . All of Her Ways Are Empty." In *Agnes Martin*, edited by Barbara Haskell, 139–140. New York: Abrams.

Kang, Cindy. 2018. "Morisot on the Threshold: Windows, Balconies, and Verandas." In *Berthe Morisot, Woman Impressionist*, The Barnes Foundation, Exhibition catalogue, 117–145. New York: Rizzoli.

Martin, Agnes. 2003. *With My Back to the World*. Film by Mary Lance, New Dal Films.

Martin, Agnes and Dieter Schwartz. 1998. *Writings/Schriften*. Stuttgart: Hatje Cantz Verlag.

SECTION III
SOCIAL STRUCTURE AND POWER RELATIONS

11

Credibility

Resisting Doubts, Reimagining Knowledge

Monica C. Poole

She told the truth, and nobody believed her.

Cassandra[1] was a princess, but that wasn't her priority. Instead of partici-pating in the social life of the royal family of Troy, she committed to remain unmarried in order to be a priestess in the temple of the god Apollo.

One night, Apollo himself appeared in her room. *I will give you the gift of prophecy,* he said. *You will see the truth clearly when others cannot. You will predict the future with perfect accuracy, greater than any oracle you have ever known.*

How wonderful! This was everything Cassandra had worked for and more than she ever could have hoped for. She began to sing a hymn of gratitude.

Apollo interrupted her: *nice song, but*—he said, *you could really show your appreciation for this gift by having sex with me.*

Well, he *was* a god. What was she going to say? As he was unfastening her gown, she realized: god or not, she could say no. She pushed away his hands. *Come on,* he said, *we've already gotten started.* She said *no, I don't want to. No.*

Apollo was angry. He had given Cassandra an extraordinary gift of prophecy. Girls didn't say no to gods like him. *Ungrateful bitch. Who does she think she is?*

He wanted to take back his gift, but he couldn't. Prophetic gifts, once given, could not be taken away. Those were the rules.

But Apollo was clever; he knew how to take his revenge. He cursed Cassandra with a lack of credibility. *Go on, speak the truth, but nobody will ever believe you.*

Afterward, Cassandra couldn't bear to stay in the temple anymore. Too many memories. She moved back to the Trojan royal palace. The priestess tried to act like a proper princess, but just as Apollo couldn't take back the gift

Monica C. Poole, *Credibility* In: *Philosophy for Girls*. Edited by: Melissa M. Shew and Kimberly K. Garchar, Oxford University Press (2020). © Oxford University Press. DOI: 10.1093/oso/9780190072919.003.0012.

of prophecy, Cassandra couldn't un-see the prophetic truths that came to her. When she saw clearly what others couldn't, she spoke up.

When her brother brought home his new girlfriend Helen, runaway wife of the king of Sparta, Cassandra predicted that this would lead to the destruction of Troy. Nobody believed her. *She's always been dramatic,* her mother said, apologetically. *Don't mind her.*

Cassandra foresaw that the Greeks would invade to reclaim Helen for her husband. Nobody believed her. Later, when the Greek ships arrived on the beach, everyone was surprised. *It's like they came out of nowhere.* Cassandra wasn't surprised. She reminded them that she had predicted this, but nobody remembered. *She's just saying that because she wants attention.*

What the Greek allies lacked in strength, they made up for in strategy. Cassandra saw their clever schemes coming even before the Greek soldiers had begun to put them into practice. She tried to tell her father and brothers, but they waved her away. *We've got a war to plan! Can't she see we're too busy to listen to her daydreaming? Silly girl.*

After many years of fighting, one day, the Greeks were gone. In place of their encampment, they had left a wooden horse. A few of the Trojans argued that the wooden horse should be left on the beach, but most of them wanted to take it into the city as a trophy of war.

As they dragged it past the solid city walls, Cassandra saw the horse, as everyone else did; and she saw the elite Greek special forces hiding inside it, as nobody else could. She spoke one last warning to her people: *It's a trick. The Greeks are here. The horse will destroy us.*

Nobody believed her. Troy was destroyed.

11.1 She Is Disbelieved

Credibility—or lack thereof—is at the center of Cassandra's story. In philosophy, credibility is a topic within *epistemology*, a field of philosophy devoted to questions about knowledge and truth. When philosophers examine credibility, we explore questions about who should be believed and who should be doubted, what counts as a legitimate source of knowledge, and which knowledge really matters.

Think about what is considered "common knowledge." For example, the planet Earth is approximately 93 million miles from the sun. Maybe you knew that already. If so, how did you know? Did you go out into space with a measuring tape? Did you do the astronomical observations and calculations to figure it out? I didn't. I read it in a book, or looked it up online, or learned it in school. We call that *testimonial knowledge*. For philosophers working on knowledge, "testimony" doesn't just refer to testimony in a court of law; it can refer to any knowledge one gets through someone else.[2] Most of what we call "common knowledge," we know through testimony. When gathering knowledge by hearing or reading testimony, a person must decide whether that testimony is credible.

Let's also think about doubt. Maybe I thought the speaker was untrustworthy, or maybe I just thought they were mistaken. Regardless, I evaluated their testimony and I decided not to believe it. In order to know things outside our direct, personal experience, we need to rely on testimony, and in order to rely on testimony, we must make decisions about what to believe and what to doubt. These are judgments about credibility. Judgments about credibility are made in contexts of social power, and often, they are shaped by social inequity.

Accordingly, epistemology is not apolitical. Linda Martín Alcoff observes that epistemology is deeply entwined with social and political issues, operating within cultural, ideological, and political contexts.[3] Social prejudices "cause a hearer to give a deflated level of credibility to a speaker's word," writes Miranda Fricker, characterizing this as one of many forms of *epistemic* injustice: injustice related to knowledge.[4] Further, Lorraine Code argues that our judgments of credibility are applied "unevenly across the social order."[5] Some people are unfairly "disqualified" from full membership as truth-tellers. Their credibility is deflated, not because of what they know, but because of who they are or, more accurately, who others see them to be. Many elements of social power might unfairly deflate a person's credibility, including but not limited to gender, race, age, education, physique, and language.

Social power dynamics can cause us to give a deflated level of credibility to some people, and to give an *inflated* level of credibility to other people. If we imagine credibility as seats on an airplane, credibility inflation is like getting an upgrade to first class. Maggie Nelson recalls her mother asking her to change to a TV channel with a male weatherman, because, according to her mother, "they usually have the more accurate forecast." Nelson objected that all the TV stations are using the same script, with the same weather forecast, regardless of whether the TV presenter is male, female, or otherwise. Her mother shrugged, "It's just a feeling."[6] That "feeling" represents an artificial inflation of men's credibility, reflecting broader social dynamics that tend to give men more power than they have earned. Likewise, suppose a person has an impressive title or a prestigious academic degree; what they say is often taken more seriously, even when they are talking about a subject unrelated to the degree they have earned.

While choosing one weather forecast over another might be trivial, the consequences of credibility deflation and inflation are often much greater. Psychiatrist Judith Herman describes how abuse perpetrators discredit their victims: "The more powerful the perpetrator, the greater is his prerogative to name and define reality, and the more completely his arguments prevail."[7] In countless situations, a victim claims that they were harmed, and a perpetrator denies it. Often, it's the victim's word against the perpetrator's, and a community needs to decide whom to believe, and whom to protect. Abuse perpetrators tend to be in positions of power (bosses, doctors, teachers, parents) relative to their victims, and often, with that comes inflated credibility: the power to get others to believe their version of "reality," even if it is not actually true. Sometimes, unfairly inflated credibility becomes a risk to personal and community safety.

When two speakers are competing to be believed, differences in social power might be combined to inflate one person's credibility and deflate the other's, increasing the "credibility gap" between the two speakers. For example, in 1991, Clarence Thomas was nominated to serve as a Justice of the US Supreme Court, and during his confirmation hearings, a professor of law, Anita Hill, testified that Thomas had sexually harassed her when he had been her boss. Leigh Gilmore describes this "he said, she said" situation as a case of credibility deflation and inflation working in tandem. Like a balance scale that is rigged on both sides, what "he said" was given extra weight, and what "she said" was given less weight, creating an insurmountable credibility gap. Professor Anita Hill was doubted; Justice Clarence Thomas was confirmed.[8]

The tragedy of Cassandra is that she spoke vital truths, and her people did not believe her. Her credibility was deflated by the revenge curse inflicted by the god Apollo. The tragedy of our own world is that people often tell the truth and are not believed; not because of divine intervention, but because of social inequity. Social biases exclude many people from "full membership" as truth-tellers, deflating their credibility even before they have spoken.

11.2 She Is Serious

Philosophers who work on epistemology inquire into what counts as knowledge, whose testimony should be believed, and the importance of the knowledge in question. While adult women's credibility is often attacked, girls' credibility is often a nonstarter.[9] Some of the most powerful tactics used in deflating girls' credibility mix doubt and trivialization. In other words, girls' insights are often dismissed as silly or trivial, even before their truth is evaluated; if what a girl says is unimportant, what need is there to think about whether it is true? Before a girl can even begin to defend the veracity of her statements, she must get past her hearers' belief that what she says should not be taken seriously.

Every few years, a publication treats girls as serious readers and writers, and nongirls are astonished. When *Teen Vogue* shifted its editorial perspective in 2016 to feature critical feminist takes on current events, many people (mostly adult men) were baffled. Seeing incisive political coverage alongside makeup tutorials didn't match up with the notion that girls' interests were silly and insignificant. The girls who were the primary audience of *Teen Vogue* were not baffled, though, because they didn't subscribe to that notion in the first place. As journalist Sophie Gilbert reflected, "If [*Teen Vogue*] is finally gaining recognition among adults for its thoughtful, nuanced coverage of topical issues, it's less surprising to teen readers who've been for months taking in (and sharing) stories about the Standing Rock Protests or Texas's campus-carry laws."[10] *Teen Vogue* was "taking [young women]—and their manifold interests—seriously."[11] What a radical idea.

The deflated credibility of girls is contagious: music, movies, and fiction popular with girls tend to be dismissed as trivial, trashy, or otherwise not-serious.[12] From the Beatles to Taylor Swift, teen girls have been influential in pop music, yet musicians often distance themselves from their appeal to teen girls, because, as one journalist puts it: "[Young] female fans are seen as less legitimate, so their adoration is an instant credibility-killer."[13] This reflects a broader social prejudice that teen girls "are incapable of the critical thinking their older, male counterparts display" in evaluating music and other media; an album might be a hit with teen girls, but it is accorded artistic "legitimacy" only once adult men recognize it.[14]

Naturally, some of the most cogent critiques of this prejudice have been written by girls. For example, Adrianna Radice, a senior contributor to the newspaper of her all-girls high school, explores the long-term effects of training teenage girls into a deflated sense of their own credibility. A society that fails to "assure women at arguably the most formative time in their lives that their opinions hold the same value as the men around them" should not be surprised to see internalized misogyny and self-doubt in adult women.[15] Radice's article offers a valuable perspective, and, moreover, its very existence testifies to girls' capacities for serious argumentation and critical thought.

11.3 She Doubts Herself

Cassandra's persistence is impressive. Doubted by her community again and again over the years, she continues to speak her prophecies. Nobody she knows regards her as credible, but she never seems to falter. Yet Cassandra's persistence is also eccentric. For most of us, when we tell the truth again and again, and other people fail to believe us again and again, eventually, we give up. Sometimes, when others repeatedly deflate our credibility, we even lose credibility with ourselves. Perhaps it is less painful to learn to doubt oneself than to remain alone in seeing a truth that everyone else denies.

"Gaslighting" is a phenomenon where a person's trust in their own credibility is steadily eroded. Often, but not always, women and girls are the targets of gaslighting. In her philosophical analysis of gaslighting, Kate Abramson describes it as follows:

> [A] form of emotional manipulation in which the gaslighter tries (consciously or not) to induce in someone the sense that her reactions, perceptions, memories and/or beliefs are not just mistaken, but utterly without grounds—paradigmatically, so unfounded as to qualify as crazy. Gaslighting is, even at this level, quite unlike merely dismissing someone, for dismissal simply fails to take another seriously as an interlocutor, whereas gaslighting is aimed at getting another not to take herself seriously as an interlocutor.[16]

This phenomenon is named for a movie, *Gaslight* (1944), in which a husband deliberately undermines his wife's confidence in her accurate perception of reality by manipulating her, her friends, and her surroundings. He dims the gaslights in the house, and when she notices the dimmed lights, he says she must be imagining things. He confides to their friends that he is worried that she is becoming mentally unstable, and he sets up situations to demonstrate her supposed instability. For instance, he tucks his watch in her purse, accuses her of stealing it, and then, when they are with friends, he "discovers" his watch in her purse. She doesn't remember taking his watch, *because she didn't*. She thought she saw the lights dim, *because she did*. Maybe her husband is right, she wonders; maybe she really isn't thinking clearly.

Some might object that only weak-minded or unintelligent people could be convinced to doubt their own credibility. The ideas of "weak-minded" and "unintelligent" are a shaky foundation in any case, but those critiques remain beyond the scope of this chapter. Regardless, geniuses are not immune to gaslighting. When her social circle chipped away at her self-confidence, one of the most famous twentieth-century women philosophers became unsure of her very ability to think.

Simone de Beauvoir was taught to doubt herself in the summer of 1929. That spring, she had taken the first part of the competitive exam to be certified as a philosophy teacher in France. Her essay had impressed the examiners, and now the philosophy community in Paris was buzzing: Who was this girl? Nobody had ever seen her in the elite exam-prep schools. She was only twenty-one years old, and if she passed the second part of the exam later that year, she would be the youngest person ever to receive the certification. Jean-Paul Sartre was one of the most popular philosophy students in Paris, and was also taking the same exam that year. He decided he needed to meet the new girl, and de Beauvoir and Sartre quickly became friends. One summer morning, they met in a quiet nook in the Luxembourg Gardens. As de Beauvoir describes it, she eagerly shared with her friend a theory of moral philosophy she was working on:

> He ripped it to shreds. I was attached to it, because it allowed me to take my heart as the arbiter of good and evil; I struggled with him for three hours. In the end I had to admit I was beaten; besides, I had realized, in the course of our discussion, that many of my opinions were based only on prejudice, bad faith or thoughtlessness, that my reasoning was shaky and my ideas confused. "*I'm no longer sure what I think, or even if I think at all,*" I noted, completely thrown.[17]

In her memoirs, de Beauvoir recalls that she spent most of that summer with Sartre and his friends, and she felt "uncertain of [her] true abilities" as she spent more time with them. Among these new so-called friends, de Beauvoir came to doubt herself, her acute insights, and her talents as a philosopher.

Not long after that, the students took their oral exams, the second part of the certification. Students' scores were published and ranked. It was close, but Sartre took first place, with de Beauvoir coming in second. Perhaps their positions would have been reversed if de Beauvoir had scored higher on the oral exam—and perhaps she would have performed better in the oral exam if she hadn't spent the summer with "friends" who had eroded her self-confidence. Unlike Cassandra, most of us cannot resist self-doubt when the people around us deflate our credibility.

11.4 She Gets Emotional

Emotions are weaponized against the credibility of women and girls. When speaking unwelcome truths, women and girls are often accused of being "crazy," "shrill," "manipulative," and "irrational." Related to a word for the uterus (as in "hysterectomy"), the word "hysterical" was coined to discredit women, characterizing them as "unstable" and rendering their testimony "unreliable." If a woman is white, middle-aged, upper-class, thin, straight, cisgender, and formally educated, she might still be called "hysterical." If she doesn't fit that profile—and most women and girls don't—it is even more likely.

A woman might start out speaking in a "respectable," "reasonable" way, but when someone calls her "hysterical" to try to silence her unwelcome truths, she might find it impossible to maintain a perfectly calm voice and pleasing facial expression. Contemporary philosopher Veronica Ivy (formerly known as Rachel McKinnon) describes a vicious "feedback loop": when a speaker is dismissed because they are supposedly "too emotional," that itself tends to provoke emotion—including anger, frustration, and despair—and those expressions of emotion are used as further ammunition to discredit them. Ivy calls this the "epistemic injustice circle of hell."[18]

Many credible sources experience intense emotions, and the expression of those emotions may be a vital part of the truth they are conveying. Brittney Cooper, a philosopher, professor, and self-described "fat Black girl" calls attention to how the "Angry Black Woman" stereotype has been used to discredit Black women as "irrational, crazy, out of touch, entitled, disruptive, and not team players."[19] She analyzes how Black women have managed their speech and behavior in a politics of respectability and "rage-management" to try to avoid credibility deflation within a white-dominated culture.[20] Cooper lifts up the value of rage, recalling how a Black female student praised her lectures as "the most eloquent rage ever," and describing how she continues to grapple with embracing her "messy" anger as a "feminist superpower."[21]

Far from discrediting a speaker, honest expressions of rage (and many other emotions) can be essential parts of credible testimony. Patricia Williams argues that freeing ourselves from the myth that objectivity is a criterion of credibility will improve social responsibility and intellectual honesty.[22] Openly acknowledging our subjective perspectives and how who we are shapes the truths we know makes it harder to hide harmful biases and festering feelings. Cassandra's hearers complain about the "hysterical clang" of her "prophetic voice."[23] Yet sometimes, those "messy" emotions are part of speaking the truth.

11.5 She Reimagines

When the Greeks take Troy, Cassandra runs to the temple for sanctuary. She prays to Athena, goddess of wisdom, war, and independent young women, but Cassandra's plea for protection fails; one of the Greek military officers rapes her in the temple—a public act of sacrilege. The other Greeks excuse their battle companion's misconduct: *He just got carried away; don't ruin a good guy's life; we all make mistakes.* Athena punishes the Greeks, but that does not rectify the harm done to Cassandra. Perhaps, just as Cassandra's people had refused to heed her prophecies, Athena did not heed Cassandra's prayers until it was too late.

Cassandra is well-known as a tragic heroine, but she is also an agent of resistance and reimagining. After the fall of Troy, she is captured and enslaved as a sex partner to the highest-ranking Greek military commander. She uses her prophetic speech to destabilize her captors' confidence, needling them: "Greek commander, you think you did something great?"[24] She counts up the Greek losses: a generation of young men buried in foreign soil, never to return to their families at home, all because of this supposedly "glorious" war. When they take her away to the Greek ships, she promises vengeance: "Troy, dear country, brothers, father beneath the earth;/soon I shall join the dead. I'll come victorious,/ruining the house that ruined us."[25] We, too, can be agents of resistance.

Credibility needs a gut renovation; we cannot build new façades on old structures. The criteria of credibility have been defined by people who doubt girls before they have even spoken.[26] Instead of trying to fulfill their criteria, we must work together to remake knowledge and credibility, using what José Medina calls our "resistant imaginations."[27]

Philosophers working on feminist epistemologies have been reshaping how academic philosophy understands knowledge. One key element in knowledge is *lived experience*, which means considering a person's memories and personal experiences to be a valuable source of knowledge. Patricia Hill Collins's framework for a Black feminist epistemology was foundational in establishing lived experience as not only a viable source of knowledge, but, specifically, a "criterion for credibility."[28] Grounded in the epistemologies of Black women, lived experience has become a cornerstone of feminist epistemology as a whole.

Another important component of feminist epistemology is dialogue. Knowledge is made in dialogue between people, and in dialogue between different parts of one person's self. Silvia Rivera Cusicanqui draws on her knowledge as a mixed-heritage woman *(mestiza)* of the Aymara indigenous people to develop a theory of *ch'ixi*: interwoven-ness: the "parallel coexistence of multiple cultural differences" in a sometimes-contentious, always-valuable "creative dialogue," a fabric woven of many colors and textures.[29] While *ch'ixi* remains distinctive to Aymara culture, Rivera Cusicanqui's theory offers broader lessons relevant to everyone.[30]

Girls[31] reading (and writing) this book enter philosophy classrooms with prior academic knowledge as well as knowledge from lived experiences. Many women philosophers recall moments when their lived experiences were not regarded as "credible" or "legitimate" sources of academic knowledge. Yet like Cassandra, we were able to see what others around us could not, and we knew that we had valuable truths to contribute, even if others doubted us or dismissed our concerns as trivial. Cassandra tried to tell her difficult truths to other women in her community—her mother, her fellow priestesses, even the goddess Athena—but they failed to hear her. As girls doing philosophy, we seek out wise companions: teachers and mentors, classmates and peers, and even writers whom we might never meet in person. We speak our many different truths in dialogue with each other. Hopefully, unlike the women in Cassandra's life, we do not fail to listen, even when our companions speak truths that are difficult to hear. We define our own criteria for validating knowledge. We integrate knowledge from our lived experiences and more typically recognized academic knowledge; we contribute to a plurality of truths in a living philosophical dialogue; and, in so doing, we remake credibility in our own images.

Notes

1. I am far from the only writer to connect Cassandra to philosophical discussions of credibility. Although my interpretations differ from theirs, two key examples are Solnit (2014) and Townley (2011), 44–45. Classical written sources for Cassandra's story include Homer, *The Odyssey*; Lykophron, *Alexandra*; Euripides, *The Trojan Women*; Aeschylus, *Agamemnon*; Virgil, *Aeneid*; Quintus Smyrnaeus, *The Fall of Troy*. I have also incorporated visual depictions, medieval and modern retellings of Cassandra's story, and my own imagination, including or omitting elements and weaving them together with purpose, just as the ancient storytellers did.
2. Lackey (2008).
3. Alcoff (1999, 74).
4. Fricker (2007, 1).
5. Code (1995, 58–59).
6. Nelson (2015, 38).
7. Herman (1997, 8).
8. Gilmore (2016, 50).
9. For works that address how girls negotiate epistemic authority in specific contexts, consider Mwita and Murphy (2017); and Skapoulli (2009). Carel and Györffy (2014) principally focuses on children, not adolescents, yet remains relevant as one of a very small number of works that address credibility deflation in young people. Mitchell and Moletsane (2018) is rare in its conscious analysis of epistemic injustices done to girls, *and* in its reparative choice to feature girls not only as subjects but as authors in this collection.
10. Gilbert (2016).
11. Ibid.
12. Chaney (2016).
13. Lancaster (2015).
14. Ibid.
15. Radice (2019).
16. Abramson (2014, 2). On self-doubt and self-silencing, see also Dotson (2011) and Manne (2018, 3–18).
17. Beauvoir (1958). I use the translation provided by Trista Selous in her translation of Le Doeuff (2007, 136).
18. Ivy [McKinnon] (2017, 169). The context of this is relevant: Ivy is analyzing how cis women use the "too emotional" excuse to silence unwelcome concerns expressed by trans women.
19. Cooper (2018, 2). Cooper draws significantly on Audre Lorde's theory of rage expressed in her keynote address at the National Women's Studies Association (1981).

20. Cooper (2018, 151 and throughout).
21. Cooper (2018, 2–5).
22. Williams (1991, 11).
23. Aeschylus (2009, 52).
24. Euripides (2016, 653).
25. Ibid., 654.
26. The foundational work on this is the discussion of knowledge-validation processes controlled by a white male academic establishment in Collins (2000 [1991]), especially chapter 11, "Black feminist epistemology."
27. Medina (2012).
28. Collins (2000 [1991]), 257.
29. Cusicanqui (2012, 105).
30. As a white, Anglo-American US citizen, it would be both ethically and intellectually irresponsible for me to take Rivera Cusicanqui's Aymara concept of *ch'ixi* and use it as if it belonged to me. When a person carelessly and unjustly uses language, art, theories, or other elements belonging to a culture not their own, we call that "cultural appropriation." Often, cultural appropriation involves taking elements of culture out of context, failing to give credit to the people who constructed them, and exoticizing, patronizing, or trivializing the culture in question. Responsible scholarly work must avoid cultural appropriation. However, that doesn't mean we are forbidden to learn from cultures other than our own! Indeed, while cultural appropriation violates academic integrity, *intercultural learning* is necessary in philosophy and many other fields. While the concepts of intercultural learning and cultural appropriation are relatively clear, putting them into practice is complicated, ambiguous, and imperfect. Philosophers and others continue to grapple with how to responsibly learn from cultures not their own; scholars who belong to historically dominating cultures overrepresented in academia (such as white Americans) must be especially careful in this respect. Cultural appropriation and intercultural learning are important issues in epistemology, and in philosophy more generally, but a full consideration of these issues is beyond the scope of the present work. Readers who wish to learn more might begin with Nittle (2018), Acquaye (2018), and Matthes (2018).
31. For many people—including the author of this chapter—"girl" and "woman" are not a perfect fit to describe who we are, but we still feel a sense of belonging in things like women's colleges, women's sports teams, all-girls high schools, and projects like *Philosophy for Girls*. Gender is complex and evolving, and a gender binary of "female" and "male" doesn't work for everyone. Readers who wish to learn more might begin with Dembroff (2018).

Bibliography

Abramson, Kate. 2014. "Turning Up The Lights on Gaslighting." *Philosophical Perspectives* 28: 1–30.

Acquaye, Alisha. 2018. "White People Need to Learn How to Appreciate a Different Culture Without Appropriating it." *Teen Vogue.* August 23. https://www.teenvogue.com/story/cultural-appropriation-appreciation-kim-kardashian.

Aeschylus. 2009. *Agamemnon.* In *An Oresteia,* translated by Anne Carson. New York: Farrar, Straus and Giroux.

Alcoff, Linda Martín. "On Judging Epistemic Credibility: Is Social Identity Relevant?" *Philosophic Exchange* 29, no. 1, article 1: 73–93.

Beauvoir, Simone de. 1958. *Mémoires d'une jeune fille rangée.* Paris: Gallimard.

Carel, Havi, and Gita Győrffy. 2014. "Seen But Not Heard: Children and Epistemic Injustice." *The Lancet* 384, no. 9950: 1256–1257.

Chaney, Alexis. 2016. "Swooning, Screaming, Crying: How Teenage Girls Have Driven 60 Years of Pop Music." *Vox,* January 28. https://www.vox.com/2016/1/28/10815492/teenage-girls-screaming.

Code, Lorraine. 1995. "Incredulity, Experientialism, and the Politics of Knowledge." In *Rhetorical Spaces: Essays on Gendered Locations,* 58–59. New York: Routledge.

Collins, Patricia Hill. 2000 [1991]. *Black Feminist Thought: Knowledge, Consciousness, and the Politics of Empowerment.* Second edition. New York: Routledge.

Cooper, Brittney. 2018. *Eloquent Rage: A Black Feminist Discovers Her Superpower.* New York: St. Martin's Press.

Dembroff, Robin. 2018. "Why Be Nonbinary?" *Aeon,* October 30. https://aeon.co/essays/nonbinary-identity-is-a-radical-stance-against-gender-segregation.

Dotson, Kristie. 2011. "Tracking Epistemic Violence, Tracking Practices of Silencing." *Hypatia* 26, no. 2: 236–257.

Euripides. 2016. *The Trojan Woman.* Translated by Emily Wilson. In *The Greek Plays: Sixteen Plays by Aeschylus, Sophocles and Euripides,* edited by Mary Lefkowitz and James Romm. New York: Random House.

Fricker, Miranda. 2007. *Epistemic Injustice: Power and the Ethics of Knowing.* Oxford: Oxford University Press.

Gilbert, Sophie. 2016. "Teen Vogue's Political Coverage Isn't Surprising." *The Atlantic,* December 12. https://www.theatlantic.com/entertainment/archive/2016/12/teen-vogue-politics/510374/.

Gilmore, Leigh. 2016. *Tainted Witness: Why We Doubt What Women Say About Their Lives.* New York: Columbia University Press.

Herman, Judith. 1997. *Trauma and Recovery: The Aftermath of Violence—From Domestic Abuse to Political Terror.* New York: Basic Books.

Lackey, Jennifer. 2008. *Learning from Words: Testimony as a Source of Knowledge.* Oxford: Oxford University Press.

Lancaster, Brodie. 2015. "Pop Music, Teenage Girls and the Legitimacy of Fandom." *Pitchfork,* August 27. https://pitchfork.com/thepitch/881-pop-music-teenage-girls-and-the-legitimacy-of-fandom.

Le Doeuff, Michèle. 2007. *Hipparchia's Choice: An Essay Concerning Women, Philosophy, etc.* New York: Columbia University Press.

Lorde, Audre. 1981. "The Uses of Anger: Women Responding to Racism." *Women's Studies Quarterly* 9, no. 3 (Fall): 7–10.

Manne, Kate. 2018. *Down Girl: The Logic of Misogyny.* New York: Oxford University Press.

Matthes, Erich Hatala, 2018. "The Ethics of Cultural Heritage." In *The Stanford Encyclopedia of Philosophy.* https://plato.stanford.edu/entries/ethics-cultural-heritage/

Ivy, Veronica. [formerly McKinnon, Rachel V.] 2017. "'Allies' Behaving Badly: Gaslighting as Epistemic Injustice." In *The Routledge Handbook of Epistemic Injustice*, edited by Gaile Polhaus Jr., Ian James Kidd, and José Medina, 167–174. New York: Routledge.

Medina, José. 2013. *The Epistemology of Resistance: Gender and Racial Oppression, Epistemic Injustice, and Resistant Imaginations*. Oxford: Oxford University Press.

Mitchell, Claudia, and Relebohile Moletsane (eds.) 2018. *Disrupting Shameful Legacies: Girls and Young Women Speaking Back Through the Arts to Address Sexual Violence*. Leiden: Brill/Sense.

Mwita, Emiliana J., and Susan P. Murphy. 2017. "Challenging Hidden Hegemonies: Exploring the Links Between Education, Gender Justice, and Sustainable Development Practice." *Ethics and Social Welfare* 11, no. 2: 149–162.

Nelson, Maggie. 2015. *The Argonauts*. Minneapolis: Graywolf Press.

Nittle, Nadra. 2018. "The Cultural Appropriation Debate has Changed. But is it for the Better?" *Vox*. December 18. https://www.vox.com/the-goods/2018/12/18/18146877/cultural-appropriation-awkwafina-bruno-mars-madonna-beyonce.

Radice, Adrianna. 2019. "Why Society Hates Teenage Girls." *ACHONA: School Newspaper of the Academy of the Holy Cross*, January 22. https://achonaonline.com/top-stories/2019/01/22/why-society-hates-teenage-girls-opinion/.

Rivera Cusicanqui, Silvia. 2012. "*Ch'ixinakax utxiwa*: A Reflection on the Practices and Discourses of Decolonization." *South Atlantic Quarterly* 111, no. 1: 95–109.

Skapoulli, Elena. 2009. "Transforming the Label of Whore: Teenage Girls' Negotiation of Local and Global Gender Ideologies in Cyprus." *Pragmatics* 19, no. 1: 85–101.

Solnit, Rebecca. 2014. "Cassandra Among the Creeps." *Harper's Magazine* 329, no. 1973 (October): 4–9.

Townley, Cynthia. 2011. *A Defense of Ignorance: Its Value for Knowers and Roles in Feminist and Social Epistemologies*. Lanham, MD: Lexington Books.

Williams, Patricia J. 1991. *The Alchemy of Race and Rights*. Cambridge, MA: Harvard University Press.

12

Language

Power Plays in Communication

Elisabeth Camp

LANGUAGE is indisputably the more immediate province of the fair sex: there they shine, there they excel. The torrents of their eloquence, especially in the vituperative way, stun all opposition, and bear away in one promiscuous heap, nouns, pronouns, verbs, moods and tenses. If words are wanting (which indeed happens but seldom) indignation instantly makes new ones . . . Nor is the tender part of our language less obliged to that soft and amiable sex; their love being at least as productive as their indignation . . . I remember many very expressive words coined in that fair mint. I assisted at the birth of that most significant word, FLIRTATION, which dropped from the most beautiful mouth in the world . . . Some inattentive and undiscerning people have, I know, taken it to be a term synonymous with coquetry; but I lay hold of this opportunity to undeceive them . . . that FLIRTATION is short of coquetry, and intimates only the first hints of approximation, which subsequent coquetry may . . . end in a definitive treaty.[1]

Words are used to do many things: to describe, plan and promise, invite and command. They are also used words to wound—to demean, insult, and exclude. In this 1754 letter in the British magazine *The World*, the statesman Lord Philip Stanhope apparently undertakes to praise women for their verbal aptitude, especially for linguistic innovation in the service of insults and subtle indirection in the service of courtship. But in so doing, he himself deftly deploys eloquence, expressive words, and indirection to mock these

Elisabeth Camp, *Language* In: *Philosophy for Girls*. Edited by: Melissa M. Shew and Kimberly K. Garchar, Oxford University Press (2020). © Oxford University Press. DOI: 10.1093/oso/9780190072919.003.0013.

very same "female" ways of speaking, and to cast women in general as silly creatures obsessed with petty passions about social trifles.

The fact that words can have such potent, pernicious effects is puzzling, because they are, after all, just words. As the schoolyard chant goes, "Sticks and stones may break my bones, but words can never hurt me." Words do hurt though—not only our feelings, but our social status, even our basic dignity as human beings. How can sounds and shapes do all that? Many philosophers have thought of language as a kind of game. Both games and language are complex, abstract structures that we deploy strategically to achieve serious goals, as well as for fun. Thinking through some of these similarities can illuminate how something so intangible can have such powerful effects. And seeing how people wield that power for malicious ends can reveal how to turn the tables and fight back.

12.1 Power Plays and Weapon Words

Like basketball, language involves arbitrary rules. Where basketball's conventions specify how to use the ball, linguistic conventions specify default ways of using words. Many of these conventions are fairly straightforward: naming objects ("apple") and properties ("red"), and combining them into sentences to express propositions that represent the world and communicate information that is true or false. However, words can also conventionally perform other functions: they can express feelings ("Hooray!"), evaluations ("good"), and recommendations ("should"). They can also work to manage social status. Thus, titles like "Sir" honor their applicants, while epithets like "Boy" diminish them. We sometimes use diminutive epithets to build intimacy ("You go, girl!"). But they are often used to enforce power differences. In 1967, psychiatrist Alvin Poussaint recalled an experience in his hometown of Jackson, Mississippi:

> As I was leaving my office . . . a white policeman yelled, "Hey, boy! Come here!" Somewhat bothered, I retorted: "I'm no boy!" He then rushed at me, inflamed, and stood towering over me, snorting, "What d'ja say, boy?" Quickly he frisked me and demanded, "What's your name, boy?" Frightened, I replied, "Dr. Poussaint. I'm a physician." He angrily chuckled and hissed, "What's your first name, boy?" . . . As my heart palpitated, I muttered in profound humiliation, "Alvin." . . . "Alvin, the next

time I call you, you come right away, you hear? . . . You hear me, boy?"
My voice trembling with helplessness, but following my instincts of self-
preservation, I murmured, "Yes, sir." This had occurred on a public street
for all the local black people to witness, reminding them that *no* black
man was as good as *any* white man. All of us—doctor, lawyer, postman,
field hand and shoeshine boy—had been psychologically "put in our
place."[2]

The use of "boy" as a put-down may seem to belong to a bygone era (though
note that the US Supreme Court ruled in 2006 that it may constitute evidence
of racism). Nonetheless, other verbal tools for putting people in their place
are very much alive and well.

In particular, slurs—that is, derogatory terms for categories defined by
ethnicity, gender, sexual orientation, occupation, etc.—are powerful tools for
social oppression, particularly when hurled as epithets ("You S!"). Even if we
would never use the word ourselves, and even if we reject the aptness of its
applicability to the person at whom it's aimed, the very fact that we recognize its meaning achieves some of its intended effect, because its currency
demonstrates that enough other people do buy into its associated perspective
for it to achieve that public status. In 1940, Langston Hughes described the
social force marshaled by what is now typically called "the N-word" (though
note that Hughes himself actually mentioned the word, in order to dramatize
its visceral effect):

> The word $n{***}r$, you see, sums up for us who are colored all the bitter years
> of insult and struggle in America: the slave-beatings of yesterday, the
> lynchings of today, the Jim Crow cars . . . the restaurants where you may not
> eat, the jobs you may not have, the unions you cannot join. The word $n{***}r$
> in the mouths of little white boys at school, the word $n{***}r$ in the mouth of
> the foreman at the job, the word $n{***}r$ across the whole face of America!
> $N{***}r!$ $N{***}r!$[3]

As with "boy," we may hope that this slur is less prevalent now than in 1940.
And today as then, this particular slur is especially incendiary, because of the
uniquely institutionalized racial oppression of African Americans. All slurs,
however, have palpable power because they demonstrate to the target, and
those around them, that "people" think that members of the targeted group
deserve low status, that social mechanisms exist to enforce that status, and

that the speaker is prepared to invoke those mechanisms to push the target into their "proper place."[4]

12.2 Frames and Stereotypes

Not all utterances containing slurs are "fighting words," or weapons hurled directly at their targets. Some, like "That's where the Ss all hang out," primarily inform a hearer of some (supposed) fact, leaving the slur's perspective off to the side as color commentary. These informational uses are still jarring, though, given slurs' status as taboo words. But taboo is not necessary for enforcing social norms: "polite" terms can also have this as an aspect of their conventional function. Thus, nouns like "prude," "tease," and "spinster" encode assumptions about proper expressions of female sexuality. By using them, speakers do not just express their own personal feelings; they demean the women to whom they are applied for having violated public norms of female sexuality, and enforce those norms as regulative for everyone else. Other terms, like "demure" or "jailbait," enforce the same sorts of norms through a kind of praise. While the praise may make them feel better in the short run, it still locates their targets in a "place" that has been deemed appropriate for them, and disparages those who do not conform. Words can even function regularly to enforce norms for a group without being conventionally restricted to that group. Thus, in principle terms like "bossy," "abrasive," "strident," "aggressive," "emotional," and "irrational" can apply to anyone, regardless of gender. In practice though, they are overwhelmingly applied to women: a 2014 analysis in *Fortune* of 248 performance reviews from 28 companies found that "all of these words show up at least twice in the women's [performance] review[s] . . . *Abrasive* alone is used 17 times to describe 13 different women. Among these words, only *aggressive* shows up in men's reviews at all. It shows up three times, twice with an exhortation to be more of it."[5]

Two features of "thick" terms like these, or words that combine description and evaluation, make them especially conversationally powerful. First, they *presuppose* social norms, presenting them as being accepted by "everyone" as uncontroversial. As we have seen, the word's very public currency already supports this assumption. But presenting those norms as already established rather than new information also makes them harder to challenge within the conversation. If someone says "The bank is closed," we can deny that claim just by saying "No it's not." By contrast, denying a presupposition requires refocusing the conversation, saying something like "Hey wait a minute! When you call Jane a spinster, you're assuming that women are defined by their marital status! That's not true!" Often, it is easier to go along with the conversational flow, especially if the word's descriptive conditions (say, being unmarried) are satisfied.

Second, even if one is prepared to derail the conversation, it is hard to identify precisely what the thick term's objectionable presupposition *is*. If I say "George managed to solve the problem," I presuppose that the problem took some effort for George. This proposition might be false, but it is at least something one can identify and disagree with. Slurs and thick terms are not like that. Instead, what they presuppose is a complex, open-ended bundle of thoughts, images, emotions, and evaluations—a *perspective*. For any particular assumption to which we might point, the speaker can plausibly deny having meant *that*, without undermining the perspective as a whole. Further, because images and feeling cannot be true, they cannot be straightforwardly rejected as false but have to be dislodged as inappropriate in some other way.

The perspectival quality of thick terms' presuppositions makes them powerful cognitively as well as conversationally. By evoking stereotypes soaked in images, feelings, and evaluations, they frame their subjects at a deep intuitive level, guiding what we notice and remember about them, how we explain what they do, and what we expect from them in the future. As Claude Steele puts it, such stereotypes are "a threat in the air."[6] Worse, this threat is self-fulfilling, because it can cause us to act in ways that conform to the stereotype—say, to underperform on math tests. The effects are most dramatic, and most directly damaging, for members of the targeted group. But by framing the thinking of everyone within a conversation, thick terms make even sympathetic "allies" unwitting collaborators in enacting the demeaning perspectives they evoke.

Finally, even words with purely descriptive meanings can function as frames in certain types of sentences. Thus, by itself "girl" doesn't encode a rich gender stereotype: we can say "There are seven girls and five boys in my class" without committing to anything about how girls are or should behave. (It is more controversial how the ascription of gender relates to biological sex.) But sentences like "Girls are bad at math" or ""Boys will be boys," in which "girl" and "boy" are used as *generic* terms, frame girls and boys as a group in terms of an intuitive stereotype, with the same threat-inducing effects as a thick term would have. Sentences that use generic structure are especially powerful because they encode generalizations in a way that tolerates exceptions, making them relatively impervious to counterevidence. Especially in application to social kinds, this seems to be because generics impute *essences*: unobservable properties that make a thing be what it is and generate dispositions to behave in certain ways. The intuitive pull of essentialist thinking has been shown to lead us to overestimate statistical correlations and impute nonexistent causal connections, and to treat certain attributes as natural, normal, and "fitting" for members of the group, even when there is no scientific basis for such a connection.[7]

12.3 Saying and Un-Saying

So far, I have focused on language as similar to games in being built out of conventional rules that invest arbitrary actions with social significance, and especially on how those conventions enforce norms regulating social roles. A second strand of analogy focuses on turn-taking. As in chess, conversations involve sequences of alternating moves. As in baseball, conversations involve different types of moves, with different moves being possible depending on the stage of the conversation, with the effects of any one move depending both on general conventions and on the conversation up to that point. And as in poker, participants may play strategically; but it is not legitimate to break the rules, for instance by lying or saying something totally off-topic.

Further, in both games and language, participants can exploit the assumption that they are following the rules in order to accomplish something other than the conventional meaning of their move. Thus, just as a bridge player might lead with a low heart to signal to her partner that she is thin in the suit and that her partner should take control, so might a teenager answer the question "Where is your brother?" with "Out," to communicate that they do not know, or will not say, anything more informative. In such cases, the speaker constructs her move by assuming that the hearer will assume that the speaker is indeed following the rules, and so will reinterpret an apparently illegitimate or irrational move in such a way that it makes sense after all.

This sounds complicated, but it is something we do all the time, often without noticing it. If you ask me to go to a concert on Thursday night and I say I have an exam Friday, my response does not itself answer your question, but if you add in the assumptions that I have to study for the exam and that this means I am busy, then you can figure out that I am declining your invitation. Philosophers call this meant-but-not-said meaning an *implicature*. But why would we communicate indirectly, without saying what we mean? As the example of the declined concert invitation illustrates, one reason is that it is more efficient to bundle several moves together. Another is that leaving our meaning unstated can be more polite, softening the blow of explicit rejection or criticism. In some contexts, like a conversation between friends, this is an act of kindness. In others, like a salary negotiation, it may enable the speaker to get away with a move that would be impermissible given the participants' respective social roles.

If a speaker constructs her utterance carefully, leaving her main point unsaid can also afford her *deniability* about what she meant. If the hearer, or someone else, challenges her, asking something like "Hey wait a minute! Are you suggesting that you should get a raise when John and Alice, who've worked here longer, shouldn't?" the speaker can respond with a demurral like "No, I was just pointing out that I've been putting in a lot of hours. I know everyone here works hard." Such a denial allows the speaker to avoid being held to account for her meaning—even when it is obvious to everybody that she really did mean it. (As we might put it, "plausible deniability" is often not very plausible.) Alternatively, the speaker can shift interpretive responsibility onto the hearer: "You said it, not me."

Deniability is especially useful when a conversational move is socially risky, involving high stakes or uncertainty about how it will be received. Navigating the tricky power dynamics of romantic and professional relationships is one common motivation for communicating through deniable insinuation. Threats are another. For instance, in 1926 *The Ludington (MI) Daily News* ran the headline "Detroit Bandits Use Psychology in Bank Robbery. Pick Cashier Up on Street and Bring Him to Verge of Hysteria with Questions," where the questions were superficially innocent inquiries like "How are your children now? You think a lot of them, don't you? You have a nice little family, haven't you? Wouldn't it be a pity if anything happened to break it up?"

Finally, as Lord Stanhope's opening disquisition on female eloquence both literally says and indirectly shows, we often prefer to frame insults in veiled terms. Paul Grice illustrates the core idea of implicature with a letter of recommendation stating in its entirety "Mr. X's command of English is excellent, and his attendance at tutorials has been regular. Yours, etc."[8] In effect, the writer of such a letter weaponizes the grandmotherly adage "If you can't say something nice, don't say anything at all." More explicitly, since the writer is the candidate's teacher, they must know more than the letter actually says;

and since the purpose of such a letter is to provide as much relevant information as possible, the writer must be refusing to say anything more informative because whatever they would say would be negative. By assuming that their readers are clued into the normal expectations for such letters, the writer can communicate "Don't hire this guy!" without saying it.

Alexander Pope recommended this same technique of insinuation via conspicuously mild compliment back in 1734:

> Damn with faint praise, assent with civil leer,
> And without sneering, teach the rest to sneer;
> Willing to wound, and yet afraid to strike,
> Just hint a fault, and hesitate dislike.[9]

Pope's strategy goes beyond Grice's general technique for imparting risky information, to advocate "sneering" in particular Because implicatures are implicit, they are especially apt for sneering by framing their targets under the amorphous, open-ended denigration that can be accomplished using perspectives. Consider, for instance, a speaker who utters "Barack Obama's middle name is Hussein. Just saying," On the surface, they merely state a fact. But indirectly, they present it as a "telling detail": as the surface symptom of a cloud of unspecified, sinister attributes purportedly associated with people named Hussein. Like thick terms, then, framing insinuations enable a speaker to inject objectionable unarticulated assumptions into the conversation, where the very fact that the hearer can identify those assumptions lends them credibility, making them seem like something "out there" that "everyone knows."

In insinuation, speakers craft their conversational move so they can insist (disingenuously) that they only meant the innocent thing they actually said. Typical cases of sarcasm, like "What a cool outfit! It's so . . . vivid" or "That's . . . different" push this strategy further, presupposing an unstated social norm and insinuating that the target violates it, without undertaking any commitment to what is said. Similarly, the (bad) joke, "Why can't Helen Keller drive? Because she's a woman," presents it as common knowledge that women are terrible drivers, so much so that being female is a worse impediment than blindness. With both sarcasm and jokes, a speaker can deflect criticism from their utterance on the ground that they were "just kidding," and accuse the objector of being humorlessly literalistic, while the very fact that the objector "gets it" again demonstrates that there's *something* apt about the utterance and adds further pressure on the hearer to "play along."

In all these varieties of implicit speech, all parties to the conversation recognize what the speaker really meant, even if they deny it or cannot articulate exactly what "it" was. Insinuation, sarcasm, and jokes can also speak to multiple audiences, appearing sincere and literal to one while communicating deniable hidden messages to another. For example, at one point in Jane Austen's *Pride and Prejudice*, Mary Bennett has been singing wretchedly, oblivious to eye-rolling and mocking by the Bingley sisters. After a beseeching look from Mary's sister Elizabeth, their father intervenes, saying, "That will do extremely well, child. You have delighted us long enough. Let the other young ladies have time to exhibit." He intends for Mary to take his utterance sincerely, but also for Elizabeth, and perhaps the Bingleys, to hear "delight" as meaning something closer to its opposite, torture.

A similar effect can be achieved in public contexts through "dogwhistles," in which speakers articulate their real message so as to restrict it to "those who have ears to hear." For example, on its face George W. Bush's invocation in his 2003 State of the Union address of the "power, wonder-working power, in the goodness and idealism and faith of the American people" offers an inclusive testimony to American resilience. But by employing a fundamentalist Christian trope, Bush at least signals his affiliation with that group, and perhaps promises to institute Christ-centered values in his government.[10]

12.4 Fighting Fire with Fire

In explaining the various conventional and conversational mechanisms language offers for enacting power plays and enforcing social norms, I have emphasized how those mechanisms exploit presupposition and perspectival framing in ways that make it difficult for hearers to resist. This situation can make it seem that hearers are passive victims at the mercy of manipulative speakers. But this obviously cannot be the whole story, not least because conversations typically involve taking turns speaking. More importantly, the same techniques that lend speakers power also create conversational vulnerabilities, which hearers can exploit to fight back. In effect, an insinuating, sarcastic, or joking speaker attempts to avoid conversational accountability by engaging in a kind of communicative bluff that shifts interpretive responsibility onto the hearer. As a result, successfully implementing Pope's advice to "just hint a fault" when one is "afraid to strike" a more open blow requires treading a delicate line: making one's meaning obvious enough that the hearer recognizes it as what was meant, but not so obvious that it undermines deniability.

More specifically, if an insinuating speaker manages to be subtle enough to avoid the peril of overobviousness, she risks miscommunicating by undersignaling in one of two different ways. On the one hand, her utterance might be taken as just a sincere statement of its surface meaning. On the other, it might be assigned a different meaning than she intended, one that relies on an alternative set of implicit assumptions. Both sorts of miscommunication can occur simply because the hearer is flat-footedly oblivious. But just as speakers can pretend not to have meant something that they really did mean, so too can hearers pretend not to grasp a meaning that they really do get. For instance, the rejected concert inviter might respond to the addressee's statement that they have an exam Friday by saying, "Great! The concert doesn't start till 10, so you'll have plenty of time to study. How about I come by at 9:30?"—even though they fully realize that the addressee intended their statement as a (polite) refusal. Alternatively, hearers can not just ignore, but willfully reinterpret the speaker's meaning. Thus, the salary negotiator might respond to the boss's implicit accusation of selfishness by saying "Actually, I was hoping that you could find a way to offer all three of us an increase." Both willful obliviousness and willful reinterpretation shift the interpretive pressure back onto the speaker: obliviousness by refusing to acknowledge the speaker's implicit meaning, and reinterpretation by twisting it to the hearer's own ends.

Conventional means for enacting power plays, such as thick terms and generics, leave less room for strategic speaker denial and hearer reinterpretation, precisely because they rely on conventional meaning, which all parties acknowledge as part of their competence with the language. But hearers can still use these same basic techniques to challenge speakers' attempts to sneak in objectionable assumptions. Thus, a hearer can use willful incomprehension, along the lines of "Hey wait a minute! I don't understand. What do you mean when you call her a slut/prude/shrill?" in order to deny uncontroversial status to the speaker's attempted presuppositions, thereby forcing her to either articulate and defend them explicitly or else to abandon them as governing the conversation.

Alternatively, a hearer may be able to twist the speaker's literal words by imposing an alternative perspectival frame on them. The most dramatic cases of this involve appropriated slurs like "queer." Members of the targeted group have combatted the slur's demeaning status by embracing its associated stereotype as a badge of honor rather than shame, as in this 1979 letter from the editors of *Lesbian Tide*:

> What men have meant when they call us dykes is true: we ARE uncompromising (where loving women is concerned), we ARE ugly (when beauty is measured in rigid stereotypes or in passivity), we ARE frightening (to those who fear independent women), we ARE unpleasant (when silence and smiles are pleasing).[11]

However, re-appropriation is also risky. First, the strategy cannot be undertaken by a single individual: it must be waged politically, and requires widespread cultural acceptance for success. Second, success itself is dangerous, because it risks reinforcing the slur's underlying essentialist thinking. Part of what makes thick terms like "slut" and "prude" problematic is that they focus attention on a category that does not warrant any distinctive social status, high or low. Appropriation doubles down on the underlying category, merely shifting its associated cognitive and social valuation.

In this chapter, I've surveyed a range of ways in which speakers can use language to enact power dynamics and enforce social norms, either wittingly and unwittingly, and a range of ways in which hearers are pressured to comply, but can also resist. Given the risks of denigration and manipulation, how should sincere, well-meaning speakers and hearers proceed? Philosophers especially might think the solution is to avoid appeals to murky implicit assumptions, by saying exactly what we mean and meaning all that we say. However, our discussion shows that this is not a viable option. For one thing, we could never finish talking if we had to state everything explicitly. Every conversation must start somewhere, and we need ways to bundle many moves together. For another, sometimes inexplicitness really is beneficial, for speaker or hearer or both, by protecting against hurt feelings and social backlash. Further, even total explicitness cannot guarantee successful uptake. In *Pride and Prejudice*, Elizabeth Bennett repeatedly rejects Mr. Collins's proposal of marriage, but is summarily dismissed each time: since he believes that "it is usual with young ladies to reject the addresses of the man whom they secretly mean to accept, when he first applies for their favour; and that sometimes the refusal is repeated a second, or even a third time," he is "therefore by no means discouraged by what [she has] just said, and shall hope to lead [her] to the altar ere long." When Elizabeth finally pleads, "Can I speak plainer? Do not consider me now as an elegant female, intending to plague you, but as a rational creature, speaking the truth from her heart," Mr. Collins simply responds, "You are uniformly charming! . . . And I am persuaded that when sanctioned by the express authority of both your excellent parents, my proposals will not fail of being acceptable." Any degree of literal clarity and direct speech on Elizabeth's part merely serves as further grist for Mr. Collins's self-confirming interpretive mill. And while, as with slurs and "Boy," we might hope that such exchanges belong to a bygone era, #MeToo and "No means No" demonstrate that such cases of "silencing" are still quite common.

The most important reason not to "go literal," though, is that it is not viable given how human minds actually work. The intuitive perspectives associated with thick terms, insinuations, and jokes are pervasive in our thinking, and they can be triggered both intentionally and accidentally by a wide range of cues including literal speech and nonverbal situational features. Once evoked, they do not just guide the conversation, but persist in our minds, affecting our judgments and actions in ways we do not fully recognize until they are dislodged.

Given this, the best strategy is often to deploy frames (and presupposition, and implicature) ourselves, but in a critical, flexible way. We should be on the lookout for framing speech, especially smuggled in at the edges of conversation. Silent accommodation of objectionable presuppositions is tantamount to acquiescence, and we have an epistemic and moral obligation to rebut presupposed frames that we think distort and demean. Explicit, literal articulation and critical interrogation are important tools for doing this, although they risk lending those presuppositions undeserved legitimacy. However, "pure reason" is unlikely to convince our antagonists, or to carry the day with neutral parties. Worse, given existing stereotypes, it can make us appear shrill and humorless. Instead, successful parrying of accountability-avoiding meaning often depends at least as much on wit and social dynamics as on logic and justice. We need to enter into our interlocutors' perspectives enough to grasp what they will be able to hear. We need to marshal intuitive images and tropes to make them recognize the legitimacy of our operative assumptions and norms. And we need to muster allies who will stand with us in embracing and enforcing those assumptions and norms. Finally, rather than falling into the trap of dogmatically assuming that our own norms are natural and therefore right, we need to cultivate imagination and epistemic humility—without abandoning our moral compass.[12]

Notes

1. Fitz-Adam (1754, 606).
2. Poussaint (1967); quoted in McConnell-Ginet (2020).
3. Hughes (1940, 268–269); quoted in McConnell-Ginet (2020).
4. Lynne Tirrell (1999, 2012) analyzes the social effects of slurs and other derogatory expressions in terms of inferential language games. Mary Kate McGowan (2019) explains a wide variety of forms of harming speech as exercises of linguistic and conversational power to enact social norms. Rae Langton (2017) treats hate speech as a tool for exercising social authority through presupposition accommodation. Sally McConnell-Ginet (forthcoming) offers a compendious and accessible, empirically informed overview of power dynamics in language.
5. Snyder (2014).
6. Steele (1997).
7. Susan Gelman (2005) argues that essentialist thinking is deeply embedded in human thought, originating early in childhood. Claude Steele (2011) argues that "stereotype threat" can be triggered in many ways, and affects our behavior in many situations. Sarah Jane Leslie (2017) argues that judgments about generics are driven by and reinforce intuitive, affectively loaded stereotypes. Cordelia Fine (2010) analyzes ways in which scientific findings are commonly interpreted by journalists, laypeople, and scientists as supporting biological essentialism about gender.
8. Grice (1975).
9. Pope (1926 [1734]).
10. I discuss insinuation as a form of Gricean speaker's meaning that exploits presuppositions which are not acknowledged in the common ground in an article (Camp 2019). Jennifer Saul (2019) analyzes coded political speech, including the quote from Bush, as dog whistles.
11. "Dyke" (1979); quoted in Tirrell (1999).
12. Thanks to Ernie Lepore, Jonna Perrillo, Gregory Ward, Nancy Yousef, and especially to Mary Kate McGowan and Sally McConnell-Ginet for discussion. Thanks to audiences at Arkansas University, the Chapel Hill Colloquium, Colgate University, Columbia University, Southern Methodist University, Vassar College, and the Yale Humanities Program for useful and enjoyable discussion.

Bibliography

Camp, Elisabeth. 2019. "Insinuation, Common Ground, and the Conversational Record." In *New Work on Speech Acts*, edited by Daniel Fogal, Daniel Harris, and Matt Moss, 40–66. Oxford: Oxford University Press.

"Dyke: A History of Resistance" (Editorial). 1979. *The Lesbian Tide*, no. 8 (May/June): 21.

Fine, Cordelia. 2010. *Delusions of Gender: How Our Minds, Society, and Neurosexism Create Difference*. New York: Norton.

Fitz-Adam, Adam. 1754. *The World* vol. 101: 606.

Gelman, Susan. 2005. *The Essential Child: Origins of Essentialism in Everyday Thought.* Oxford: Oxford University Press.

Grice, Paul. 1975. "Logic and Conversation." In *Syntax and Semantics, Vol. 3, Speech Acts,* edited by P. Cole and J. L. Morgan, 41–58. New York: Academic Press.

Hughes, Langston. 1940. *The Big Sea: An Autobiography.* New York: Knopf.

Langton, Rae. 2017. "The Authority of Hate Speech." In *Oxford Studies in Philosophy of Law,* Vol. 3, edited by John Gardner, Leslie Green, and Brian Leiter, 123–152. Oxford: Oxford University Press.

Leslie, Sarah Jane. 2017. "The Original Sin of Cognition: Fear, Prejudice, and Generalization." *Journal of Philosophy* 114, no. 8: 393–421.

McConnell-Ginet, Sally. 2020. *Words Matter: Meaning and Power.* Cambridge: Cambridge University Press.

McGowan, Mary Kate. 2019. *Just Words: On Speech and Hidden Harm.* Oxford: Oxford University Press.

Pope, Alexander. 1926 [1734]. *Epistle to Dr. Arbuthnot.* Oxford: Clarendon Press.

Poussaint, Alvin. 1967. "A Negro Psychiatrist Explains the Negro Psyche." *New York Times Sunday Magazine,* August 20.

Saul, Jennifer. 2019. "Dog Whistles, Political Manipulation and the Philosophy of Language." In *New Work on Speech Acts,* edited by Daniel Fogal, Daniel Harris, and Matt Moss, 360–383. Oxford: Oxford University Press.

Snyder, Kieran. 2014. "The Abrasiveness Trap: High-Achieving Men and Women Are Described Differently in Reviews." *Fortune,* August 26. http://fortune.com/2014/08/26/performance-review-gender-bias/.

Steele, Claude. 1997. "A Threat in the Air: How Stereotypes Shape Intellectual Identity and Performance." *American Psychologist* 52, no. 6: 613–629.

Steele, Claude. 2011. *Whistling Vivaldi: How Stereotypes Affect Us and What We Can Do.* New York: Norton.

Tirrell, Lynne. 1999. "Derogatory Terms: Racism, Sexism, and the Inferential Role Theory of Meaning." In *Language and Liberation: Feminism, Philosophy and Language,* edited by Kelly Oliver and Christina Hendricks, 41–79. Albany: SUNY Press.

Tirrell, Lynne. 2012. "Genocidal Language Games." In *Speech and Harm: Controversies Over Free Speech,* edited by Ishani Maitra and Mary Kate McGowan, 174–221. Oxford: Oxford University Press.

13

Race

The Ontological Crisis of the "Human"

Shannon Winnubst

You have been invited into this volume through Persephone, a myth-ical woman who was abducted as a girl. The prologue, rightfully, brings Persephone to life as a young woman in transition. While painfully ripped from the comforts of her childhood home, her abduction by Hades also sets her free from an overbearing mother, Demeter. This dynamic between mother and daughter has absorbed a great deal of attention from European and European-descended women in philosophy, as the prologue shows. With not a mention of the sexual aspects of her abduction, the prologue invites you into this volume through this mythical girl, sitting at the threshold of her entry into adulthood, seeking "to know the full extent of our (human) condition."

To begin this chapter on the vexing, powerful concept of race, I introduce you to a different girl who was also abducted. This girl, who is both mythical and historical, was also stripped from the comforts of home, taken merci-lessly away from everything that is familiar and safe. But rather than awak-ening in an ornate bed and discovering a regal feast, this girl descends into a living, human-made hell. She is forced to march, with many other abducted victims, miles and miles toward the ocean, where she is warehoused in a cav-ernous stone barracoon. Thrown with strangers into this pestilent holding cell with a floor covered in feces, urine, and vomit, the girl will wait days and days or even weeks and weeks, watching as others fall prey to infections and succumb to death. Finally, she will be forced onto a ship, crowded with hun-dreds of other abducted bodies, sloshing about an open sea amidst a shared, wide-open fear for life itself. She loses everything: her mother, her family, her friendship, her security, her dignity, her sense of the world and everything that matters. She loses herself. The ship, ruled by crass men drunk on power and greed, becomes the site of a mythical and historical transformation: the

Shannon Winnubst, *Race* In: *Philosophy for Girls*. Edited by: Melissa M. Shew and Kimberly K. Garchar, Oxford University Press (2020). © Oxford University Press. DOI: 10.1093/oso/9780190072919.003.0014.

girl is no longer a girl, no longer a daughter or a sister or a friend. Entered into the ledgers of the ship for the purposes of economic transactions and insurance contracts, she becomes a unit of cargo: "4'6" x 1'0."[1] The girl is no longer human.

This abduction and this girl cross a different threshold from the one on which the prologue leaves Persephone perched. The difference is one that philosophers might call "ontological." Derived from the Greek *onto-*, an ontological distinction indicates a difference in "being." By calling this difference "ontological," I argue that the difference between these two thresholds indicates a difference in kind, not merely a difference of degree. While the prologue concludes with Persephone standing on the threshold of early adulthood, seeking "to know the full extent of our (human) condition," this girl, whom we might name "Venus," is forced across a threshold that strips her humanity from her. The moment she is forced out of the pestilent barracoon onto the slave-trading ship, she crosses a threshold that transforms her from a human being into an object of commerce. Poet Dionne Brand calls this threshold "a door of no return" (Brand 2001); it changes not only the girl's existence, but the existence of all peoples descended from those millions and millions of persons transported as cargo across the Atlantic Ocean for 450 years.[2]

The stakes of this claim that the abduction of this girl ontologically changed the meaning of "human" are very high. Philosophy, as a discipline, still needs to consider more deeply the possibility of ontological change forced by material violence and economic greed; philosophy needs to consider both this specific instance and the more general challenge that it presents to traditional understandings of "ontology." For most philosophical approaches, especially those that dominate philosophy in the United States, ontological characteristics are immutable. To claim that a characteristic is ontological is precisely to differentiate it from other characteristics that are historical, sociological, and cultural. The ontological designation, for example, is precisely the one used to indicate that the same "human-ness" exists across widely different human cultures. When I argue, along with many other scholars, that the transatlantic slave trade transformed abducted people from humans into cargo, I am arguing that it enacted an ontological transformation in the meaning of "human."

As the extensive work of Sylvia Wynter frames it, the advent of the transatlantic slave trade, which roughly coincides with the fifteenth-century emergence of Renaissance Humanism in Europe, produces the figure she names

"Man1" (Wynter 2003). With this name, Wynter argues that a new form of "the human" emerges explicitly through the exclusion of all "black" bodies from it. The designation of some populations as "black," which is an historical invention driven by economic power and greed, produces an ontological change in the meaning of "human": while the claim to be "human" still poses as a simple claim to universality, it actually becomes a central weapon in the dividing of global economies between "human" and "black" ("nonhuman") populations.

The difficulty of conceptualizing an ontological change as produced through historical, economic conditions for many traditions of philosophy calls upon us to remember that philosophy—Western philosophy—is a discipline rooted in Greek and European texts and traditions, and that these are the cultures of the people who abducted Venus and reduced her to a commodity. This does not mean, however, that we should not continue to try to engage philosophy in our efforts to understand this transformation and its profound impact on the course of human history. Rather, it shows us that we need new philosophical tools, borne of the twenty-first century, to grasp this ontological transformation. My hope is that you will join us in this demanding, ethical, and existential task of conjuring, creating, and employing these new tools.

Let us return to Venus. Why have I suggested this name? We have the stories of Persephone through the canonical authority of Greek myths and Euro-North American literary reflections, but there are no archives that record the life of this girl abducted into a global slave trade. We know that it happened: the holding cells are called "slave castles" and dot the western coast of Africa; the ships' captains kept meticulous ledgers, often for insurance contracts, and the shipmates wrote letters from various ports; there are even legal cases documenting criminal trials of captains accused of "throwing cargo overboard" or otherwise harming the promised economic returns of the voyages.[3] There are also rare documents written by the enslaved themselves that offer brief accounts of the violent mistreatment of the captives, including the regular raping of the women and girls.[4] But there is no record of the girl's voice or her experience: not a diary, not a note passed to another frightened captive, not a single shred of historical evidence of how she might have felt or what she might have thought amidst the horrors. And there is certainly no record of her name.

In naming her "Venus," I follow the groundbreaking work of black feminists to understand that this girl, whom we can never fully conjure from the archives of the transatlantic slave trade, is both historical and mythical. She existed historically, without a doubt. But we know nothing at all about her historical existence. We know nothing of its texture: its hopes, worries, desires, fears, fantasies, pleasures or loves. And we will never know any of this. Given the singularity of this particular catastrophe that is the transatlantic slave trade, this is not only a matter of a life being erased. The vast majority of human lives, after all, have not left any historical record. Despite or even through her complete absence in any historical record, this girl—who emerges from the transatlantic slave trade marked as a "black" girl—lives on as the myth that sediments the logic of anti-blackness at the core of European and Euro-descendant cultures, especially the United States.

More specifically, I name this girl "Venus" to follow the remarkable work of Saidiya Hartman.[5] As Hartman explains, the individual girl who is abducted is never named; rather, she is subsumed into an endless list of names that do not designate anything about the individual girl, but tell us everything about the violence and mendacity of the culture built upon her systematic abduction. As Hartman writes,

> Variously named Harriot, Phibba, Sara, Joanna, Rachel, Linda, and Sally, she is found everywhere in the Atlantic world. The barracoon, the hollow of the slave ship, the pest-house, the brothel, the cage, the surgeon's laboratory, the prison, the cane-field, the kitchen, the master's bedroom—turn out to be exactly the same place and in all of them she is called Venus. . . . One cannot ask, "Who is Venus?" because it would be impossible to answer such a question. There are hundreds of thousands of other girls who share her circumstances and these circumstances have generated few stories. And the stories that exist are not about them, but rather about the violence, excess, mendacity, and reason that seized hold of their lives, transformed them into commodities and corpses, and identified them with names tossed-off as insults and crass jokes. (Hartman 2008, 1–2)

The listing of names persists into our contemporary times. Hartman is influenced by the work of Hortense Spillers, who begins one of the most important essays of the late twentieth century, "Mama's Baby, Papa's Maybe: An American Grammar Book," with this personal meditation:

> Let's face it. I am a marked woman, but not everybody knows my name. "Peaches" and "Brown Sugar," "Sapphire" and "Earth Mother," "Aunty,"

"Granny," God's "Holy Fool," a "Miss Ebony First," or "Black Woman at
the Podium": I describe a locus of confounded identities, a
meeting ground
of investments and privations in the national treasury of rhetorical
wealth.
My country needs me, and if I were not here, I would have to be invented.
(Spillers 2003, 203)

For the figure of the black girl in the cultural imaginary spawned by the
transatlantic slave trade, there is no proper name. Marked by this new category that emerges with the transatlantic slave trade, "black," she is barred
from the patriarchal lineage that is required for that kind of individual life;
she never has a last name. Reduced to cargo in the holds of the slave ships,
raped and assaulted onboard those ships and on the plantations where she
finally landed, she never has been and still is not fully human. To call this
girl "Venus" is to recognize that the endless list of names given to black girls
and women, in both the past and the present, never refers to any individual
human. And, yet, the lists persist, standing at the center of the cultural imaginary of the many, many cultures still benefitting from the transatlantic
slave trade. Functioning as a myth that covers over the systemic violence that
erases her historical existence, "Venus" animates these cultural imaginaries,
while simultaneously being erased and silenced by them.

13.1 A Brief Tale of Two Categories: "Black" and "Race"

From this originary scene of the transatlantic slave trade, we inherit two categories that continue to shape cultures across the globe: "black" and "race." For
most of us, these categories are lumped together. We assume that "black" is
a racial identification, just like "white," "Native American," "Latinx," "Asian,"
and so on in a list of constantly changing racial categories. Especially for those
of us who are racially identified as "white," we are not forced or encouraged
to give any serious thought to these categories, since the privilege of being
white does not make them seem important to us. This is, after all, how social
privilege works: boys and men are not encouraged to think about gender;
straight people don't go through a painful "coming out" process about their
sexuality; cis-gendered folks rarely think about how their gender identification lines up with their biological certification of sex at birth; able-bodied

persons don't often consider the inaccessibility of built environments; and so on. The general assumption that "black" is just like "white" and all the other particular identifications of "race" is, I argue, part of the obfuscating work of "race" in the post-transatlantic slave trade world. This confusion allows the fundamental logic of anti-blackness to persist.

In an effort to intervene in this confusion, I turn now to a story of how both "black" and "race" emerge out of the transatlantic slave trade and begin to travel along various routes into our contemporary world. This is, of course, a portrait painted with very broad brush-strokes: there is far more gritty historical detail than I can offer here. Moreover, we must also be mindful of our own assumptions and habits as readers in the twenty-first century. Especially as readers of English, which is still the language of empire, we are very prone to read the past through a narrative of progress. That is, we are very prone to read the past as naïve and riddled with mistakes that we would never commit now. This response, which is most often unconscious, signals a kind of quiet arrogance, a resounding assumption that we have grown out of the silly childishness of our forbearers. It is a remarkably sly way that we consistently let ourselves "off the hook," reassuring ourselves that things are always, necessarily getting better. Moreover, this belief in progress as a natural given of human development is also a habit that has often upheld the racial hierarchy that claims European superiority.

Scholars widely agree that the transatlantic slave trade marks a break unlike any other in human history. While slave trades and their horrors have existed across human cultures, including African cultures, this systematic transportation of humans as cargo to cultures across the Atlantic Ocean formed a singular catastrophe that still shapes the contemporary world. The transatlantic slave trade set circuits of trade and capital into motion across the globe.[6] Happening alongside the massive European colonizing of the Americas, large parts of Asia, and Australia, the circuits of the slave trade exerted an unforeseen economic force that produced global structures of inequality. Consequently, those cultures benefitting from this capitalist extraction of labor from "human cargo" needed a way to make sense of this new world order. How to justify the systematic reduction of human bodies to cargo and commodities? What kind of explanations could justify the enslavement of millions and millions of bodies?

From the fifteenth through the eighteenth centuries, the authoritative voice of religion offers a clear way to explain the division of the world into "civilized" and "savage" regions. Grounded in Christian theology and doctrine, European colonizers carved the world easily into those who have and those who have not been "saved" by the truth of Christianity. Colonization was thereby framed not as a violent system of conquest and exploitation, but as an evangelical mission of civilizing and saving the world in the name of the Christian God. As Charles Mills reminds us in his ground-breaking philosophical work, *The Racial Contract*, the European assumption that Christianity was the undebatable and singular Truth ensured that any resistance to it immediately signaled a savage, even bestial, lack of rationality, even if the Christian message was delivered in a foreign language. As Mills relates, "In the case of the Native Americans this acceptance [of Christian rule] was to be signaled by their agreement to the *Requerimiento*, a long statement read aloud to them in, of course, a language they did not understand, failing which assent a just war could lawfully be waged against them" (Mills 1997, 22). On the basis of religious authority, therefore, European superiority justified both the colonization of indigenous peoples and the abduction of Africans. While there are a very large number of differences between these two systems, the general category of "race" emerged in these centuries as a way to distinguish Europeans from those colonized and enslaved "others," who were racialized as nonhuman.

Fast-forward to the period of the seventeenth to nineteenth centuries, a period known as "the Enlightenment," and reason emerges as the highest authority and firmest foundation for systems of human judgment. With democracy and modern science slowly developing, the singular authority of religion in Europe begins to unravel. This dissolution presented fresh challenges for the concept of race. The appeal to Christianity to justify the superiority of European cultures was no longer sufficient. Especially as the nineteenth century brings the abolition of slavery onto the horizon, the racial hierarchy that posits European superiority required novel justifications. Modern science provided them immediately in a field known as "scientific racism," which arguably birthed the concept of race that we still hold in the twenty-first century.

As Stephen Jay Gould explains, the scientific work of the early and mid-nineteenth century in the United States and Europe produced a new line of defense for the racial hierarchies sedimented by the transatlantic slave trade and colonialism. Even before Charles Darwin's 1859 publication of *On the Origin of Species*, which would present the first scientific account of evolution, scientists were already struggling to account for racial differences without recourse to theologies of creationism. With the authority of religion eclipsed by science and reason, the colonial transatlantic slave trade's racial hierarchy faced a central challenge: Are all human bodies descended from the same source? In other words, are non-European, "nonwhite" bodies human?

Gould focuses on the early nineteenth-century field of craniometry in the United States. Bringing together new practices of anatomy and nascent theories of cognitive science, craniometry isolated the skull as the primary site of intelligence, personality, and behavior. The scientists thereby developed a critical new aspect of the concept of race: they tested their theories on physical bodies. For example, through various forms of "experimentation" and "data analysis," American craniologist Samuel George Morton, who was widely hailed as one of the greatest scientists of his time and who directly influenced eugenic practices of twentieth-century Nazi Germany, collected skulls from all over the world to prove that racial hierarchies were scientifically sound. Through extensive comparisons and meticulous methods of measurement, Morton concluded that the white race is the most superior form of the human species and the Negro race is the most inferior form, with indigenous "Indians" just above them. That is, through a "rational scientific method," Morton produced a scientific hierarchy of the races based on the evidence of skulls.

While Stephen Jay Gould thoroughly exposes the errors in Morton's methods, he refuses to conclude that Morton consciously and intentionally manipulated his data. Rather, Gould argues that the cultural context of our intellectual practices, including science, profoundly shape our conclusions. Therefore, when we find ourselves appalled by Morton's manipulation of measurements and data in order to uphold the white race as superior, we should be very careful about what this says about our contemporary culture. We may want to believe that we have progressed past this kind of unabashed racial hierarchy, especially as we are called to be "colorblind" and "celebrate diversity." I argue, though, that we share three aspects of Morton's research: 1) an ongoing crisis in the category of "the human" caused by racial difference; 2) the logic of anti-blackness that always places blackness at the bottom of all racial hierarchies; and 3) the persistent claim that racial difference is located in the body.

This concept of race produced by modern science reverberates across the twentieth century in both the United States and Europe. In the United States, W. E. B. DuBois declares in 1903, following Frederick Douglas's essay of 1881, that "the problem of the twentieth century is the problem of the color line" (DuBois 1994, 1), while also describing race as a matter of hair, skin and bone. Alongside his astute analyses of the ongoing economic, political and psychological impact of racial hierarchies on black communities, DuBois always recognized that race was a concept rooted in an arbitrary emphasis on particular bodily traits. In Europe, early eugenics practices from the United States develop into the horrors of the Holocaust and World War II. It is abundantly clear in the first half of the twentieth century that, despite the abolition of slavery, race persists as the most powerful and violent concept of the modern world.

However, as the civil rights movements of the 1960s sweep across the United States and Europe, the legal connotations of race as a problem to be overcome appear to gain the upper hand over these scientific concepts that locate race firmly in biological hierarchies. The progress narrative of classical liberalism firmly takes hold here, portraying the problem of racism as an error of the past that will eventually be corrected. As people in the late twentieth century and early twenty-first century embrace multiculturalism, colorblindness, and diversity across the United States and Europe, the claim of legal progress becomes so widely circulated that it produces a cultural slumber about the ongoing reality of the stark economic and legal disparities between white and nonwhite communities and lives. For example, in the 1980s and 1990s, as multiculturalism and diversity became the way we talked about race, mass incarceration in the United States skyrocketed to unforeseen heights precisely through the disproportionate incarceration of black and brown persons.[7] Trapped by both the language of progress and "celebrating diversity," we find ourselves lacking the language to confront the ongoing, persistent power of the transatlantic slave trade that began six centuries ago.

13.2 What Is the "Human?"

In this narrative, we can see how the concept of race supports and perpetuates the logic of anti-blackness in several manners: 1) it distinguishes kinds of human beings in the service of a racialized hierarchy; 2) it attaches to any kind of justification, whether religious, scientific or legal; and 3) since the nineteenth century, it attaches arbitrarily to particular aspects of the body (DuBois's "hair, skin and bones"). In each of these, the concept of race supports and perpetuates the racial hierarchy that locates European and European-descended peoples, who are identified as "white" at the top and

Africans and African-descended peoples, who are identified as "black" whom the at the bottom. In other words, the concept of race enables and perpetuates the ontology of anti-blackness spawned by the transatlantic slave trade six centuries ago.

This becomes even more problematic when we realize how much energy continues to be spent on the question of whether "race" is biological. As the brief history I have sketched shows, the concept of race attaches directly to bodily characteristics in the early nineteenth-century scientific theories and practices. While craniometry attaches it to skulls, racial difference gets located in a variety of biological characteristics across European and North American practices: the texture of hair; the shape of noses, eyes, lips, and genitalia; and, of course, the color of skin. Across the array of characteristics, we begin to understand that the biological trait that is designated as the locus of "race" is arbitrary. Moreover, as the study of genetics emerges in the late twentieth century, the racial trait does not even need to be visible: the search for "the race gene" and genetic markers of racial difference remain a very hot pursuit. Across all of these arbitrary biological markers, the need to secure the racial hierarchy persists.

Consequently, we find ourselves in the midst of a profound ethical problem. The material "evidence" of this racial hierarchy that upholds the superiority of European and European-descended persons, communities, populations, and cultures continues to pile up all around us. Whether poverty and wealth rates, school-to-prison pipelines, maternal mortality, health-care disparities, food insecurity, environmental racism or some other aspect of contemporary society, black persons, communities and populations continue to be systematically disenfranchised and subjected to explicit state and nonstate violence, while white persons, communities and populations continue to benefit from systemic economic and cultural advantages. However, if we stay inside of the language of "race" to address this ethical problem, then the debate continues to focus on whether and how race is biological. The language of race cannot sufficiently address persistence of the racial hierarchy itself.

As awareness of the systematic character of racism grows, contemporary cultures are struggling to find the language through which to address these unethical structures. As part of that effort, I return to the language of ontology that I introduced at the beginning of the chapter. Recall that, amidst the story of Venus, the category spawned most directly and immediately in the transatlantic slave trade was "black." As bodies were abducted, reduced to the numerical measurements of cargo, and transported as cheap commodities that were regularly tossed overboard, living humans were stripped of their humanity. The designation that carried this violent stripping of humanity was "blackness."

This new category, "blackness," designates the ontological transformation of humans to objects: to be called "black" is to be barred from the category of "human." The category of "black" is capacious and can apply to the wide range of bodies and populations who are racialized as nonwhite and, thereby, designated as nonhuman. When the concept of race begins attaching arbitrarily to various parts of the human body, it is the rendering of these bodies as "black" that matters. "Black" bodies are framed as the ones that are "the problem," freighted with their own victimhood. "Black" bodies are framed as the ones that deviate from the norm, leaving nonblack bodies as "simply human," who rarely think of themselves as even having a race. In order to interrupt the systemic persistence of the racial hierarchy, we must address this ontological transformation in the category of the human. The problem of racism is not merely an accident of the past, nor is it a question of locating racial differences more precisely. The persistent, global problem of racism is the effect of the anti-black ontology that was put into motion in the colonial transatlantic slave trade. This ontological division of bodies into "human" and "nonhuman" continues to structure our contemporary worlds; it has not been addressed, much less remedied.

To take up this ontological crisis in the category of the "human" and to frame racism as the system of ontological anti-blackness is, I argue, at the heart of all ethical challenges facing us in the twenty-first century. It will require immense courage and fortitude, as well as delicate intellectual work to navigate the deep social, psychological, and economic structures that would be uprooted by such an effort. It will involve taking Dionne Brand's "door of no return" as a fundamental structure of our shared cultural consciousness and filtering every event, great or small, through it. It will be immensely difficult, but it is also the path toward reclaiming a true "humanity" in our world. I invite you to join us in that struggle.

Notes

1. Hortense Spillers provides these measurements in her groundbreaking essay "Mama's Baby, Papa's Maybe" (2003).

2. Scholars generally agree that the slave trade was initiated with Portuguese voyages to Africa in 1415. In 1888, Brazil became the final nation benefiting from the transatlantic slave trade to abolish slavery.
3. See Hartman (2008).
4. See Equiano (1995). This is the most well-known narrative written by a formerly enslaved man and offers accounts of the violence that are not framed by sentimentality or presumed knowledge of the experiences of those undergoing the violence; it was originally published in 1789.
5. Hartman chooses the name "Venus" based on the actual documents of a court trial of a captain accused—and exonerated—of discarding property from his slave ship. However, "Venus" is also the name of one of the most famous cases of an African girl abducted for the delights of European culture: Saartje Baartman was called "Hottentot Venus," and was paraded through European salons and circuses as a "freak show."
6. See Lowe (2015) for an excellent account of how European colonialism affected cultures and economies across the globe, including the continent of Asia.
7. See Alexander (2010) for a thorough account of the explosion of the prison industry in the United States since 1980 through the disproportionate incarceration of black and brown persons.

Bibliography

Alexander, M. 2010. *The New Jim Crow: Mass Incarceration in the Age of Colorblindness.* New York: The New Press.

Brand, D. 2001. *A Map to the Door of No Return.* Toronto: Vintage Canada.

DuBois, W. E. B. 1994. *The Souls of Black Folk.* Chicago: Dover Thrift Editions.

Equiano, O. 1995. *The Interesting Narrative of the Life of Olaudah Equiano.* New York: Penguin.

Hartman, S. 2008. "Venus in Two Acts." *Small Axe* 26 (June): 1–14.

Lowe, L. 2015. *The Intimacies of Four Continents* Durham, NC: Duke University Press.

Mills, C. 1997. *The Racial Contract.* Ithaca, NY: Cornell University Press.

Spillers, H. 2003. "Mama's Baby, Papa's Maybe: An American Grammar Book." In *Black, White, and in Color: Essays on American Literature and Culture,* 203–229. Chicago: University of Chicago Press.

Wynter, S. 2003. "Unsettling the Coloniality of Being/Power/Truth/Freedom: Towards the Human, After Man, Its Overrepresentation—An Argument." *CR: The New Centennial Review* 3, no. 3: 257–337.

14

Gender

To the Binary and Beyond

Charlotte Witt

In her 1969 science fiction classic *The Left Hand of Darkness,* Ursula Le Guin describes a culture that is called *Gethen* or *Winter,* in which binary sex differences and binary gender roles are unknown. In Winter, all beings are *ambisexual* as opposed to being categorized in binary terms as male or female, man or woman.

As ambisexual, everyone is capable of *becoming* male or female for the purposes of reproduction during the fertile period of the month, called *kemmer*. But at other times, everyone is androgynous (i.e., exhibiting neither explicitly masculine nor feminine characteristics). When a partner is found during kemmer, hormonal dominance is established by one person, the other takes on the opposite role, and there is no social status associated with either position. (Occasionally the kemmer partners are same sex.) Le Guin writes, "Normal individuals have no predisposition to either sexual role in kemmer; they do not know whether they will be the male or the female, and have no choice in the matter."[1] The female role continues through the period of breast-feeding. In Winter, a single individual could be the biological mother of several children and the biological father of several more. The traditions of kemmer shape all the institutions of the society; their commerce, size of settlements, stories and social structures, but there is no biological sex difference, nor gender difference and associated gender dominance, for most of the month (the time outside of kemmer).

Since anyone is liable to play the female role in procreation, the role is both less restrictive and less limiting. In our society, biological mothers are usually assumed to provide the ongoing care of emotional and social mothering. In other words, gendered assumptions about mothering are assumed to match up with biological mothering. Likewise, fathering is assumed to correlate with the contribution of genetic material by the biological father. In Winter,

Charlotte Witt, *Gender* In: *Philosophy for Girls*. Edited by: Melissa M. Shew and Kimberly K. Garchar, Oxford University Press (2020). © Oxford University Press. DOI: 10.1093/oso/9780190072919.003.0015.

however, the burdens associated with mothering—that is, gender role assumptions—are shared and distributed among the citizens without one group (biological women) being designated to bear them. This has the consequence that anyone can play any gender role in society. "There is no division of humanity into strong and weak halves, protective/protected, dominant/submissive, owner/chattel, active/passive."[2] Interactions with the people in Winter cannot follow our expectations and pattern of socio–sexual relations because they see each other neither as sexed in a binary way (as male or female), nor gendered in a binary way (as men or women). The visitor notes that on Winter, "One is respected and judged only as a human being. It is an appalling experience."[3] It's appalling because the visitor is accustomed to benefitting from various privileges associated with his sex and gender and is utterly shocked that he does not maintain the same privileges in Winter. Le Guin imagines an egalitarian society in which sex differences simply don't matter because they are transitory. Everyone will eventually play, or might eventually play, each role during *kemmer*.

In contrast, in our society, gender has been historically understood to be binary. That is, a person must be a woman or a man, and there is no other alternative. Binary gender roles have traditionally (and incorrectly) been attached to a binary understanding of biological sex. Social standing and privilege is powerfully encoded in our binary gender roles such that men and women are expected to—and do—act in certain ways.

While Le Guin's imaginary society comments on our world of binary sex and gender indirectly by describing a society without them, this chapter aims to explore gender by means of a thought experiment—in this case a parable—that illustrates the way that gender organizes our social lives today. Like Le Guin's description of Winter's ambisexual culture, my thought experiment is intended to raise questions and to provoke thought about our gendered world, and the future, rather than to provide neat and easy answers.

14.1 The Parable of the Talls and the Shorts

Imagine a human culture in which the physical trait of height was socially significant, and people in that culture were divided into Talls and Shorts.[4] There were a number of arbitrary rules, and even physical interventions, that pushed people of average or unstable height in one direction or the other. This was ostensibly done for their own good. Some rebels refused to identify as either Tall or Short, and they walked on tiptoe or with bent knees to parody and destabilize the culture's binary height categories. Some rebels also posed intellectual difficulties by pointing out that the designations "Tall" and "Short," although apparently labels for objective and physical characteristics of individuals, were actually culturally variable terms that encoded and reinforced cultural norms. In other words, what counts as Tall and Short is completely dependent upon who else is around because Tall and Short vary drastically from group to group.

Imagine further that necessary social functions in this culture were shaped by elaborate norms reflecting the distinction between Talls and Shorts. Dining is one example. Talls always ate before Shorts, who served them and then ate what was left. Perhaps this set of dining norms originated because the Talls were bigger than the Shorts; perhaps the norms were thought to make sense because the Shorts were closer to the table, and hence it was easier and more natural for them to place items on the table. Maybe it was the psychology of the Shorts, who after all were servile, that explained the apparent solidity and good sense of the social practice. Perhaps there was a religious justification in that their deity, the Giant, resembled Talls more than Shorts. Maybe the dining roles persisted because of the common understanding that Talls needed more food than Shorts and had difficulty controlling their impulses. Without the existing dining norms, the Talls might simply take the food from the Shorts and not even leave them leftovers, so the social norms governing dining were truly in the best interests of everyone. Since their science, religion, and politics served to reinforce the height-based social hierarchy, its contingency and its unfairness were largely invisible both to Talls and to Shorts. The dining norms seemed utterly and completely "natural" and they could not imagine dining in any other way.

The Parable of the Talls and the Shorts is intended to mirror and illuminate our social world in which gender identity, historically considered in terms of the categories of men and women, is a basic ordering principle. Like Height Society, our culture organizes many of its most important activities around a binary gender division. Consider the differences between men and women's sports and activities, clothing, presumed interests and aptitudes, roles in the family, depictions in the arts and media, political power and roles in traditional religions. Indeed, in many cultures, including our own, women traditionally prepare and serve food to men and children before sitting down to eat themselves. And, finally, notice that like the Talls and the Shorts, men occupy a privileged position in relation to women in terms of income, political power, and other markers.[5] In our social world the question "What is gender?" immediately transforms into a question about the gender binary, the division of human beings into men and women.

Given the deep social groove worn by the gender binary, it is surprising to learn that there is significant overlap between women and men on a number of important metrics, and significant differences among women and differences among men on a wide range of measures.[6] Moreover, recent work in neuroscience attempting to establish the existence of male and female brains is not persuasive.[7] There is thus good reason to question the basis for a strict gender binary that cleanly divides persons into women and men where that division tracks important functional differences in our brains or in our capabilities beyond reproduction. The question of reproductive ability, though, brings us to the issue of the assumed binary, biological sex differences on which gender is often presumed to be grounded. Perhaps the gender binary rests on an underlying biological division into female and male human beings.

Traditionally, a man is considered to be a male human and a woman is considered a female human. This way of defining gender bases gender on biological sex differences that are, as mentioned earlier, problematically assumed to be binary as well. Early feminists thought that gender was the social meaning of sexual difference. Consider Simone de Beauvoir's famous line in which she asserts "One is not born, but rather becomes, a woman." In other words, one might be born female but one becomes a woman through sociological training. Two assumptions underlying this line of thought are worth a closer look.

The first assumption is that sexual differentiation in humans is binary. Male and female humans are differentiated from one another by several features: chromosomes (XX female humans and XY human males), hormone levels (lower average testosterone levels in females), and primary and secondary sex characteristics (uterus, penis). As it turns out these features do not always align in an intersex individual who may be born with a chromosomal identity other than XX or XY or with genitalia that is not considered strictly male or female. There is a small percentage of babies born who would not count as either male or female by the biological features I just mentioned. We cannot go directly from a binary sex difference to a binary gender difference because sexual difference itself is complex and does not fall into a neat binary. Human biology suggests that we cannot simply base the gender binary on a more basic, underlying binary sex difference.[8]

The second assumption is that sexual difference determines gender difference. Feminist philosophers like Judith Butler have pointed out that the gender binary actually is so very powerful that it drives the medical profession (and parents) to intervene medically in order to remake intersex babies into facsimiles of one sex or another, presumably so they will then also be one gender or another.[9] These philosophers doubt that there is a clear biological level of binary sex differences distinct from the gender binary. Not only is sex difference not a binary but neither is the dichotomy between gender and sex if binary sex differentiation requires social intervention. The simple idea that women are female humans and men are male humans is not so simple after all, and maybe not satisfactory on closer inspection. What, then, is gender?

Let's return for a moment to Height Society. Just as some in our society would define a woman as an adult female human, in Height Society a Short is defined in terms of their small stature. A person's social role status (that is, being a woman or being a Short) is based on a physical or biological fact about the individual (sex or stature). However, just as with the complexity of sex determination in our world, there are problems with pinpointing exactly what counts as stature, and there are interheight cases that do not fit easily into the binary of small stature/tall stature. Further, because Height Society bases a central social function—dining—on a binary height system, some individuals are given growth hormones or suppressants so that they fit the dichotomy of Talls and Shorts as well as possible. That is, sometimes there is medical intervention in being a Tall or a Short just as there can be medical intervention in being a woman or a man in our society. In sum, it is just as difficult to simply ground being a Tall or Short with having a certain stature as it is to ground gender in biological sex differences.

But there is another, more significant problem to consider. The attempt to base gender on sex difference, even if it all lined up neatly, does not really capture what many feminist and other social theorists are interested in understanding, which is the social meaning of gender differences. For social constructionists about gender, like myself, the object of study is the social role of gender, which includes being a woman or being a man but need not be restricted to the binary. Gender roles are multiplying beyond the binary to include genderqueer, transgender, and other identities.[10] In the Height Society parable, genderqueer people are those that destabilize the binary of Talls and Shorts by parody, or by simply rejecting the social role of being a Tall or being a Short, by alternating heights or mixing attributes. Trans height individuals do not identify with the height they were originally assigned.

Social constructionist views about gender can take a wide range of approaches from those who understand gender as a performance, and emphasize the nonsubstantial, ungrounded character of gender roles to those—like me—who focus on the normative dimension of being gendered. By this I mean a focus on all the norms (or informal rules or "ought tos") that make up gendered social roles, the reasons why they apply to us, and how they impact our actions and activities. In the simplified terms of Height Society this is a focus on why the Talls and Shorts are responsive to and can be judged according to the norms that structure their dining behaviors. In Height Society we wonder why ought a Short dine after a Tall and why Shorts should be subservient to the Talls. Similarly, in our culture we might wonder why a woman ought to be maternal or why a man ought to avoid emotional expression.

More recently, an idea of gender has emerged as neither rooted in biological sex differences nor in gendered social roles but rather as a matter of gender identity. In the Height Society equivalent, these theorists reject both the idea that being a Tall or a Short is a question of physical stature as well as the idea that it is a matter of the social role one plays in dining (server or served). Instead, height is a question of "sincere avowal," or self-identification, or self-understanding as a particular gender.[11] This understanding of gender intentionally casts a large net and is, in principle, inclusive of individuals who understand themselves as women or men or genderqueer or transgender, but who might not be recognized by others as that gender. Some question, though, whether even this net is wide enough; after all there are women who might not be capable of sincerely avowing their gender identity. Would we want to deny that a woman with Alzheimers disease is a woman?[12] Another question that this approach raises concerns the content of the self-understanding. For a social constructionist like myself, this would seem to include at minimum some aspects of the normative gender role. In the vocabulary of Height Society, if being a Tall or a Short is a matter of identity, or self-understanding, then that self-understanding would seem to include eating first or second, serving or being served, or being a master or being subservient. Otherwise, why is it the self-understanding of being a Tall or of being a Short? Gender identity, the relevant self-understanding, might require an internalized gendered script, where the content of the script is fixed in relation to gendered social roles. Call this the gender identity plus social role view of gender (and notice that it could apply to nonbinary genders like being genderqueer).[13]

So far I have been using the Parable of Height Society, with its central dualism of Talls and Shorts, to illustrate various ways in which one might approach and unpack the concept of gender. The Parable is useful in so far as it allows us to radically simplify the social world along just one axis and one, albeit important, social activity. Of course our world is much more complicated with regard to the multiplicity of social practices, the multitude of social roles, and the existence of overlapping dominant and subaltern communities often with differing sets of social norms or required behaviors. In the real world the genders do not appear in isolated splendor but rather are intermixed with racialized groups, religious communities, nationalities and the like. It is time to complicate things.

One approach to addressing the complexity of human social worlds uses the notion of intersectionality. According to Kimberlé Crenshaw, who introduced the concept: "Intersectionality is a lens through which you can see where power comes and collides, where it interlocks and intersects. It's not simply that there's a race problem here, a gender problem here, and a class or LBGTQ problem there. Many times that framework erases what happens to people who are subject to all of these things."[14] An intersectional view of gender recognizes the complex overlap among various axes of oppression and privilege that can serve to occlude or omit entirely the experiences of some individuals. Crenshaw is particularly concerned to highlight the experience of black girls and women, which can disappear from view when the focus turns either to race alone or to gender alone. Intersectionality is an idea with broad reach and many applications and it can be used to analyze both theoretical and public policy gaps. Some feminists use the concept of intersectionality to express a view of the self as complex and multiple.

The Parable of the Talls and the Shorts has been useful to consider because it helps us to see how a contingent social practice, like the dining practices of the Talls and Shorts, might seem natural, correct, and unalterable to members of that society—but not to us readers. That their dining practices are arbitrary, and indeed unjust, is not apparent to the citizens of Height Society because they have no alternative to consider. The same might be said of our culture, and the practices surrounding gender and gendered social roles. They seem to be natural, correct, and unalterable. To see that they are not, it would be useful to find or to imagine an alternative society with very different practices of gender.

14.2 A Return to Ambisexuality

Le Guin imagines a society in which there are no genders in that there is no social elaboration of binary gender roles. For most of the time there is simply no differentiation into male and female human beings or into men and women, nor are social roles prescribed by those differentiations. Winter is an androgynous, ambisexual culture populated by human beings. It is an egalitarian vision in which gender difference simply doesn't matter because it is transitory. Everyone will play, or might play, each role during *kemmer*. Winter society, like Height Society, is a creation of the imagination, and we might well wonder about its relevance to our own culture and lives. After all, we earth humans don't have the flexible hormonal bodies of Winter society, and we are (arguably) not fixated on dining like the denizens of Height Society. Nonetheless, each scenario challenges us to think critically and reflectively about our own culture, the gender binary, and gender norms.

The Parable of the Talls and the Shorts was intended to help us to see what a binary role society organized around a central social function looks like, and the way it invites inegalitarian practices. It presents a pared down version of our own culture that allows certain features to emerge that might otherwise remain invisible because they are so pervasive. For example, the focus on physical stature raises important questions about the relevance of physical features to social status and standing. The practice of allowing just two categories of height and ignoring differences also emerges as a site of injustice. The way in which religion, science, and psychology are marshaled in support of Height dining practices mimics the ideological support offered to gendered norms and hierarchical structures in our own world. We might wonder whether the unequal status of Talls and Shorts could be changed simply by changing their dining practices but retaining the height categories, or whether subordination and oppression are so integral to the categories themselves that they should consider a politics of height eliminativism or the abolition of height categories altogether. In a similar fashion, gender eliminativists argue for the erasure of the gender binary, and the elimination of gendered social roles because they are an integral part of gender hierarchies and gender injustice.

Le Guin's description of Winter provides a fitting counterpoint to the Parable by giving us an alternative vision of a genderless society. She imagines a society in which reproductive roles do not determine gender roles. More precisely because there are no fixed reproductive roles, any citizen can, and most likely will, be both a female parent and a male parent, there are no gender roles. What remains is a society of human beings, not demarcated into genders and not ordered by hierarchies of value: strong and weak, protective/protected, dominant/submissive, owner/chattel, active/passive. Looking at Winter, we are prompted to ask about our own culture: How closely tied is gender to engendering or socially mediated reproduction? If future artificial reproductive technology (e.g., cloning) allowed us to reproduce in a way parallel to Winter, would gender roles and dualisms simply become irrelevant and wither away? Does a society that values equality among its citizens need to consider becoming more and more androgynous? Should we eliminate gender categorization? Or should we strive for a society with a less hierarchical gender structure?

14.3   Conclusion

I began with the deceptively simple question "What is gender?" Readers expecting a concise answer to this question will have been disappointed. Rather than simplify the question to fit a simplistic answer, I played the philosopher's favorite card trick and began to multiply the questions. For a concise definition of gender, I recommend a dictionary. But for thinking deeply about what gender is and the ways in which it orders and permeates our social lives, we need to use our philosophical imaginations to construct alternative realities that illuminate not only how things are in our society today, but also how they might be.

Notes

1. LeGuin (1969, 91).
2. LeGuin (1969, 94).
3. LeGuin (1969, 95).
4. The first three paragraphs of this parable are taken, with minor changes, from my book (Witt 2011, 27–28).
5. Witt (2011, 27–28). A contemporary snapshot of gender inequality worldwide can be found in a 2019 article from *The Economist*, https://www.economist.com/graphic-detail/2019/06/05/the-world-is-a-long-way-from-meeting-its-gender-equality-target?fbclid=IwAR0NK8dnxl1tEv-uM16cKtTRryymJUfwFeQZKXGYF0Ncjw30IWZfFTJwm_4.

6. For a useful overview of similarities among women and men on a wide array of physical, psychological, and intellectual characteristics, and differences among women
and among men on those same features, see Rhode (1997).

7. Fine (2010) is a useful critical discussion of what she labels "neurosexism," the attempt
to ground gender difference in neuroscience and in brain and cognitive differences
between men and women.

8. For a discussion of the complexity of human biological sex see Fausto Sterling (2000).

9. For an elaboration of Butler's criticism of the distinction between sex and gender see
Butler (1990).

10. Dea (2016) is a useful discussion of the complexity of gender identification.

11. The term "sincere avowal" was coined by Bettscher (2014).

12. For more on difficulties with the idea that gender identity is necessary and sufficient
for being a gender, see Barnes (2019).

13. For a discussion of the gender identity plus internalized gender "map" account of
gender see Jenkins (2016).

14. Crenshaw (2017

Bibliography

Barnes, Elizabeth. 2019. "Gender and Gender Terms." *Nous* 54, no. 1: 1–27.

Bettcher, Talia. 2014. "Feminist Perspectives on Trans Issues." *The Stanford Encyclopedia
of Philosophy* (Spring Edition), edited by Edward N. Zalta, https://plato.stanford.edu/
archives/spr2014/entries/feminism-trans/.

Butler, Judith. 1990. *Gender Trouble: Feminism and the Subversion of Identity.*
New York: Routledge.

Crenshaw, Kimberlé. 2017. "Kimberlé Crenshaw on Intersectionality, More than Two
Decades Later." Cloumbia Law School. https://www.law.columbia.edu/news/archive/
kimberle-crenshaw-intersectionality-more-two-decades-later, accessed June 2019.

Dea, Shannon. 2016. *Beyond the Binary: Thinking about Sex and Gender.*
Ontario: Broadview Press.

Fausto-Sterling, Anne. 2000. *Sexing the Body: Gender Politics and the Construction of
Sexuality.* New York: Basic Books.

Fine, Cordelia. 2010. *Delusions of Gender: How Our Minds, Society and Neurosexism
Create Difference.* New York: Norton.

Haslanger, Sally. 2000. "Gender and Race: (What) Are They? (What) Do We Want Them
To Be?" *Nous* 34, no. 1: 31–55.

Jenkins, Katherine. 2016. "Amelioration and Inclusion: Gender Identity and the Concept
of Woman." *Ethics* 126, no. 2: 394–421.

LeGuin, Ursula. 1969. *The Left Hand of Darkness.* New York: Penguin.

Rhode, Deborah. 1997. *Speaking of Sex.* Cambridge, MA: Harvard University Press.

Witt, Charlotte. 2011. *The Metaphysics of Gender.* Oxford: Oxford University Press.

15

Recognition

Living a Queer-Alien-Mixed Consciousness

Shanti Chu

I am a mixture.

—Frida Kahlo (Ankori 2013, 21)

Frida Kahlo explored a mixed self graphically in her painting *The Two Fridas*. In the painting, Freida[1] and Frida simply stare at the viewer in a stoic yet inviting manner. Reflective of their unity, they hold a haunting, firm gaze framed by their distinct unibrow that is enamoring and mysterious. To utter everything and nothing with a distinct glance characterizes Freida and Frida, who seem lost in their realities. Their lips are red and luscious, lightly enveloped underneath their notable, faint mustache, which is more distinct on the Frida to the right.

On the left, Freida is a bride on her wedding day. She wears a well-fitted white blouse and a white skirt with ornate flowers on the bottom that has been stained with blood as she loosely holds scissors on her lap with her right hand. The scissors touch the red artery that arbitrarily wraps around her neck and connects Freida's deconstructed heart to the broken heart of Frida on the right. The thin and delicate artery is positioned at the center of the photo, yet it easily gives way to the hybridity of the two Fridas. Frida's left arm is partially shackled by her dark red artery as it holds a barely recognizable, tiny egg-shaped child portrait of Diego Rivera, who has deeply and infinitely betrayed her.

While this Frida is older and has experienced more pain, she is donning bright, colorful garments. She wears a vivid, loose fitting blue shirt with yellow stripes above a full, muted green skirt with a white trim on the bottom, reminiscent of a Tehuana mother characterizing her mestiza identity as the daughter of a half-Spanish, half-indigenous Tehuana woman and a German-Hungarian,

Shanti Chu, *Recognition* In: *Philosophy for Girls*. Edited by: Melissa M. Shew and Kimberly K. Garchar, Oxford University Press (2020). © Oxford University Press. DOI: 10.1093/oso/9780190072919.003.0016.

Jewish father. She is "mestizaje" in every sense of the word: a queer, multira-cial, uniquely abled artist who painted herself because she spent her days alone, alienated even in the company of others (Ankori 2013, 22). Her duality be-came her friend. Her other self was a place of comfort in a binary world that she could not inhabit, so Frida constructed an imaginary friendship with herself as the "source of her doubled self" (50). Her imagination told the story of her loneliness and otherness in almost every aspect of her being.

The Freida to the left is not solely the Frida that Diego had loved; she is also the Frida who attempted to conform more to her traditional roles as a woman and a wife, which tormented her throughout her life. Freida's clothing is more European in appearance as she navigates her identity as a European, indige-nous, Mexican, Jewish woman. Freida became Frida further into her adult-hood as she more deeply connected with her mestiza identity, represented by her Tehuana clothing that made Frida recognizable. Her facial hair is more distinct as she continues to question and reject the societal expectations as-sociated with being a woman, wife, and mother. She polices her body less.

The Fridas are both symmetrical and asymmetrical, conveying how Frida can be something and nothing by breaking the rules of logic and dualistic thinking. As Frida herself reflected, "Do I contradict myself? Very well then I contradict myself . . . I enjoyed being contradictory" (Ankori 2013, 19). Her hybridity and chronic pain characterized her identity, which is exhibited through these two distinct women, Freida and Frida, who define the woman we know today as Frida Kahlo. Her identity is interwoven with her pain, her resistance, her alienation, and her internal and external fragmenta-tion that threatens the gender, racial, and bodily borders. In her paintings she is connected to her multiple selves, which sometimes take the form of the human, the animal, and the plant. These multiple forms of embodiment challenge our notions of being, agency, and recognition of the "other."

The Two Fridas tells us a story about Frida that can be disturbing to see yet ultimately liberating from the caricature of oppositional embodiment and identity. The Fridas embody order and chaos. We use order to make sense of the objects in the painting; however, the objects disrupt our thinking of traditional human identity in the sense that one body can only contain one self, one race, one culture, one gender, one sexual orientation, and ultimately one way of being in the world. We see an ontological disruption of self and an epistemological chaos of how to think and what to know.

The life of Frida was heartbreaking but also inspiring, especially to those who live their own hybridity, otherness, and mixed consciousness. The Two

Fridas paints a messy, gruesome story of growth and change. It is a vessel, a voice for a new way of being and understanding the world. It marks self-discovery through the heartbreak of a betrayed self whose identity is multi-layered and fluidly shifting into someone who is more intimately connected to her ever-changing selves.

15.1 Race in the United States

Frida Kahlo's story as a multiracial, queer, distinctly abled woman can open the doors for many of us who experience a sense of otherness and hybridity. In the United States, the multiracial population is growing and this trend is projected to continue far into the twenty-first century ("Census Race Categories" 2015). Nonetheless, there is still an absence of community, representation, and stories that embody the multiplicity of multiracial identity. Like Kahlo, a multiracial person, especially a multiracial girl growing up in a patriarchal society, can feel alienated from the world. She can feel othered in a myriad of social spaces because she embodies everything and nothing. She is not enough of *this* but she is too much of *that*.

How can a person attain a sense of comfort and being in a world that prescribes monoraciality and whiteness? We can understand racial identity and multiracial identity through philosopher Linda Alcoff's framework of racialized identities in *Visible Identities* and *The Future of Whiteness*. A person constructing her own perception of what is beautiful, worthy, and intelligent can enable her to attain a sense of being and comfort in the world. Further, Gloria Anzaldúa's "mestiza consciousness" from *Borderlands: La Frontera* and Sarah Ahmed's notion of "queerness" from *Queer Phenomenology* are tools to reclaim one's identity in creative and multifaceted ways that challenge stability, wholeness, and straightness. The multiracial girl is everyone and no one. She is a bridge to multiple ways of being in the world, and like Frida she understands herself as many selves within a singular body.

15.2 Multiracial Identity

While multiracial identity is a global reality, I will solely focus on multiracial identity in the context with which I am most familiar: the United States. Multiracial identity is defined as belonging to more than one racial group.

Race is a social construct, but it is a real, lived existence and informs our experience of the world. Racial categories, as constructed, shift and evolve in light of demographic changes and transformative socioeconomic realities. While discourse around multiracial identity can sometimes be applied to multiethnic and multicultural identities, I am discussing a specific type of "mixedness," one that relates to how race is constructed in rigid ways. In American[2] society, race tends to be understood as binary and essential.

In any case of racial otherness, that is, nonwhiteness, racial constructs have been projected upon less dominant groups by those in positions of power. This otherness is compounded when it comes to multiracial identity as multiracial individuals are neither viewed as white nor do they fit within other constructed racial identities. Given the lack of agency nonwhite individuals have historically had in the United States when it comes to racial identification, reclaiming one's agency and constructing one's identity can be a form of liberation. We must consider how racial identities are initially constructed and formed in order to understand how multiracial identities can be created.

15.3 Race and Multiracial Identities

In a country like the United States where white supremacy still reigns and is woven into our cultural fabric, nonwhite racial identities are constructed in opposition to whiteness. Our understanding of race is intersubjective, a combination of our upbringing, culture, and geographical location (Alcoff 2015, 125). How we understand ourselves is influenced by how people understand us. The meaning of the experienced world changes as it is filtered through the experiences and concerns of historically embedded individuals; knowledge and recognition are embodied and embedded through this process.

Alcoff discusses how racial identities can be "perceived quite differently and entirely misperceived" (Alcoff 2015, 49). Since racial identities are fluid, sometimes contradictory, and changing, they can be easily misperceived and interpreted in different ways depending upon the context. One's racial identity may be misperceived by others because she has "confusing features" or seems "out of place." For example, I identify as someone who is biracial: both white and Asian Indian. If someone else categorizes me as solely Indian, this is a misperception. While I, as the subject, can define myself as both white and Indian, that does not prevent others from misperceiving me as solely one or the other (or something outside of my racial identification). While

I technically can define my racial identity, others' perceptions of me can be different from my own. This process of misperception can render one's own racial identification as meaningless insofar as others' interpretations do not always cohere with the subject's own racial identity. This sense of meaninglessness can be amplified when someone is misperceived cumulatively throughout their life. Therefore, we cannot ignore the reality that we are interconnected beings and thus we inevitably internalize how we are seen and understood by others.

Others can see us as embodying contradiction through comments such as "that's an interesting mix" or "what are the chances of being . . . !." If one is both white and nonwhite, then it is seen as contradictory by people given the rigid racial classification system I previously discussed. We are often socialized into thinking that if we embody one characteristic, then we cannot embody another characteristic; that quality x and y are mutually exclusive. It's easy to see one's multiracial identity as a curse and a burden. However, this binary polarization is harmful and unrealistic. In the case where a multiracial person is white as part of their multiracial being, this bipolar rigidity may cause her to want to pass as white. On the other hand, white supremacy and "cultural imperialism"[3] may cause the part-white multiracial person to resent the nonwhite aspects of oneself.

Cultural imperialism results in what W. E. B. DuBois calls "double consciousness," whereby a person understands herself through the dominant group's perspective and from her own perspective (DuBois 1969, 45). She experiences "this sense of always looking at one's self through the eyes of others" (45) where she measures herself in relation to whiteness. If a multiracial person grows up in a white supremacist society that privileges straight hair, light skin, a small nose, and so on and renders her "nonwhite" features as inferior, she may internalize that inferiority and yearn for whiteness while resenting her nonwhite features. The multiracial person can be "rejected by the dominant race as impure and therefore inferior, but they are also sometimes disliked and distrusted by the oppressed race for their privileges" (Alcoff 2006, 267). The multiracial person not only has to navigate being an "other" in a racially hierarchical society, she also has to navigate the politics of her oppressed racial identity with a sense of guilt or shame for a privileged racial identity that she didn't choose. Furthermore, the multiracial person may come to feel that she embodies a sense of nothingness, that is "without a coherent identity, an individual can feel an absence of agency" (269). How can someone be hypervisible and invisible at the same time? One can be hypervisible because they are read as standing out or not belonging in whatever social space they occupy, which is signified by a stranger asking "what are you?" But they can also feel invisible because their own agency to define their racial identification is not recognized by others. For example, you tell the stranger your racial identification and they respond with "oh well you look more like x than y." Even if one technically has their own agency, they can feel as if it is not recognized by others. An absence of agency is a deprivation of autonomy, which is a sacred characteristic of humanity further embodying this sense of nothingness and lack of subjectivity.

Multiracial persons can experience a triple-consciousness in the sense that they see themselves through the lens of the dominant group (Alcoff 2006, 278), nondominant group, and their own lens. Their particular form of racialization is not socially recognized, which can lead to a stifling alienation fueled by their triple-consciousness. Their very existence challenges the dominant societal notion of a stable and singular identity. Alcoff describes this alienation in *Visible Identities*:

> Without a social recognition of mixed identity, the mixed race person is told to chooseone or another perspective. This creates not only alienation, but the sensation of having a mode of being which is an incessant, unrecoverable lack, an unsurpassable inferiority, or simply an unintelligible mess. This blocks the possibility of self-knowledge: the epistemic authority and credibility that accrues to nearly everyone at least with respect to their "ownmost" perspective, is denied to the mixed race person. (Alcoff 2006, 279)

Social recognition of multiracial identities is essential in order for the mixed-race person to have a social reference point from which to understand her own racial identity and triple-consciousness. This reference point grounds the mixed-race person insofar as she sees herself as an efficacious subject with agency. It is not enough for mixed-race persons to create their own racial identification because of how easily the social recognitions of mixed-race people can turn into misrecognitions (Alcoff 2006, 288). As with all other aspects of identity, if we are to create new social meanings for racial identity *and* a recognition of multiracial identities, there must be an interplay of individual and long-term societal effort. Alcoff applies her call for a substantive concept of multiracial identity to her own mixed and "mixed up" racial identity. While being mixed can carry a form of existential anxiety and alienation, it can also provide a new way of being in the world that is informed by "seeing through multiple lenses" (Alcoff 2015, 173). We will now turn to Ahmed's and Anzaldúa's works to understand this new way of being.

15.4 A Queer, Alien-Mixed Consciousness

In a racially hierarchical society, one's proximity and relation to whiteness informs how one is read and recognized. As Ahmed discusses in *Queer Phenomenology*, "Things are shaped by their proximity to other things" (Ahmed 2006, 124). Bodies do not always choose their proximity to other objects. If a body seems "distant" and out of place, then the body is perceived as "strange," as mediated through skin and flesh. The flesh becomes representative and connected to one's perceived history, one's community, and one's family through the idea of representing a "racial origin." We inherit "forms of bodily and social distance: those that are 'at home', but who are marked as 'further' away even in the face of this proximity" (Ahmed 2000, 127). Even if one is "at home," her bodily appearance and presence within the social space she occupies can be viewed as being distant from her home. If one's body is not conforming to the preexisting social meanings of rigid racial and gender categorization[4] and is additionally viewed as a subordinate body within the racial and gender hierarchy of the United States, then one's body will be read as "strange" or "queer." "Bodies stand out when they are out of place" (Ahmed 2006, 135) and whiteness becomes normative, or a kind of a straightening device (137), by which all other bodies are assessed and forced to conform. We all know the cliché of the nonwhite and multiracial person being asked "where are you from?" which ultimately can turn into an interrogation about why the "stranger" does not look "white." The "stranger" is hypervisible and exposed, rendering her body as out of place because she is perceived to be outside the bounds of whiteness. A heightened self-awareness and hypervigilance of how one appears and is interpreted by others in any type of social space serves as a form of alterity, or otherness, for the multiracialized other. A mixed-race identity becomes a failed orientation and identity because there are no socially recognized, multiracial concepts from which to interpret and understand the mixed-race body.

For the multiracial person who is also white, the cultural history of white supremacy and contradictory reception means that she is simultaneously fetishized and not living up to the standards of whiteness in society.

The mixed-race person may then become obsessed with or fantasize about being like the white parent. For Ahmed, she wanted to be white and identified with her white mother earlier on in her life (2006, 144). According to her, "Wanting to be white for the mixed-race child is about the lived experience of being white even when whiteness is 'at home' . . . The desire for whiteness . . . is expressed as a murderous rage against part of one's inheritance or genealogy. In my own body memory, that wish for disappearance took the form of a desire to give up my proximity to my father's body" (146). Reading Ahmed's account of wanting to be in closer proximity to her white mother and further proximity from her brown father harkened back to my own lived experiences growing up in white suburbia as a half white (Hungarian) and half Asian (Indian) girl. My parents were divorced and I lived with my white mother. Though I was in closer physical proximity to whiteness, I did not feel like I was fully oriented toward it. I cursed my nonbutton nose, my nearly black hair, and my olive-skin, wishing I were white with smaller features that didn't make me stand out. When people would ask me "what" I was, I would hide my Indian-ness and pretend I was fully white. I thought that they were not entitled to know since my racial identity is no one's business. But my "little lie" negated part of my racial identity and I struggled with self-hatred. Whenever someone called me "exotic," I detested it and felt like I failed at being white, I felt strange. My desire to be white was also complicated by the fact that I was socialized in a society that renders a woman's value as primarily contingent upon her beauty. While I excelled in school, I was haunted by not being white enough and not being pretty enough in the mainstream way my mother and peers were. My beauty felt like a deviation from what I was supposed to be: white. I was grappling with patriarchal beauty standards and white supremacy, which were complicated by my primary role model embodying the ever-so-lauded white beauty ideals. I felt I had a mutation because I could not live up to those standards that my white mother met, even though I was oriented toward them.

If I had a "substantive" social understanding of mixed-race identities, perhaps I, as a mixed-race person, could have created my own healthy racial identity and beauty in a way that is socially recognized. Ahmed discusses mixed-race identity as an orientation, a way of being in the world in relation to others while also recognizing the different forms of proximity to whiteness and nonwhiteness a mixed-race body occupies. "A mixed orientation would not simply take each side and bring them together to create a new line. A mixed orientation might even preserve the secrecy of the other side, as the 'side' that is behind what we face, even at the very moment we turn around to face what is behind us" (Ahmed 2006, 153). Ahmed's mixed orientation gave her a unique direction from which to understand her racial identity in relation to others, but her whiteness was not something that could be solely owned. This notion of having multiple orientations is akin to Anzaldúa's "outsider within status" that gave her a special ability, "la facultad" (Anzaldúa 2007, 7). This gift is inherited by those "who are exposed to multiple social worlds, as defined by cultures, languages, social classes, sexualities, nation states, and colonization, develop the agility to navigate and challenge monocultural and monolingual conceptions of social reality" (7). "La facultad" allows the border crosser to see through the "eyes of others" while embodying a flexible disposition. As I grew older, I started to become open to my Indian-ness and started identifying as a woman of color. Some people saw me as a woman of color. Others did not, and I grew aware of these differing perceptions others had of me in different social spaces instead of seeing it as a personal failure. I learned how to perceive myself in the white spaces in which I grew up, but I also was attuned to how others of South Asian descent would recognize me. While other people's curiosity about my racial identity is pesky, I started to reframe their curiosity as a way to embrace my otherness. I knew the language of whiteness even though I am not at home with whiteness, but at the same time, I am also not at home with nonwhiteness. I was essentially cut off from my Indian/nonwhite side for most of my life, which resulted in me identifying as neither white nor Indian. I gave up on trying to be at home. My home is ambiguity and hybridity. I embody contradiction and that is okay.

A mixed-race identity is not exclusively oriented toward whiteness or nonwhiteness, as it can be both and neither in a way that parallels queerness. Having a mixed-race identity is a failure to embody monoraciality and whiteness in a similar way to how queerness is a failure to embody heterosexuality and the gender binary. One's gendered and racialized body is read as crossing into multiple identities when border crossing is not a socially recognized action. "There is something already rather queer about such an orientation. I am not sure that being mixed race is what makes me queer . . . Instead, I would say that the experience of having a mixed genealogy is a rather queer way of beginning, insofar as it proves a different 'angle' on how whiteness itself gets reproduced" (Ahmed 2006, 154). A mixed genealogy is a genealogy that is outside of the boundaries of racial categories. It is slanted and slightly "off." A mixed genealogy cannot be straightened or easily understood given our present racial categories. Anzaldúa also made this connection between her mixed-race identity and queerness. She declares that she made the "choice" to be queer since being a "lesbian of color" is the "ultimate rebellion she can make against her native culture" (Anzaldúa 2007, 41). For Anzaldúa, being a queer woman of color enabled her to conceptually exit the patriarchy where "males of all races hunt her as prey" (42). Clearly her racial and cultural alienation are intimately connected to her alienation as a queer woman of color. Perhaps her alienation as a woman of color opened the doors for her to understand herself in queer ways that transcend straightness. When one aspect of your identity is distinct from that which is normative, it can be easier to recognize other aspects of your identity that deviate from already existing social categories.

Ascribing a queer genealogy to one's identity can be liberating because queerness is a concept that transcends categorization. It embraces ambiguity and multiplicity. While queerness is a nondominant identity, it *is* a socially recognized concept. Multiracial identity, however, remains unrecognized socially as an organizing concept. Nonetheless, there are a number of parallels that can be helpful in understanding what we hope multiracial recognition might become. Queerness, as does multiracial identity, rejects dualistic and oppositional thinking about racial purity. Queerness affords one the space to be white and nonwhite, neither or both, without having to quarantine one's different selves. To be queer and mixed-race for Anzaldúa is a form of resisting the "absolute despot duality that says we are able to be only one or the other . . . But I, like other queer people, am two in one body, both male and female. I am the embodiment of *heiros gamos*: the coming together of opposite qualities within" (Anzaldúa 2007, 41). The queer, mixed-race woman embodies oppositions in a way that disrupts numerous binaries. She has accepted the contradictions within herself.

We can return to the painting *The Two Fridas* for a visual representation of this queer duality, the internal meeting of opposite qualities, and the feeling of being alien. To be a border crossing alien is painful, but at the same time, one has multiple frameworks through which to understand herself and the world. The new "alien race" serves as a challenge to the fantasy of racial purity and is a theory of inclusivity and multiplicity (Anzaldúa 2007, 99). "At the confluence of two or more genetic streams, with chromosomes constantly 'crossing over,' this mixture of races . . . provides hybrid progeny, a mutable more malleable species with a rich gene pool . . . an 'alien' consciousness is presently in the making—a new *mestiza* consciousness . . . It is a consciousness of the Borderlands" (99). Being a "mestiza" is full of contradictions and is something entirely new that challenges racial purity and opens the doors for a queer way of being. To be internally unified and adhere to solely one form of identification is a form of effacement for the multiracial woman. The "mestiza consciousness" allows her to think in different ways that disrupt the rules of Western rationality and oppositional thinking. This consciousness is a form of coping with the internal struggles and a lack of external recognition from others. It is a form of agency as she determines her own consciousness. She claims her consciousness by developing a "tolerance for contradictions" and "a tolerance for ambiguity" (101). Through developing this tolerance she is able to dismantle subject-object duality by transcending her own subject-object duality. As an autonomous human, she is a subject while also seeing herself as an object through her triple-consciousness. In finding her own mestiza-consciousness, she breaks with oppressive traditions such as patriarchy and heteronormativity and embodies this rupture. Anzaldúa firmly believes that this consciousness must occur *prior* to societal change (109), which slightly differs from Alcoff's call for a *simultaneous* social recognition of mixed-race identities with a need for a mixed-race consciousness. I argue that both solutions need to simultaneously occur as it would seem impossible for them to occur individually. Mixed-race consciousness like "mestiza consciousness" requires an internal revolution of consciousness with an external societal recognition.

Part of internalizing this mixed-race consciousness allows us to give up on having a home and instead embrace something more fluid and less foundational. For Alcoff, her peace as a multiracial woman is finding a lighthouse instead of a permanent home:

> I am not simply white nor simply Latina . . . I cannot bridge the gap, so I negotiate it, standing at one point here, and then there, moving between locations as events or other people's responses propel me. I never reach shore: I never wholly occupy either the Anglo or the Latina identity . . . Peace has come for me by no longer seeking some permanent home on shore. What I seek now is no longer a home, but perhaps a lighthouse that might illuminate this place in which I live. (Alcoff 2006, 284)

A lighthouse gives her a 360-degree perspective where she engages with reality from multiple vantage points. Alcoff's use of a lighthouse helps us understand multiracial identity as "la facultad," a gift, a unique ability to navigate different worlds. I will never have a home or a unified self, but I do have different parts and pieces of me that I can cultivate and recognize.

15.5 Conclusion

Mixed-race consciousness requires an internal revolution of consciousness that embraces and plays with fluid and contradictory aspects of one's racial identity. An internal revolution of consciousness liberates the mixed-race person from the stifling barriers of racial categorization and dualistic thinking. An upheaval of consciousness allows the multiracial person to embrace having multiple perspectives instead of cursing this multifaceted way of being. Freed from her internalized chains of desiring whiteness, she seizes her lack of belonging. She is proudly at the lighthouse where she has a comprehensive view of her shifting and changing reality. An internal revolution of consciousness allows her to recognize her queer genealogy that transcends subject-object duality, borders, and oppositional thinking. Being mixed-race does not have to be solely pervaded by alienation, self-hatred, and misrecognition.[5] She sees herself as adopting a special, new, alien way of existing in the world that can be a means of reclaiming agency amidst the flourishing of bountiful social meanings of multiracial identity.

Through this internal revolution of consciousness, the mixed-race person recognizes and embraces her split personalities and orients her racial identity as being on top of a lighthouse where she can see a vast, rotating landscape. She constructs and plays with her own ambiguity while peering at the world that is simultaneously overwhelming and available to her. She will not find a home because the notion of a home is repressive to her. Her lighthouse is a temporary resting place as she continues to understand and define herself. As Kahlo stated, "I am a mixture." I have no home nor community, but I do have the gift of an orientation that transcends oppressive borders and rigid categories. I can create my own beauty and ways of knowing while shifting and moving. I am now undergoing an internal revolution of consciousness and recognize myself as a plurality.

Notes

1. Frida Kahlo used to spell her name as "Freida," reflecting her German heritage. It wasn't until her twenties when she started going by Frida, which reflected a change in her cultural identification. I refer to Freida as the woman to the left and Frida as the woman to the right.
2. Prior to 1960, census-takers had the power to identify *another* person's race ("Census Race Categories" 2015). It also wasn't until 2000 where Americans could self-identify

as belonging to more than one race. On many job applications and surveys the term "other" is often the only option for those of us whose identity doesn't neatly fit into the present racial categories, which further instills one's otherness and alienness.

3. Iris Marion Young establishes how cultural imperialism is the "universalization of the dominant group's experience and culture, and its establishments as the norm" (2004, 54). The dominant culture expresses their own understanding of reality as the universal interpretation rendering other interpretations as deviant and factually wrong.

4. Racial categorizations of white or nonwhite and gender categorizations of man or woman.

5. Of course these feelings will continue to exist, but they do not have to dominate the mixed-race experience.

Bibliography

Ahmed, S. 2000. *Strange Encounters: Embodied Others in Post-coloniality.* London: Routledge.

Ahmed, S. 2006. *Queer Phenomenology.* Durham, NC: Duke University Press.

Alcoff, L. M. 2015. *The Future of Whiteness.* Cambridge, MA: Polity Press.

Alcoff, L. M. 2006. *Visible Identities.* New York: Oxford University Press.

Ankori, G. 2013. *Frida Kahlo.* London: Reaktion Books.

Anzaldúa, G. 2007. *Borderlands La Frontera: The New Mestiza.* San Francisco, CA: Aunt Lute Books.

"Census Race Categories: A Historical Timeline." 2015. Pew Research Center's Social & Demographic Trends Project. June 11, https://www.pewsocialtrends.org/interactives/multiracial-timeline/.

Dubois, W. E. B. 1969. *The Souls of Black Folk.* New York: New American Library, Inc.

Young, I. M. 2004. "The Five Faces of Oppression." In *Oppression, Privilege, & Resistance,* edited by L. Heldke and P. O'Connor, 37–63. Boston: McGraw Hill.

SECTION IV
CONTEMPLATION IN ACTION

16

Anger

Embracing the Medusa Trope as an Act of Resistance

Myisha Cherry

My name is Medusa. You may have heard of me. I was once the protector of
the Temple—a job assigned to me by the goddess, Athena. But no jobs last
forever. After a violent encounter with Poseidon (this is an understatement,
but I don't have much time to go into it here), Athena decided that I should
be fired. Her motive is unclear. Some think it was out of jealousy. Others
surmise that it was outrage over my inability to protect the Temple's sanctity.
In either case I was fired, let go, dismissed. Well, *punished* is a better word
for it. The punishment: my long hair would become threads of snakes and
any man who looked upon my face would be turned into stone. I'm sure you
have seen my image or read about men who dared to make my acquaint-
ance. The typical story goes as follows: a man attempts to pass my way, but
then I turn in rage, catch his eye and you know the rest. He turns into stone.
I'm that dangerous, they say. I am so dangerous that even after I'm defeated
in death, my decapitated yet raging head is used to protect others in battle.
Anyone who possesses my head can use me—my rage and my powers—to
turn their enemies into stone. My name is Medusa. You might think that because you, my fellow sisterly comrade, have a different name that you are different from me. But maybe we are not so different. I am Medusa. Although
I was a victim of a crime, I became blameworthy for it. I am Medusa. I was
full of rage and as a result was perceived as dangerous. You might think that
because thousands of years have passed since I roamed this earth that we are
different. But maybe, my sisterly comrade, we are not.

The Medusa story is an interesting one particularly because, like most
good stories, it is not just about the main character. As Medusa hints or warns
at the end of the anecdote mentioned here, her life is not so different from the
lived experiences of many women and girls. To lay out exactly what such a

Myisha Cherry, *Anger* In: *Philosophy for Girls*. Edited by: Melissa M. Shew and Kimberly K. Garchar, Oxford University
Press (2020). © Oxford University Press. DOI: 10.1093/oso/9780190072919.003.0017.

life comprises, it is best to see Medusa's as the following: a woman is a victim of a crime but is declared blameworthy and must be punished. As a result, she is full of rage and perceived as dangerous. A combination of her blame-worthiness, angry emotion, and dangerous perception provide reasons for why she must be conquered and controlled. We can describe the perception of such a life as conforming to the *Medusa formula* or, more precisely, the *Medusa trope*. Now, the trope is not perfect with how it latches on to every detail of Medusa's life, but I think it gives us valuable insight into a certain perception and treatment of women today. The Medusa trope depicts women who are angry as having no real reason for being angry since, more often than not, they are not really victims. (Note that Medusa is punished for being a victim of Poseidon's violence against her.) The trope also depicts such angry women as dangerous, and society concludes that these angry, blameworthy women must be conquered and controlled through patriarchal norms, laws, expectations, and hostility.

In what follows, I describe the reality of such a trope for many women and girls. I then discuss some implications of it, particularly the urge for women and girls to escape features of the trope in order to escape being conquered and controlled. I also wonder to what extent it is possible to escape the trope, and I offer some reasons for why women should not escape it, even if they could. I conclude by arguing why and how women and girls can embrace the Medusa trope as a form of resistance against sexism and misogyny.

16.1 The Facts on the Ground

While Medusa's story may sound like a mythological tale that appeals to our fascination with monstrous villains, for many, it may speak to and about our current world. If we look closely, we can see that the ways in which the gods and warriors treated and perceived Medusa are not so different from the experiences of many women and girls today. A common trope that besets lots of women is that when it comes to moral wrongdoing against them, they are blameworthy and not "real victims." They are angry and dangerous, and therefore, they must be conquered and controlled. Let's address each of these elements in turn to provide some detail for how each plays out in contemporary times.

First, what causes societies to judge women as blameworthy for mistreatment directed toward them? The answer to this question depends on the nature of the crime, the social position of the particular woman as well as the perpetrator, and the type of society that is often judging front and center as well as from the sidelines. For example, some perceptions are racialized. A society might struggle to view black women as victims given stereotypes about their inability to experience pain. Other judgments depend on the crime and the perpetrator. We are likely to blame women for their own domestic abuse and sexual assault then we are to blame a male victim for his own homicide. When women report being victims of inequality, mistreatment, and violence at the hands of men, they are not often perceived—at least as a default position—as victims. This might be is due to our oversympathy for men as well as our oversexualization of women.

In many cases, women and girls are either seen as complicit in the wrongdoing or are thought to be lying about the event. Responses such as "she knew what she was getting into" or "why was she wearing that dress?" are examples of accusations of complicity. These accusations can point to either direct or indirect complicity, for she can either be viewed as someone who had a direct hand or agreement in the act, or someone who did not do enough to ensure that she would not be a victim. Indirect complicity is the responsibility we put on women to prevent being victimized, to "be safe" (as if their victimization is always the result of their unwillingness to properly act). Soraya Chemaly points out, though, that the admonishment to be safe is never really about safety, since we do not teach boys the same lesson. It is about social control (Chemaly 2018, 130). More on this later.

In the 2018 documentary *Surviving R-Kelly*, when black women accused the singer of abuse, online responses such as "they were of consenting age" and "they should have paid attention to the previous accusations" were rampant, proving that the complicity accusation around victimization is not just a theme in Greek mythology. Further, when women are not viewed as complicit, they are often depicted as liars. When Anita Hill brought accusations of sexual harassment against supreme court nominee Clarence Thomas in 1991, she was accused of not telling the truth and "trying to bring a black man down."

When charges of complicity and lying prove inadequate, an act of mistreatment directed at a woman is often minimized by questioning the extent to which the act was actually wrong or harmful to begin with. It was not surprising that when Dr. Christine Blasey Ford made public her allegations of sexual assault against supreme court nominee Brett Kavanaugh in 2018, many wondered "why did she wait so long?" The thinking, although irrational, was that assaults only have strong moral weight if they are reported by the victim within a particular time frame. Based on this kind of thinking, if reports of mistreatment do not meet a hypothetical timestamp, nothing "wrong" or "harmful" has actually occurred.

Even when there is consensus that a wrongdoing has occurred, in some cases the effects of that wrongdoing are not taken seriously. For example, we often do not take the physical pain of women seriously. Women are frequently viewed as hysterical, dramatic, or just weak. The pain they experience is not "real" in the way that men's pain is. To wit, implicit bias studies show that women are treated differently than men by health professionals; women usually wait more time in the emergency room than men, and their reports of pain are often dismissed if they look healthy or pretty (Samulowtiz 2018). This type of treatment is not limited to responses to physical pain but psychic pain as well. When women report sexual harassment, for example, their reports of pain are often dismissed. If women are perceived as weak and hysterical, then if Anita Hill did experience sexual harassment at the hands of Clarence Thomas, it was not the kind of wrongdoing that deserved an attentive moral response from the public, for Hill only perceived it as a wrongdoing because she was not "strong enough" to let certain office banter go. (At least this is how the thinking goes.) If sexual harassment made her feel uncomfortable, it was only due to her own susceptibility and not to any objective act of wrongdoing.

As I have argued elsewhere, there is a connection between value, respect, and anger (Cherry 2020). When we judge that someone is valuable, we think they have claims to—that is, they deserve—respect. When that valuable person is disrespected through wrongdoing, our anger in response to that wrongdoing is justified. If women were valued and respected in the same way that men are, they would be justified when becoming angry in response to mistreatment and violence, as well as the dismissal of their reports of such. However, unlike their male counterparts, women's anger is often not taken seriously. This situation arises partially because in a sexist and misogynistic society, women are thought to have no inherent value but only value in respect to men. Thus, when women are disrespected (which, of course, occurs frequently in sexist and misogynist societies), they have no right to anger. When women are angry in these societies, their claims to anger stand in contrast to patriarchal norms and expectations, and they will be considered a danger to the status quo. Like Medusa, women's anger in response to their own mistreatment is unacceptable in misogynist societies.

Instead, women will be taught to comply to patriarchal norms by thinking that their anger is always inappropriate. It is not surprising that a 2010 study found that only 6.2% of women (yes, women) in America and Canada view the expression of women's anger as ever appropriate (Praill 2010). Judgments of inappropriateness in turn cause negative emotions for the angry woman. Psychologist Ann Kring (2000) reminds us that although women and men experience anger in similar rates, women report feeling shame about their angry experiences. In scholarship on the philosophy of emotion, "appropriate" is used to describe emotions that fit the occurrence. We might say that sadness is an appropriate response to death and joy is an appropriate response to a job promotion. Likewise, we tend to think that anger is an appropriate response to wrongdoing. However, when we leave the world of the theoretical and examine the ways in which we actually evaluate the emotional responses of certain socially positioned people, we discover that the emotions we typically label appropriate do not always fit the neat formula mentioned here.

Although anger is indeed a fitting response to wrongdoing, women's anger is often judged to be inappropriate. It is viewed as inappropriate not because it is anger, but because it belongs to, is in response to, and protests treatment of and defends women. To this end, some suggest that we should get rid of the term "appropriate" all together. Chemaly writes, "If there is a word that should be retired from use in the service of women's expression, health, well-being, and equality, it is appropriate—a sloppy, mushy word that purports to convey some important moral essence but in reality is just a policing term used to regulate our language, appearance, and demands. It's a control word. We are done with control" (2018, 261).

While I agree with Chemaly's analysis, I do not fully agree with her prescription. While it is indeed true that the term "appropriate" has been used as a form of control, we can also use the term to refute the control and criticize the critics who deem women's anger as inappropriate. Evaluations of the appropriateness of certain emotions are not random, subjective assessments. Certain requirements must be met for an emotion to be judged appropriate and they are fairly simple: the emotion must match a particular occurrence. An emotion need not occur in a particular, socially positioned body to be deemed appropriate. When there is wrongdoing, anger is appropriate. End of story. Any other assessment provides us with evidence that the evaluation of appropriateness is indeed a misuse of the term. It also provides women with an easy way to detect schemas of patriarchal control, for where we see this misuse, we can be more confident of its patriarchal roots and intent.

According to the Medusa trope, women's anger in their own defense is not only inappropriate, but its inappropriateness also provides reasons to view such women as dangerous. I am not claiming that women who are angry are perceived as dangerous. Rather, I am claiming that *women's anger* is perceived as dangerous. For example, I can be angry at the injustices of others. As a black woman, I can be angry that black men are being systematically shot by the police. I can be angry that my best friend did not get the promotion he deserved. In these cases, my anger is what Audre Lorde describes as being "in the service of other people's salvation or learning" (2007, 132). There is nothing conceptually wrong with this type of anger; it can show solidarity with other groups as well as motivate us to act in support of them. I am not considered dangerous when I am angry for reasons like these. In a patriarchal society, though, women are often encouraged to be angry at the injustices of others, particularly men, but not at the injustices that they experience themselves. Recall that when Perseus cuts Medusa's head off, he doesn't bury it. He keeps it and uses it for future battles. Note the irony. While it is not acceptable for Medusa to use her rage for herself, it is acceptable, and is even ingenious, for Perseus to use her raging head in the service of his own goals.

"Women's anger" is different from "the anger of women." Women's anger is not anger in response to men's pain or injustices suffered by them. Women's anger is, instead, a woman's response to her and other women's experiences of pain and the suffering of injustice. Women's anger makes demands not that men get relief, but rather that women do. In a male-dominated culture, this is a radical act. Women's anger focuses on and thus centers women. Women's anger does not support patriarchy. It challenges it.

If women's anger is perceived as dangerous, women must then be controlled and conquered to alleviate the danger. The control of women, and thus control of their anger and its dangerous potential, is manifest in patriarchal norms, expectations, punishments, and rewards. Consider, for example, the infamous street harassment call for women to "smile, baby, smile." This admonishment highlights the inability of some men to risk the existence of women's anger, even when such anger is not directed his way. When such a woman is spotted in public, the "smile, baby, smile" encouragement is a call for her to remember her "emotional place." It also provides comfort to men who, if only briefly, may see signs of a potentially dangerous woman because of her anger.

This form of control does not only manifest on public streets, but as we saw in the 2010 study cited earlier, it is also internalized. Women and girls themselves will begin to think that only a smile, not a frown, is an appropriate expression. This internalization often arises quite early for girls as a result of punishment and rewards systems imposed by adults in early childhood. We punish and reward young girls and boys differently when it comes to negative emotions such as anger. Recognizing the difference in the ways that adults and peers respond to their anger and the anger of boys, girls begin to conform to gendered emotion norms. They learn to "put on a pretty face" (Chemaly 2018, 7). While little girls can be sassy, teenage girls learn quickly that they are less cute when they are angry. They also learn that their anger may be dismissed as just a "teenage raging hormone stage." Boys are not treated in the same way. Girls consequently learn to self-police their anger so that they will not be perceived in a negative light.

Continuing into adulthood, women are continually punished for their anger. These forms of punishment are not only retributively directed at the woman whose indignation roars, but they are also deterrently directed; these punishments are a societal way to suppress the anger of all women. We punish women for their anger by labeling them as bad, misinterpreting their expressions, and depicting them in sexist stereotypes. While we allow the anger of men to work on their own behalf, we make the anger of women work against them. Angry men are viewed as passionate and fierce leaders. Angry women are irrational bitches. Women learn that their anger cannot be expressed like their male friends and colleagues, and the others watching them learn this as well. All women are likely to self-police their anger as a result.

While I am highlighting restrictions on anger and anger expression in the public sphere, there is a distinct moral nature of these restrictions that should not get lost. The punishment and policing of anger has a particular ethical and social significance because a person's anger makes claims about value and protests injustice (in this case, disrespect, sexism, misogyny, etc.). When we try to control women's anger and angry expressions, we are not just prohibiting their freedom of expression. We are also attempting to control and refute their claims to value, equality, and respect, which is morally troubling. Control is about making women stay in their place and can be achieved through rewards, punishments, stereotypes, double standards, internalization of sexist standards, and self-policing. The Medusa trope operates to ensure that women are and remain subservient, silent, and never a threat to patriarchy.

16.2 The Escape Option

If angry women are viewed as dangerous and must be conquered, then a woman who does not want to be conquered might think that if she escapes the trope, or the parts of it she can control, she can also escape domination by others.

How might a person go about escaping the trope and the conquering fate? A woman could act contrary to the trope in hopes that she will be a recipient of different treatment. While a woman might not be able to escape being a victim, perhaps she could choose to not respond with anger and therefore be perceived as less dangerous. If she is less dangerous, perhaps she can escape being conquered. The logic is quite similar to respectability politics in the African American community, an option originally proposed by black men and women thinkers in the late nineteenth century. The logic of respectability politics suggests that if blacks act respectable (e.g., don't drink, dress well, keep their surroundings clean, act moral, and work hard), then they will win the respect and thus the same rights and equality of those of the dominant society, whites.

Similarly, a woman might attempt to escape the trope by not getting angry. Or if she is angry, she could try not to express her rage. She might deny that she is angry. She could excuse the wrongdoing of others as a way to not have reason to be or remain angry. She might continue to question her own assessment of the wrongdoing, preferring to stay in a state of confusion or doubt rather than moral judgment—a judgment that could result in anger. She might "wear" a smile when there is no reason to have one so that her mere appearance will not figuratively turn others into stone. She may intentionally misidentify her emotions to make members of the dominant group feel less threatened. She may prefer to describe her emotions as disappointment or sadness instead, for surely, no one would ever find a sad woman threatening. A woman could also decide to maintain and express her anger but do so in ways that she believes conform to the standards of rationality, discipline, virtue, and femininity imposed by the patriarchy. Conformation to these norms, she thinks, might convince others that she is not dangerous.

There is no direct, empirical evidence that shows any of these strategies work in the context with which we are concerned, though. While there are many examples of them working, there are a seemingly equal number of counterexamples. We can see this in the respectability politics examples. For as many black women and men that we can find who were not harassed by the police because they were wearing professional clothing, we can find counterexamples of professional black folk getting harassed.

Psychologists often suggest strategies to counter tropes and stereotypes, but the strategies are usually not directed at those who are said to embody the stereotype or trope. Instead, they are directed at the stereotyper. Consider scholarship about implicit bias. In order to lessen implicit bias, psychologists do not offer suggestions for the stereotyped. They do not suggest that women never get mad, for example. Instead, researchers suggest that stereotypers expose themselves to more positive images of women. In our case, a psychologist might say that a way to escape the conquering and dominating consequence of the trope is for the stereotyper to challenge his own idea of women and girls as outraged, hysterical, dangerous, and in need of control. This solution is not one that the angry woman can affect. It is the job of those who believe in the Medusa trope to somehow unlearn the same trope.

Lack of empirical data aside, some women and girls might still think that they can escape domination by being a "good girl," and a person might be particularly persuaded by this if she thinks that misogyny only targets folks like Medusa, women who act out in rage. In her 2017 book on the logic of misogyny, *Down Girl*, Kate Manne agrees that misogyny "typically differentiates between good women and bad ones, and punishes the latter," but she also points out that misogyny is not just about what we do to "bad women." Misogyny is about "rewarding and valorizing women who conform to gendered norms and expectations" (Manne 2017, 72). Escaping punishment for our lack of outraged expressions is not the only form of patriarchal control. Being rewarded for our lack of rage or outraged expression is also a form of control.

Additionally, one need not be perceived as Medusa in order to be considered a threat and thus subject to control and domination. As Manne explains, "Since one woman can often serve as a stand-in or representative for a whole host of others in the misogynist imagination, almost any woman will be vulnerable to some form of misogynist hostility from some source or other" (2017, 68). Mocking, shaming, vilifying, and condemning are examples of forms of hostility that serve to punish, deter, and warn all women. Manne uses Elliot Rodger's violence as an example. His victims on that dreadful day in 2014 were not his actual targets. Rodger's violence was motivated by his feelings of neglect and humiliation he felt were brought on by certain kinds of women. When he arrived at the Alpha Phi sorority house near the University of Santa Barbara, he was not targeting any particular "bad woman." His victims that day were not his actual targets but only representatives of the kinds of women he believed treated him in a certain way. Those women paid for the so-called sins of others (2017, 53).

Patriarchal domination need not target every individual, twenty-first-century Medusa who roams the earth. Misogyny operates in such a way that it targets actual, perceived, or representative challenges to or violations of patriarchal norms. Even if a woman were to cleanse herself of any feature of the Medusa trope, she will still remain vulnerable to perceptions of danger as well as patriarchal control because of the way misogyny operates at a social level. Thus, even if these strategies did work, women ought not use them. The trope operates to control and conquer women. It is a way for women to police themselves so they will not be a threat. Self-policing is still policing, and policing is an instrument of control. It is a task that the dominant class does not have to directly engage in themselves, but it still manages to accomplish their aim: the control of women. When a woman monitors herself in order not to appear full of rage and therefore a threat, she is giving into the controlling and conquering efforts that the trope aims to achieve. As Manne reminds us, "Misogyny upholds the social norms of patriarchies by policing and patrolling them" (2017, 88). Its very purpose is to maintain or restore a patriarchal order and protest when it gets challenged. It develops irrespective of who is doing the policing at any particular moment.

This form of control does not just operate within the Medusa trope, but also in stereotypes like the "angry black woman" and the "sassy Latina woman," both of which feature distinctive types of the Medusa formula. If a situation calls for anger, a black woman, given the stereotype, will be less prone to express her anger because she may be afraid to give in to the stereotype. Her reasons can be praiseworthy. She may want to represent black women in the best light possible. She may not want to satisfy the negative, racist perceptions that whites may have of black women. She may want to be an individual and not a stereotype in that moment. I am sympathetic to these reasons; however, there are other results to consider when one self-polices in this way. By doing so, a woman may risk not expressing her feelings, perceptions, desires, and judgments. In addition, her unexpressed, suppressed anger is unlikely to challenge injustice, hold people accountable, and make claims of value and respect. It is more likely to compromise her physical and psychological well-being. These results are not unintentional. They are one of the main purposes of the stereotype. Sexist and racist stereotypes that deal with emotions are not just false overgeneralizations of a particular group. They operate as policing mechanisms. Anger is then unable to do the important moral work for marginalized groups that it has the potential to do in contexts of systemic injustice, oppression, and domination.

Refusing to embody any feature of the trope out of fear of how the dominant class will react is a way of surrendering to the conquering efforts of the dominant class. In fact, a person is likely to get the very results that the escape strategy is trying to subvert. However, by refusing to let go of certain features of the trope—angry and dangerous perceptions—a person resists controlling efforts. Not only does she resist the domination that self-policing aims to perpetuate, but through refusals to give up her anger, she is also able to call out controlling and conquering projects. Moral protest names injustice and shines a light on it wherever it is hidden.

16.3 The Embrace Option

If my argument for why we should not resist features of the trope sounds tenable, then a better option is to embrace the Medusa trope rather than attempt to escape it. Embracing the Medusa trope is the opposite of the strategies mentioned in the previous section. Embracing it includes expressing one's rage, identifying oneself as angry, refusing to give up one's anger in order to appease misogynists or silence racists, and being a danger to oppression by refusing to give in to its demands and perceptions of women. In this view, a person acknowledges and calls out moral wrongdoing enacted on women while refusing to be vilified by such wrongdoing. In embracing the Medusa trope, women and girls can also recognize their power to resist domination and therefore embrace the danger they pose to it. Embracing the trope of an angry, dangerous woman does more than just contribute to the "bad woman" perception. By embracing the Medusa trope, women and girls are also able to control their own narrative instead of allow dominating systems to do so. Unlike the first-person anecdote that begins this chapter, the story of Medusa has never been told from her point of view. The narrative of Medusa has been told by others. Men were warned by others not to look upon her face. Others declared she was guilty and dangerous. Her story was supposed to be a cautionary tale about the danger of women. However, it is contemporary feminists, not ancient storytellers, who have decided to reimagine and reinterpret Medusa. Argentine-Italian artist Luciano Garbati asked a question before he began sculpting "Medusa" in 2008: "What would it look like, her victory, not his? How should that sculpture look?" (Griffin 2018). What he created was an image where Medusa is victorious over Perseus. It is she that beheads him. In 2018, that image became an avatar for women's rage in the wake of the #MeToo movement. Likewise, by embracing the trope, women can reinterpret what it means be a victim, angry, and dangerous.

16.4   Conclusion

As argued throughout this chapter, anger at patriarchal norms and misogynistic hostility is an act of moral protest. It brings attention to moral wrongdoing enacted on women, making that which is invisible, visible. It declares that these are injustices that should not be permitted. In doing so, the angry woman resists logics of domination by refusing to accept sexism and misogyny as the norm. Since anger is connected to certain perceptions of value and respect, embracing the option declares that girls and women, regardless of background, have inherent value and deserve respect despite their compliance or noncompliance to patriarchal norms and expectations. A woman who is angry at misogyny does not just express an emotion at injustice or gender mistreatment. She calls injustice out, points us to its unfairness, makes claims to the value and respect of women, and demands change. Since anger motivates us to act in the world and affects our beliefs and risks we are willing to take to actualize certain goals, it can help women engage in actions and projects where they can challenge our current world and create a better one.

Any woman or girl who does these things are indeed dangerous, but such an angry agent, in the spirit of Medusa, knows that this danger is not pejorative but necessary and even beautiful. She also knows that she is just as or even more heroic than the mortal men who seem to demand our attention as we obsess over mythological tales of gods and monsters.

Bibliography

Chemaly, S. 2018. *Rage Becomes Her: The Power of Women's Anger*. New York: Atria Books.
Cherry, M. 2020. *The Case for Rage: On the Role of Anger in Anti-Racist Struggle.* Unpublished Manuscript.

Griffin, A. 2018. "The Story Behind the Medusa Statue That Has Become the Perfect Avatar for Women's Anger." *Quartzy*, October 3, https://qz.com/quartzy/1408600/the-medusa-statue-that-became-a-symbol-of-feminist-rage/.

Kring, A. 2000. "Gender and Anger." In *Gender and Emotion: Social Psychological Perspectives*, edited by Agneta H. Fischer, 211–231. New York: Cambridge University Press.

Lorde, A. 2007. *Sister Outsider*. New York: Crossing Press.

Manne, K. 2017. *Down Girl: The Logic of Misogyny*. New York: Oxford University Press.

Praill, N. 2010. "An Evaluation of Women's Attitudes Towards Anger in Other Women and the Impact of Such on Their Own Anger Expression Style." MSW thesis, Wayne State University.

Samulowtixe, A., Gremyr, I., Eriksson, E., and Hensing, G. 2018. "Brave Men and Emotional Women: A theory-Guided Literature Review on Gender Bias in Health Care and Gendered Norms Towards Patients with Chronic Pain." *Pain Research and Management*, no. 3: 1–14.

17

Consciousness-Raising

Social Groups and Change

Tabatha Leggett

17.1 Consciousness-Raising

It was Labor Day weekend in 1967. A coalition of left-wing groups involved in the battle over civil rights and the Vietnam War had gathered in Chicago for the first ever National Conference for New Politics. There were two thousand young activists present, including Shulamith Firestone, a twenty-two-year-old aspiring artist and student at the School of the Art Institute of Chicago (Faludi 2013). As soon as Firestone saw the conference's agenda, she noticed that an important topic was missing: women's rights. With Jo Freeman, a fellow conference attendee, Firestone drafted a memo calling for equal marital and property laws, complete control by women of their own bodies, and proportional representation of women on the conference floor. When their memo was ignored by the conference's chairman, Firestone and Freeman ran to the podium in protest. "Move on little girl," said the chairman. "We have more important issues to talk about here than women's liberation" (Echols 1989, 49). Then he reached out and patted Firestone on the head. At that moment, Firestone and Freeman realized that if they were serious about fighting for their own rights, something needed to change. Inspired by the black power movement, whose members had successfully campaigned to allow black people to define their mission based on their own experiences of oppression, the women scheduled a meeting without any men present (Echols 1989, 49).

A week later, Westside was formed. The separatist group of women, who later became the Chicago Women's Liberation Unit, agreed that it was valid for women to "define the terms of their struggle" (Echols 1989, 49). They continued to meet regularly, often in Firestone's apartment on the west side of Chicago, and always in the absence of men. Their goal was simply to put an

Tabatha Leggett, *Consciousness-Raising* In: *Philosophy for Girls*. Edited by: Melissa M. Shew and Kimberly K. Garchar, Oxford University Press (2020). © Oxford University Press. DOI: 10.1093/oso/9780190072919.003.0018.

end to female oppression. Five months later, Firestone moved to New York. She settled into an apartment in the East Village where, with Pamela Allen, a civil rights activist she had met in Chicago, she began recruiting women for a new group called the New York Radical Women (Faludi 2013). Firestone launched two other women's groups in the next year: Redstockings, which she cofounded with Ellen Willis; and New York Radical Feminists, which she cofounded with Anne Koedt. These steps marked the beginning of a huge movement, and so-called consciousness-raising groups started cropping up all over America.

Consciousness-raising was a product of the radical feminist movement, which arose with second-wave feminism in the 1960s. Radical feminism followed—and differed from—liberal feminism, which focused on overturning legal obstacles to gender equality.[1] Radical feminists did not believe that changing laws was enough; they were committed to drawing a distinction between sex and gender. They understood gender as socially constructed as opposed to biological, and they were focused on liberating women from oppressive practices and the restrictions supported by traditional concepts of femininity (Stone 2007, 140).[2] A society characterized by unequal power relations between men and women in which women are systematically silenced and oppressed is called a patriarchy (Lerner 1986, 6–7). Patriarchy is what radical feminists set out to dismantle. They understood that male dominance and female oppression are so entrenched in the ordinary processes of everyday life that societal attitudes hamper equality even when the law promotes it. Their method was called consciousness-raising and its goal was to expose inequality in order to overcome it (MacKinnon 1987, 40).

Jane Kramer, a reporter for the *New Yorker*, signed up for one of Firestone's early consciousness-raising groups. Kramer was researching a feature on the women's movement and attended some of the group's meetings in a rental office in New York's upper East Side (Kramer 1996). Writing for the *New Yorker* twenty-six years after her first profile was published, Kramer describes how openly women talked in those groups: "I think it was their speaking out . . . that changed my life and, because of it, my daughter's life" (1996). Kramer's profile describes how the group operated. They would choose a topic, such as fidelity, and then share their experiences of it, questioning their own realities along the way. The goal was to break down the barriers between what was considered public and what was considered private in order to stop women unknowingly being oppressed in their private lives. They looked for common ground: common experiences, common frustrations, and eventually common objectives. They listened to each other's stories, refrained from passing judgment, and then made a plan of action (Kramer 1970, 52–55).

> In Kramer's first meeting, one attendee summarized consciousness-raising's objectives: Consciousness-raising . . . would break down the oppressive distinctions between the private and the public, the personal and the political, that women had been taught to make . . . It would uncork their anger and frustration, direct their energies toward the obliteration of the structures and institutions that had caused their problems to begin with and in general increase their sensitivity to all the various and subtle forms that their oppression took. (Kramer 1970, 52)

Consciousness-raising groups were different from the other female-only groups of the 1970s, which included lesbian retreats and Betty Dodson's pro-sex workshops. Rather than presenting them with a list of preidentified oppressions, consciousness-raising groups encouraged women to share their own experiences which allowed them to become aware of, and collectively analyze, the situation of women in general. In turn this allowed them to unlearn their oppression and ultimately channel their feelings of anger, sadness, and frustration into anti-oppressive action.

Consciousness-raising is a historically situated example of an educational method called "critical consciousness theory," which was developed by pedagogue Paulo Freire (1970, 73).[3] Freire's founding belief was that education is the key to liberation, but that traditional educational methods force learners to behave as passive receptacles of information, rather than encouraging them to investigate, analyze, and discern the realities of the world (1970, 72). As a result, education tends to uphold conventional ways of thinking that encourage indoctrination into oppressive cultures. Instead, Freire encouraged both educators and learners to systematically analyze their realities, including the reasons for—and the consequences of—thinking in certain ways. Reaching critical consciousness involves a constant and cognitive "unveiling of reality," which requires individuals to let go of any epistemological[4] and ontological assumptions[5] they may hold about the world (Freire 1970, 81).

In the case of consciousness-raising, casting aside background assumptions about the world is important precisely because these assumptions have been created and maintained by the patriarchy. Catherine MacKinnon explains: "In order to account for women's consciousness (much less propagate it) feminism must grasp that male power produces the world before it distorts it" (MacKinnon 1982, 542). Consciousness-raising is all about constructing collective knowledge, which necessarily takes time because it involves a continuous dialogue between individuals who meet regularly, rather than a theoretical abstraction.

Reaching critical consciousness requires the establishment of reciprocal, nonhierarchal relationships between educators and learners and the "conscious avoidance of the imposition of a leader" (Hart 1985, 121). It requires educators to present their materials to their learners for their consideration at the same time as reconsidering their own considerations in tandem with theirs. It is this process of constant learning and relearning that allows people to establish an "authentic form of thought and action" that isn't shaped by existing power structures and will ultimately lead to their liberation (Freire 1970, 83). Consciousness-raising groups encouraged women to concretely and systematically uncover and analyze the impact of male dominance through collectively speaking about the experience of being a woman "from the perspective of that experience" over the period of many months or even years (MacKinnon 1982, 520).

Reaching critical consciousness is a process that happens in stages, and consciousness-raising groups facilitated a version of this process. The first stage involved women opening up to one another and acknowledging their feelings (Allen 1973, 273–274). This stage was not intended to be therapeutic in any way; rather it established nonhierarchal and dynamic educator-learner relationships, whereby groups of women committed to a process of continual learning and relearning. In practice, this meant creating a democratic space in which each account was treated with equal importance; agreeing to meet regularly; and establishing a willingness to cast aside any preconceptions one may hold about the world as a group.

The second stage is sharing, which involved collectively thinking about experiences that relate to being a women (Allen 1973, 274–276). It involved women exploring and articulating their own experiences as well as listening to each other's. This enabled women to arrive at a collage of similar experiences, thus starting the process of developing a collective understanding of the common nature of women's problems. It is at this stage of the process that individual knowledge and narratives started to transition into knowledge shared by the group. Collectively thinking about their experiences allowed women to start identifying patterns of oppression. For example, discussing their relationships led some women to realize that marriage often rendered women "psychologically and financially [dependent] on their husbands" (Allen 1973, 276–277).

The third stage of the process is analysis, which included investigating and discussing the experiences that have been shared as well as addressing ontological and epistemological assumptions about the realities of the world (Allen 1973, 276–277). This analysis was more than a simple discussion of personal opinions; it was a process of collective thinking that led to collective knowledge about how the way women think is influenced by deeply held assumptions and beliefs that reflect patriarchal structures. It was not a process that was directed outward toward the analysis of an object reality, but one that was directed inward, toward the pursuit of consciousness. This is the most crucial and difficult stage of the process: it can involve women making a cognitive shift from thinking themselves valued to considering themselves oppressed. Becoming aware of one's oppression can be a painful process, which means that some women were resistive to this stage of the process. MacKinnon describes this stage as one that occurs "within yet outside the male paradigm," meaning that it is the process of reaching critical consciousness that gives women the perspective they need to start dismantling patriarchal structures:

> Proceeding connotatively and analytically at the same time, consciousness raising is at once common sense expression and critical articulation of concepts. Taking situated feelings and common detail . . . as the matter of political analysis, it explores the terrain that is most damaged, most contaminated, yet therefore most women's own, most intimately known, most open to reclamation. (1989, 120–121)

After analyzing, the fourth stage is abstracting. This involved making decisions and prioritizing the most pressing issues to work on before developing strategies with which to do so. Some of the issues identified by women in early consciousness-raising groups included accessible abortion, the availability of information about birth control, the sharing of housework, and communal child-care centers (Echols 1989, 45). The abstracting stage of the process involves agreeing on a set of principles that represents the group's shared experiences and communicates what the members of the group will no longer tolerate. At this stage of the process, where collective knowledge is collected and turned into collective action, it is vitally important that women view female oppression as a challenge to be overcome and to apprehend that challenge not as a theoretical problem, but as interrelated to other problems within a total context. This is something that Freire's educational method should enable. For example, feminists have long grappled with the problem that it is difficult to identify issues using a language which represents the world view of a patriarchy and which is limited, often derogatory, in its descriptions of women's condition. However, the cognitive shift that women undergo throughout the long process of reaching critical consciousness should enable them to recycle and recreate this limited language in order to intervene in, and challenge, their oppression.

Once women have reached critical consciousness, consciousness-raising requires that they speak out about everything they have uncovered in the hope that they will build solidarity and encourage other women to reevaluate their experiences of oppression through honest conversations in order to ultimately challenge the societal attitudes that hamper equality (Firestone 1970).

17.2 Silencing

To understand why consciousness-raising groups wanted to transform women's individual knowledge and narratives into a collective voice, it is important to understand how patriarchal structures silence women. In patriarchal cultures the voices of women are disregarded at a structural level. Kristie Dotson identifies two practices of silencing: "testimonial quieting," which occurs "when an audience fails to identify a speaker as a knower" and "testimonial smothering," which is the "truncating of one's own testimony in order to insure that the testimony contains only content for which one's audience demonstrates testimonial competence" (Dotson 2011, 242 and 244). Consciousness-raising seeks to undercut both practices.

Testimonial quieting occurs when a speaker's audience does not recognize her as a "knower," rendering her unable to offer a testimony. This happens when an identity lacks credibility, for example: Patricia Hill Collins suggests that black American women are systematically undervalued as knowers due to the social perception of black women as mammies, matriarchs, welfare mothers, and/or whores that the patriarchy upholds (Hill Collins 2000). Dotson explains that social perceptions about one's identity, and being routinely taken for a "non-knower," leads women to internalize their inferiority, undermining their intellectual courage and epistemic agency. For example, the media, the beauty industry, and celebrity culture constantly feed women the message that they are worthless if they are not beautiful (Greer 1999 in Chambers 2008, 30). Women often change the way they act in their everyday lives as a result, and their conceptions of who they are as people are affected as well. (Benson 1991, 388). In other words, messages of inferiority contribute toward testimonial quieting, and therefore silence women, when they get inside our heads.

The messages of inferiority perpetuated by the patriarchy affect more aspects of women's lives than we can imagine. For example, as well as establishing unreasonable expectations of how women ought to look, they affect the way we think about sex. Through a combination of representations of sex in the media, early education, and pornography, we are taught to value men's sexual desires above our own. MacKinnon argues that a pornified culture is a rape culture, meaning that the prevalence of pornography cultivates a culture of hypersexualization whereby women commonly find themselves subservient to men's sexual desires and subsequently find it difficult to differentiate between sex and rape (MacKinnon 2011, 9).

To this point, in a piece of fiction, Kristen Roupenian describes a woman who internalizes the message that men's sexual desires are of the utmost importance. She goes home with a man after their date and despite losing her desire to have sex with him, she allows him to penetrate her:

> The thought of what it would take to stop what she had set in motion was
>   overwhelming; it would require an amount of tact and gentleness that she felt was
>   impossible to summon. It wasn't that she was scared he would try to force her to do something against her will but that insisting that they stop now, after everything she'd done to push this forward, would make her seem spoiled and capricious, as if she'd ordered something at a restaurant and then, once the food arrived, had changed her mind and sent it back. (Roupenian 2017)

In this story the female protagonist cannot meaningfully express that she does not want to have sex. She cannot acquire what Paul Benson calls "the conceptual resources and imaginative repertoire" that would allow her to reassess the value she has assigned to her date's sexual desires (Benson 1991, 397). The reason she cannot do it is that she, like all of us, is operating from within a patriarchy that has gotten inside her head.

The second kind of silencing Dotson talks about is testimonial smothering, which is a type of coerced silencing, meaning that it requires some kind of self-silencing from the speaker (Dotson 2011, 244). Testimonial smothering occurs when a speaker omits a part of their testimony because she perceives the audience likely to fail to find it intelligible, which "runs the risk of leading to the formation of false beliefs that can cause social, political and/or material harm" (244). For example, speaking up about domestic violence is perceived to be unsafe or risky within many communities, which can discourage women from talking about it.

Consciousness-raising is a method intended to undercut these kinds of silencing, among others. It does this by encouraging women to ask ontological questions, such as 'what, if any, are the tenable distinctions between sex/gender?'; as well as epistemological questions, such as "why do people think they know what they know?" Exploring the answers to these questions within groups, in the absence of men, allows women to become aware of their own oppression; query previously unquestioned ideas, for example: that going back to a man's apartment after a date indicates willingness to have sex; and formulate agential desires. The idea behind of going through this process as a collective is that there's power in numbers: when it comes to communicating their agential desires, women have more credibility as knowers and speakers when they operate as one.

17.3 Universalization

Returning to historical accounts, though the consciousness-raising groups of the 1970s represented a huge step forward for the women's movement, they also faced widespread criticism. They were accused of drawing generalizations from the shared experiences of privileged women alone, which is called universalization. Jo Freeman, the woman who ran up to the National Conference's podium with Firestone, has written about how early consciousness-raising groups universalized the experiences of their heteronormative[6] members and excluded unmarried women (Freeman 1970, 290). Carol Williams Payne, another former member, explained how the groups' most vocal and "competitive" attendees tended to dominate meetings, meaning that some women were unable to share their experiences (Payne 1970, 290).

The groups also alienated women who were subject to additional oppression such as race and class. The idea that women experience oppression in varying configurations and in varying degrees of intensity depending on the social groups they belong to is the theory of intersectionality and was introduced by Kimberlé Crenshaw in 1989. Crenshaw explains, "The intersection of race and gender makes [Black women's] actual experience of domestic violence, rape, and remedial reform qualitatively different from that of white women" (Crenshaw 1991, 1245). If we consider consciousness-raising through the lens of intersectionality, we can see that just as some women struggled to identify their oppression in the presence of men, women facing additional oppression may struggle to identify them in the presence of those operating from within these alternate systems of power.[7] In other words, white women may occupy positions of power in racist structures even as they are relatively powerless in patriarchal structures. Moreover, the various oppression experienced by women will not necessarily be similar.

Unfortunately, early consciousness-raising groups did *not* consider their methods or goals through the lens of intersectionality and have been criticized for disproportionately focusing on white women's self-indulgences, like love and sex. Stella Dadzie, a founding member of the Organization of Women of African and Asian Descent (OWAAD), has spoken about the "navel gazing" that went on in the "white women's movement" at the expense of discussing fundamental issues "around class, around background, [around] upbringing" (Dadzie 2011). The consciousness-raising groups of the 1970s ignored the possibility that women experience oppressions in varying configurations. Mukami McCrum explains the consciousness-raising groups of the 1970s began with the presumption that everyone was equal in their oppression. These same consciousness-raising groups were ineffective in some ways because they were grounded on false premise since "equality is interpreted by people in different ways" (McCrum 2011).

Gail Lewis, a former member of the Brixton Black Women's Group (BWG), has also spoken about this problem retrospectively. Lewis explained that she was staunchly opposed to considering the BWG a consciousness-raising group, even though the BWG encouraged its members to share their experiences in order to "discern the patterns [of inequality] in the domain of the so-called private" (Lewis 2011). Despite utilizing similar methods, Lewis and other members of the BWG felt that the consciousness-raising groups of the 1970s did not represent their experiences as black women. By failing to include the perspectives of women experiencing a diverse range of oppression, the principles that were established in these early consciousness-raising groups did not represent a true cross-section of the female population. Rather, they represented a subset of privileged women.

More recently SlutWalk, a consciousness-raising movement in the form of a series of marches and protests in 2011, was criticized for universalizing and prioritizing white women's experiences. The SlutWalk began as a reaction to a Toronto police officer who told university students not to dress like sluts if they did not want to be victimized. The movement involved women challenging the misconception that women are sexually available when they dress in ways that make them feel empowered by marching in their underwear (Carr 2013, 1). SlutWalk was criticized for not being diverse enough, excluding some women, and universalizing women's experiences of oppression by parodying the white woman's experience of the word "slut" and neglecting to consider the meaning of the word in social groups where its negative connotations preclude it being reclaimed (Carr 2013, 6). Universalization was, and is, a critical problem.

17.4 #MeToo

Let's return to a more recent anecdote from 1997. New York-based activist Tanara Burke is listening to a thirteen-year-old girl talk about sexual abuse she endured. Burke is speechless. She wants to say so much but cannot find the right words: "I didn't have a response or a way to help her in that moment, and I couldn't even say 'me too'" (Garcia 2017). Burke was still thinking about her conversation with the teenager ten years later when she founded Just Be Inc., a nonprofit organization that helps victims of sexual harassment and assault. Burke named her organization's movement *Me Too*. Little did she know that twenty years after her conversation with the abused, thirteen-year-old girl, the phrase "me too" would become shorthand for a huge, decentralized movement against sexual violence.

The #MeToo movement stems from the collectively agreed-upon principle that sexual assault is unacceptable and focuses on challenging the patriarchal structures that create and sustain a rape culture.[8] The methods of the #MeToo movement bear a striking resemblance to those used by consciousness-raising groups in the 1970s. First, the #MeToo movement gave the women who had been sexually abused a collective voice with which to tell their stories so that others may realize their own false consciousness.

Like the women who met to share their experiences in Firestone's West Side apartment, women telling their stories on social media are questioning previously accepted norms and developing a collective awareness.

Consciousness-raising movements that take place on social media are even more powerful than individuals meeting to share stories because they include contributions from a greater number of women and expose their stories to a larger audience. Women are more likely to identify their own oppression when a greater number of voices contributes to the conversation. The greater the number of contributing voices, the harder it is for men and people in positions of power to silence those voices. The #MeToo movement has the potential to reach and represent a wider and more diverse group of women than the consciousness-raising groups of the 1970s. While previous consciousness-raising movements had not successfully integrated a breadth of women's experiences, #MeToo is not culturally blind. It encourages women to speak up about how patriarchal structures operate across cultures and acknowledges the types of oppression that women face vary according to any number of cultural factors (Medina 2012, 192). Thus, a truly inclusive consciousness-raising movement captures the broad range of experiences of a diverse group of women and allows them to express a wide range of emotional responses to the effects of the patriarchy before leading them to collectively agree on principles.

José Medina explains that organizing a successful consciousness-raising movement requires "network solidarity," whereby the most privileged subjects hold responsibility for including the voices of those who face a greater number of oppressions than them. This is happening within the #MeToo movement: as public figures share their experiences of oppression, as well as their experiences of identifying these oppressions, other women follow suit.

17.5 Concluding Remarks

It would be naïve to claim that talking about our experiences is all it takes to fight oppression, or that the #MeToo movement will be able to unite women across social groups in order to dismantle the patriarchy. Firestone was indeed on to something when she asked women to share their experiences and look for commonalities, though. It is also true that we have come a long way since the 1970s. The #MeToo movement is a more intersectional consciousness-raising movement that represents women across diverse income brackets, occupations, geographies, and social backgrounds. There is still a long way to go, but consciousness-raising continues to have positive effects and remains vitally important to the feminist project of overcoming oppression. The conference chairman who patted Firestone on the head was wrong: women's liberation was, is, and always will be, important. Firestone and Freeman deserved better, as do we all.

Notes

1. Liberal feminism emerged from first wave feminism in the nineteenth and early twentieth centuries. The principle behind the movement was that in order to achieve gender equality, men and women needed to have equal legal rights. This thinking inspired the suffragette movement, whose members campaigned for women's right to vote. Mary Wollstonecraft (*A Vindication of the Rights of Women*, 1792) and Virginia Woolf (*A Room of One's Own*, 1929; *Three Guineas*, 1938) are two of first wave feminism's key figures.
2. Simone de Beauvoir (*Second Sex*, 1949), Betty Friedman (*Feminine Mystique*, 1963), and Andrea Dworkin (*Pornography: Men Possessing Women*, 1981; *Intercourse*, 1987) are some of second wave feminism's key figures.
3. Paulo Freire developed critical consciousness theory in response to the illiteracy rates of impoverished Brazilian people in the early 1970s.
4. Epistemological assumptions concern the ways we acquire knowledge.
5. Ontological assumptions concern the nature of the world.
6. The term "heteronormative" refers to a world view that promotes heterosexuality as the so-called normal sexual orientation.
7. Early black feminism was separatist for this reason. Mary Ann Weathers (*An Argument for Black Women's Liberation as a Revolutionary Force*, 1969), Patricia Hill Collins (*Black Feminist Thought*, 1990), and Angela Davis (*Women, Race and Class*, 1981) are some of the black women's movement's key figures.
8. The term "rape culture" refers to a society in which our attitudes about gender normalize male force in sexual relationships and make it difficult to establish what rape is (MacKinnon 2016, 450).

Bibliography

Allen, P. 1973. "Free Space." In *Radical Feminism*, edited by A. Koedt, E. Levine, and A. Rapone, 271–279. London: Harper Collins.
Benson, P. 1991. "Autonomy and Oppressive Socialization." *Social Theory and Practice* 17, no. 3: 385–408.

Carr, J. 2013. "The SlutWalk Movement: A Study in Transnational Feminist Activism." *Journal of Feminist Scholarship* 4, no. 1: 1–9.

Crenshaw, K. 1989. "Demarginalizing the Intersection of Race and Sex: A Black Feminist Critique of Antidiscrimination Doctrine, Feminist Theory and Antiracist Politics." *University of Chicago Legal Forum* 1, no. 8: 139–167.

Crenshaw, K. 1991. "Mapping the Margins: Intersectionality, Identity Politics, and Violence against Women of Color." *Stanford Law Review* 43, no. 6: 1241–1299.

Chambers, C. 2008. *Sex, Culture and Justice.* University Park: Penn State University Press.

Dadzie, S. 2011. Interview for *Sisterhood and After: An Oral History of the Women's Liberation Movement.* London: British Library audio file, https://www.bl.uk/collection-items/stella-dadzie-black-feminist-identity.

Dotson, K. 2011. "Tracking Epistemic Violence, Tracking Practises of Silencing." *Hypatia* 26, no. 2: 236–257.

Echols, A. 1989. "Prologue: The Re-Emergence of the 'Woman Question.'" In *Daring to be Bad: Radical Feminism in America 1967–1975*, 23–50. Minneapolis: University of Minnesota Press.

Faludi, S. 2013. "Death of a Revolutionary," *The New Yorker*, April 15, https://www.newyorker.com/magazine/2013/04/15/death-of-a-revolutionary.

Firestone, S. 1970. *The Dialectic of Sex: The Case for a Feminist Revolution.* New York: William Morrow.

Freeman, J. 1970. "The Tyranny of Structurelessness." In *Radical Feminism*, edited by A. Koedt, E. Levine, and A. Rapone, 285–299. London: Harper Collins.

Freire, P. 1970. *Pedagogy of the Oppressed.* Translated by M. B. Ramos. New York: Continuum.

Garcia, S. E. 2017. "The Woman Who Created #MeToo Long Before Hashtags." *New York Times*, October 20, https://www.nytimes.com/2017/10/20/us/me-too-movement-tarana-burke.html.

Hart, M. 1985. "Thematization of Power, the Search for Common Interests, and Self-Reflection: Towards a Comprehensive Concept of Emancipatory Education." *International Journal of Lifelong Education* 4, no. 2: 119–134.

Hill Collins, P. 2002. *Black Feminist Thought.* New York: Routledge.

Kramer, J. 1970. "Founding Cadre," *The New Yorker*, November 28, http://archives.newyorker.com/?i=1970-11-28#folio=052.

Kramer, J. 1996. "The Invisible Woman," *The New Yorker*, February 26, http://archives.newyorker.com/?i=1996-02-26#folio=136.

Lerner, G. 1986. *The Creation of Patriarchy.* New York: Oxford University Press.

Lewis, G. 2011. Interview for *Sisterhood and After: An Oral History of the Women's Liberation Movement.* London: British Library audio file, https://www.bl.uk/collection-items/gail-lewis-brixton-black-womens-group.

MacKinnon, C. 1982. "Feminism, Marxism, Method, and the State: An Agenda for Theory." *Signs* 7, no. 3: 515–544.

MacKinnon, C. 1987. *Feminism Unmodified: Discourses on Life and Law.* Cambridge, MA: Harvard University Press.

MacKinnon, C. 1989. *Toward a Feminist Theory of the State.* Cambridge, MA: Harvard University Press.

MacKinnon, C. 2011. "X-Underrated: Living in a World the Pornographers Have Made." In *Big Porn Inc.: Exposing the Harms of the Global Pornography Industry*, edited by M. Reist and A. Bray, 9–15. Melbourne: Spinifex.

MacKinnon, C. 2016. "Rape Redefined," *Harvard Law & Policy Review* 10, no. 2: 431–477.

McCrum, M. 2011. Interview for *Sisterhood and After: An Oral History of the Women's Liberation Movement.* London: British Library audio file, https://www.bl.uk/collection-items/mukami-mccrum-collective-working.

Medina, J. 2012. *The Epistemology of Resistance: Gender and Racial Oppression, Epistemic Injustice, and the Social Imagination.* New York: Oxford University Press.

Roupenian, K. 2017. "Cat Person," *The New Yorker*, December 4, https://www.newyorker.com/magazine/2017/12/11/cat-person.

Stone, A. 2007. "Essentialism." In *An Introduction to Feminist Philosophy*, 140–166. Cambridge: Polity.

Westlund, A. 2003. "Selflessness and Responsibility for Self. Is Deference Compatible with Autonomy?" *Philosophical Review* 112, no. 4: 37–77.

Williams Payne, C. 1970. "Consciousness Raising: A Dead End?" In *Radical Feminism*, edited by A. Koedt, E. Levine, and A. Rapone, 282–284. London: Harper Collins.

18

Tzedek

Doing What Must Be Done

Devora Shapiro

Long ago, there was a young woman named Jael. She was clever, and she was brave, and she was good. She was also remarkable to all of her village for her beauty and her voice. Her beauty and her voice caused a stir wherever she went, but people rarely remembered her other qualities.

Her people lived in a time that was not always safe, and of late many livestock had disappeared. One afternoon, a terrifying roar was heard in the square. Jael rushed to see the cause of such a stir. There in the square was Sicera, the tiger. Sicera was a vain animal, but powerful and vicious, and he had returned to show his strength and remind the people whom they should serve.

It was Sicera who had been sampling the livestock, and he was intent on making his threat even clearer. His voice boomed from the square as he addressed the village, "I come to thank you for the delicious offerings you have left me and to discourage you from preventing my dining. Should you foolishly determine that you wish to interfere, you will find you may not like my response."

The people cowered in their places, looking desperate and unable to respond. They feared for their children and their families, worried that Sicera would turn his attention on their young ones. After Sicera surveyed the scene with satisfaction, he left the huddled townsfolk to their fear. There were those among them, though, who were brave. When they spoke, the townsfolk listened, and soon a plan was set in place. They would hunt the tiger in the night with torches and a racket, with noise and fire, and they would rid themselves of the tiger once and for all.

Jael, however, looked on with concern and raised her voice to offer an objection. "Don't be silly, precious Jael! You don't understand. Don't concern yourself with such a scary business; let those who know better take care of

Devora Shapiro, *Tzedek* In: *Philosophy for Girls.* Edited by: Melissa M. Shew and Kimberly K. Garchar, Oxford University Press (2020). © Oxford University Press. DOI: 10.1093/oso/9780190072919.003.0019.

it." Jael was quieted, and she returned to her home alone to worry. When her father returned in the morning with news that the hunting party had failed, Jael was unsurprised, and she went about her chores, singing as she often did. It was then the tiger appeared again, this time outside her home.

"What a pretty girl you are, and your voice is so pleasing to my ears. I had thought to find myself a meal, but I think I may look elsewhere just this once." Jael looked up and calmly smiled, hiding her fear and her trembling hands. "Thank you, tiger, I am pleased you enjoyed my song. It must be hard to be so fearsome, with no one to sing or entertain you." The tiger sighed and nodded slowly, but the sound of soldiers broke his gaze, and Sicera laughed and turned to roar. As he disappeared through the trees, the town erupted in chaos.

"What were you doing?" demanded her father, who had just returned to the scene. "You could have been eaten! Then what would we do? We've just found more of his victims in the field!" But Jael was undeterred now. "I know what to do!" she exclaimed, "Listen to me. I have a plan!" Still the villagers wouldn't listen, and they scolded Jael for her boldness. "Jael! Go back to your home. Let the soldiers decide what to do." So she returned to her home, frustrated but determined. That night, when the soldiers again gathered to hunt the tiger, Jael waited patiently for them to disappear. When she was certain they were gone, she prepared for action.

She gathered all her laundry and began singing as she washed outside. She danced as she sang and cleaned, and she did her best to seem relaxed and content. Just as she was finishing her work, she saw a slow and slinking movement in the field. She stretched and sang some more, and as Sicera approached, she welcomed him forward. He appeared angry and agitated, and Jael boldly asked him why. "My sleep is disrupted by your soldiers! Again they come! Though they know they cannot best me. They taunt me, and so they beg for retribution!" He shook his head and licked his lips, eyeing Jael with an appraising look.

Jael saw her danger, breathed deeply, and replied, "Such a beautiful tiger you are. Please let me comfort you." She led the tiger through the door, into her home. She brought milk and laid a blanket. "Tiger, please, won't you rest and drink my milk?" As he drank, she took her brush and began to groom him while she sang a calming song to help him rest. He soon fell asleep, purring softly. Jael laid the brush down and continued her pretty song, and slowly she reached for a long, sharp spike that her father used to anchor his tent. As she lifted the spike in one hand, and her father's mallet in the other, she sang a song to help the tiger on his way.

When the soldiers returned, they heard Jael singing. Her song was beautiful and clear, and it was strong. They came to see why she was singing late at night, and they found her sitting calmly, spike and mallet in her hands. They found Sicera at her feet, lying lifeless where he had slept. While Jael cried for her grave deed, she felt relief. She had done what she knew must be done.

18.1 Tzedek: Doing What Must Be Done

Tzedek, from the Jewish tradition, is often translated as "justice," and it is the root of Tzedakah, or "charity." These translations do not really capture the meaning of this virtue called tzedek, though. It is more significantly understood as "doing what must be done." Jael does not do what is easy; she does not hide as her elders suggest. She is told that she is not suited to fighting, that hunting is unseemly for a girl. As hard as it is to risk her father's disapproval, Jael knows that what she does is right and just, and so she does what must be done. Doing what must be done requires that we take responsibility for ourselves and our own actions. Even more, it requires us to own our actions. When we do what must be done, we are the authors of our own lives. This ownership, as we will see, is the root of our integrity.

Many of us are molded in virtue, or what we are told is a "moral life." We are encouraged to follow the directions we have been given, and praised when we model our lessons well. If we follow the path that we are taught, then when we are questioned in our actions, we can respond, "I was doing what I was taught," or "I have been raised to know that this is right." If we are afraid that we have acted wrongly, we can rely on the firm ground that has been given to us by our guides: our parents, our community, our religion, our leaders. They told us what was good, and we are doing what they have asked.

When we do what must be done, though, we sometimes stand alone. To do so requires fortification—protection—against the wave of power that comes with tradition and against the judgment that we may face. Nonetheless, we trust ourselves to know, and we know that someone must act. We must be that person. We must be those who do what must be done for ourselves and for others. As we step forward, we expect the tide of judgment to come, to wash over us, to drench us, and to weigh us down. We fear that it might drown us, yet we step into the wave and steel ourselves against it, regardless of our fear. We stand strong and then release the wave to disperse into the mist.

The wave into which we step is the power of our society and its social order. Everyone is pushed to seek her place in this order. As girls, we are told stories that help us imagine ourselves as our society would desire us: as princess, as precious, as humble, as meek, as compliant and helpful, as caring and deferential, as supportive and polite. We are told we should desire protection and wish to be cherished. We are told that our care and nurturing of others is valued. There is, after all, virtue in these socially assigned behaviors. There is virtue in caring and helping, in nurturing and supporting. Girls are also told, however, that in diverging from these social expectations, in breaking out of their place in the social order, that our actions are "bad" and "wrong" and "unbecoming of a young lady." We are shamed for our behavior. We are frightened and feel rejected. We are shunned and belittled, and this is precisely how we are meant to feel.

Shame may be warranted at times. When a person unjustly harms another or when she purposely turns away from what she knows is good, she *should* feel shame. When the threat of shame restricts girls and women to a storyline that they do not wish to follow, though, shame has been used as a means of control. Girls and women are regularly controlled through shame, but we ourselves do it to others, as well. We are socialized, all of us, to keep each other in line. We have all seen those girls on the playground, teasing another person for the way she looks or acts. We have all probably joined in at some point and made fun of someone else, relieved that we were not the target of the teasing. That's shaming. We should think seriously about those instances and ask what, exactly, the shamed person did to warrant the teasing. Perhaps she was too fat or too skinny. Maybe she was too sexy or too pretty, or athletic or boyish. She may have talked too much or too little.

Girls and women are given a set of standards and ideals of both beauty and behavior. We are convinced by our society that we will have achieved worth if we can meet them and that we have failed if we cannot. When we fail to meet these standards, we are made to feel that we are inadequate. Our inadequacy then leads to feeling ashamed. *This* shame is used to push girls and women to conform to social standards and it is a means for others to assert control. This social control is asserted over our bodies and our behavior, and the fear of shame can make it hard for girls and women to defy conformity. To do so would risk losing the acceptance of those whose approval we are taught to desire. If girls (and others) step outside the approved roles we are taught to play, we will be disciplined and ostracized, made to feel like an outsider, and alone. We are shamed into social compliance and controlled by our desire for acceptance. This demand for social conformity can be painful and demoralizing. Being virtuous does not make this pain go away, and it does not make it easier to resist the power of others' expectations or the fear of others' judgment, at least not at first. The virtue of *tzedek*, though, can aid us in claiming our own lives and resisting the force of shame meant to keep us "in our place."

There are many ways to think of what philosophers call "virtue" or "the virtues." Aristotle, an ancient Greek philosopher, developed an ethical theory founded on the importance of cultivating virtues in human life. Aristotle thought of the world as containing different *kinds* of organisms and entities. Each of these kinds contains or reflects a distinct essence proper to it, and with each unique essence comes a unique purpose or goal. When something embodies or displays its essence through functioning well, it is a virtuous example of their kind. One of these kinds is a human person, and, according to Aristotle, a person's goal is to reason well. If a person directs her life with sound reasoning and through cultivating different kinds of virtues, she will flourish. The best that a person can be, says Aristotle throughout the *Nicomachean Ethics*, is a virtuous person who has and displays, or acts in accordance with, the virtues.

Aristotle also tells us that the character traits that one must embody and practice are just those traits that lead to a good world. Philosophers disagree on what we might mean by a good, "flourishing world," however. For example, Aristotle suggests that bravery in battle is a virtue.[1] But if bravery in battle is a virtue, what does that say about a good world? If a virtuous world is brought about by bravery in battle, then that virtuous world must *include* battle. Many of us, however, would imagine a virtuous world differently: we would imagine that in a virtuous world, peace might prevail, and no fighting would be necessary. In a peaceful world, therefore, bravery in battle might be obsolete, unnecessary, or maybe even productive of the *wrong* kind of world. Moreover, since what we think is virtuous and good is just that kind of character trait that leads to, or is part of, a flourishing world, we need to agree on what that flourishing world might look like, so that we can identify the kinds of character traits that bring it about.

Julia Annas, a contemporary virtue ethicist, suggests answers to questions such as these and writes about the ways we can use a theory of virtue to guide our thinking about the good. She suggests that "virtue involves aspiring to an ideal."[2] Virtue is thus a process of learning where a person begins with the goal of becoming more virtuous, uses examples of virtue from those around her (teachers, parents, community leaders, etc.) and then begins to gain experience in virtue, developing virtue in her own way and according to her own considered judgment. Just as we learn from our experience and from our previous actions, we learn to be virtuous first by recognizing the goal of being virtuous, or good, and then by attempting as best we can to train ourselves to act in virtue: acting in ways that make real the better world we had in mind. As Annas explains, "Living in a flourishing way is an activity, the ongoing activity of a life, and living in a brave, generous, and so on way is a specification of what that is." This means that for Annas, flourishing is not an event, but instead a way of living. The virtues, then, are character traits that "embody a commitment to some ethical value, such as justice, or benevolence" so that virtue "is not merely a matter of performing actions that happen to be just, benevolent or whatever,"[3] but rather requires acting according to virtuous commitments to creating a flourishing world.

What these approaches to virtue have in common is that a virtue is part of realizing a flourishing world. We are taught virtue through demonstration, and we learn by modeling virtuous traits. When people display virtue or act virtuously, we make the world healthier for ourselves and for others. *Tzedek* is one such virtue. When people manifest *tzedek*, they lead the world toward health by doing what must be done. Not all people will exhibit this virtue alike. Some will be moved to work in the world fighting injustice in their community, while others will express this virtue by caring for those who need them. Still others will do both. There is an effort in all three to move beyond what is easy and comfortable, to push against that inertia that would keep us lazy or selfish, and to do what must be done, for others and for ourselves.

When we think, therefore, of "doing what must be done" as a virtue, we think of it as the kind of trait that people who make the world better, will often have. We will think of it as the kind of habit of character that we can aspire to and learn to better emulate. And we will think of it as the sort of character trait that when aimed at producing a flourishing world, *will* take part in bringing that flourishing world about.

Of course, the worlds in which we find ourselves are many, and the worlds that we aim to bring about are likewise numerous. *Tzedek* requires doing what we must, in the situation or place that we are in, to bring about a world that would be better for all. In *our* world, girls and women are not always respected. We can be dismissed as weak or as irrational, as frivolous or silly. We can be ignored, silenced, and diminished. Girls are expected to be strong in some ways, but we make jokes about "throwing like a girl." We say that girls can be athletes, and then tell them their performance is good "for a girl." When girls and women do succeed in stereotypically boyish or masculine physical activities, we often shame them for their prowess. We mock them for being too masculine, we call them names, we tell them that they have transgressed their rightful place, and we question whether we should count them as girls and women at all.

18.2 Integrity

Our response to these oppressive attitudes can be empowered through *tzedek*. When we act according to this virtue, we remember that others' expectations must not fully define us. We are the authors of our own selves, and each of us must define who we are and how we will live. When we do so, we display a form of integrity that arises from acting in *tzedek*; *tzedek* is a virtue that reinforces and reflects integrity. We can think of integrity as a state of wholeness or completeness, or a state of unification, solidity, and strength. Women and girls, though, are often told and trained in conflicting standards and impossible ideals such that we find it impossible to be only one person. Instead we must be many selves to fulfill the assigned roles. The encouragement we receive from parents and teachers who urge us to be exceptional students and strong leaders starkly conflicts with the seemingly benign imperative that we move aside for men who are stronger than us. Women and girls are told to make way for the men who will protect us and that we should accept that we are simply ill-suited to some tasks. When our world tells us that to be feminine is to be soft, or that to be feminine is to be attractive to boys and men, we learn that our power is in alluring and receiving attention. We are simultaneously told that to be sexually appealing makes us cheap and that to be unashamed of our bodies is indecent and diminishes our worth. Girls and women cannot fulfill both sets of expectations at the same time and are left with no path forward that does not compromise our integrity. We must be attractive, but we must hide it; we must be appealing but we mustn't reveal that we know it; we must be comforting and giving while making certain that we maintain our distance and decorum. Girls and women are told they should be a set of contradictions.

No person can play all of those roles at once. One cannot be a single unified *self* when she is expected to appease so many people and meet so many needs that are not her own. Being this unified and single self is not so difficult, though, for those who are told always to be strong, to resist conformity, and to assert their own wills. For people who are shown and taught the virtues of strength and power, the integrity of an indomitable will, an impregnable structure, and a single-minded purpose makes sense. This understanding of integrity was constructed with the ideals of patriarchy and masculinity as its guide. It was made for men and boys.

There are other ways of manifesting integrity, though. That is, there are other ways of knowing oneself, of embodying one's power, and expressing one's will in the world. Displaying the virtue of *tzedek* is part of repairing or rebuilding the world in health: by taking responsibility and ownership of oneself and by acting in the world according to one's determination of what must be done. As philosopher Lisa Tessman explains, the "task of acquiring integrity is necessary for resisting oppression and taking responsibility for—or being able to 'stand behind'—[who] one becomes."[4] Though women and girls live in—and are partially constituted, or made by—an imperfect world, we can choose the selves we wish to be and accept them as our own. To bring about a world in which people are not forced to be painfully fractured, we will need to do the work that must be done.

Integrity in this expanded sense requires thinking carefully about who we wish to be, how we wish to act, and what we need to do to become those people. As Tessman explains, "Taking responsibility for oneself in a forward-looking sense will require being able to make of oneself a person one is willing to be accountable for, a person whose values, practices, and disposition one can support, as well as a person who is capable of caring for herself."[5] This point is made in relation to feminist philosopher Claudia Card's idea that integrity rests on making deliberate choices about oneself and one's future actions, and accepting responsibility for them. This integrity is not founded on being an island, fortified against a storm, as our traditional conception would tell us. Instead, this integrity comes from a willingness to push against what others might will for us, and to *insist* that we do what must be done; that is, we do what must be done in a world where those who have the power to determine our potentials and possibilities *would prefer* for us to remain soft, silent, and deferential.

When we display the virtue of *tzedek*, convention must not turn us from our task. We resist those forces from outside that would undermine, through compulsion and coercion, our knowledge of self and weaken our will to act. For example, consider the prohibition of "hitting below the belt." To hit below the belt is, literally, to hit a person, usually a man, in his genitals. The pain delivered by such a hit is excruciating for people who have external genitalia. The phrase originates from the eighteenth century, when boxing became popular in Great Britain. It has extended to common usage to indicate an act that is unfair and now covers many kinds of examples. We are all taught that to hit below the belt is dishonorable and wrong and something only a coward would do. The prohibition against hitting below the belt is a prohibition against hitting where a man is most vulnerable. When I was young, I may have "accidentally" kicked boys below the belt in one or another playground scuffle. Winning a scuffle was how one gained entrance to the soccer game, so I obliged. At the time, I was not really smaller or physically weaker than the boys, but as I grew older, I saw my size and physical power diminish in relation to the average man, and I understood the reality of my situation. If sparring with a typical man, I would lose in a "fair fight." I then realized that a fair fight, in this case, was not fair at all. Men outweigh and outpower women on average. Perhaps the one advantage girls and women have in a physical contest against a typical man is the absence of external male genitalia and the vulnerability it creates for men. Women and girls *could* kick below the belt, and if we connect, we might "win." We have been trained to believe it is wrong, however, because the rules were structured by those who would gain protection from this prohibition: men.

The prohibition against hitting below the belt is an example of how the fear of abjection and shame can be used to preserve the privilege of some groups in our society. Training women and girls to refrain from hitting below the belt literally prevents us from defending and protecting ourselves if necessary, yet we are taught to know that such actions are out of bounds and that hitting in such a way is wrong. Consequently, many girls are socialized to think that they are powerless when physically confronted by a larger and stronger man.

In situations where we need to do what must be done, as Jael shows us, we must often disregard the judgment that will follow our action. Others may try to shame us, but we need not accept or bear the weight of this shame. As another example, consider dress codes in schools that are offered as a "solution" to boys' and teachers' purported distraction in the classroom. Girls must hide their bodies so that others are comfortable. The acceptance of this reasoning, however, makes a girl's body an object and increases the value of that object *as* an object by making it secret and taboo. Some girls may choose to resist these restrictions by engaging in policy debate. Other girls may choose to use the power they have been granted through their tabooed bodies to assert their wills more strongly through their sexuality. Each of these acts might be an expression of *tzedek* if her action is aimed toward improving the world for herself and for others.

Here we enter some tricky terrain: Can just *anything* be virtuous, so long as a person can claim it is part of the good? The answer is undoubtedly no. When we commit acts or display character traits that, if modeled by all, would lead us away from a healthy world and would harm our community's flourishing, we do not act virtuously. No individual action, whatever it might be, will alone suffice. Instead, when we look to the virtues, we look to the character traits that are cultivated and exemplified by people consistently over time and lend themselves to a better world. Merely selfish acts that are only intended to aid oneself and harm others or the world around us will never be part of virtue and would never be considered "what must be done." *Tzedek* is a virtue of those who have self-knowledge, wisdom, and determination, and it is a virtue of those who care for themselves and others. It requires compassion and thoughtfulness. When we do what must be done, we are not just benefiting ourselves. An action that must be done will be the kind of action that strengthens the doer *and* aids the world in flourishing. It will model to others the kind of person and world they are encouraged to manifest.

But still, we might wonder, how can I *know* that what I do is right? How does Jael *know* what must be done, how it must be done, and that she must be the one to do it? These are questions that do not have satisfying answers for everyone. Annas, for example, talks at length about the concerns that philosophers and others have expressed over the difficulty of *knowing* what is right.[6] There is no definitive way to know or determine which actions must be done. But as the story of Jael demonstrates, choosing to act as one believes, after consideration, is necessary for bringing about the kind of world that one aspires to create, is an essential part of realizing a virtuous world. Though we may not always *know* beyond all doubt what that ideal right action would be, the character trait of *tzedek* is one that, when practiced and improved and when aimed toward the goal of bringing about a better world, will impact the world for the better.

When Jael chooses to act on her own against convention in spite of her own fear and in a way that risks the shame of her father and her community, she embodies the virtue of *tzedek*. She acts with a force of will that stands against convention and that strays from the easier path. In doing so, Jael demonstrates an acceptance of responsibility for herself as the author of her own actions; though she has refused the admonitions of her father, and though she has committed an act that pains her deeply, she chooses to do what she has determined she must do. These features are all a part of the virtue of tzedek. When we act according to *tzedek* we risk censure, shame, and rejection because we know ourselves, we trust ourselves, and we have determined that something must be done and that we are able to do it. We act in pursuit of a world that will be better for ourselves and for others, owning our choices and accepting the consequences. *Tzedek* is not easy, as Jael shows us; sometimes it is much harder than merely doing what we are told. And yet still, sometimes, we must be the one who will do what must be done.

Notes

1. Aristotle (1999, 41–45).
2. Annas (2004, 72).
3. Annas (2009).
4. Tessman (2000, 383).
5. Ibid. Here she discusses Claudia Card's point (1996).
6. Annas (2004 and 2014).

Bibliography

Annas, Julia. 2004. "Being Virtuous and Doing the Right Thing." *Proceedings and Addresses of the American Philosophical Association* 78, no. 2 (November): 61–75.

Annas, Julia. 2009. "Virtue Ethics." In *The Oxford Handbook of Ethical Theory*, edited by David Copp, 515–536. Oxford: Oxford University Press.

Annas, Julia. 2014. "Applying Virtue to Ethics." *Journal of Applied Philosophy*. December 2014. Doi: 10.1111/japp.12103.

Aristotle. 1999. *Nicomachean Ethics*. 2nd ed. Edited by Terence Irwin. Indianapolis: Hackett Publishing.

Card, Claudia. 1996. *The Unnatural Lottery: Character and Moral Luck*. Philadelphia: Temple University Press.

Tessman, Lisa. 2000. "Moral Luck and the Politics of Personal Transformation." *Social Theory and Practice* 26, no. 3 (Fall): 375–395.

19

Empathy

Entangled Human and Nonhuman Relationships

Lori Gruen

In the first book of acclaimed African American writer Maya Angelou's seven-book autobiography, we meet three year old Marguerite (Maya) and her four year old brother Bailey as they arrive without adult supervision in Stamps, Arkansas, having been put on a train by their father after their parents split up. Marguerite and Bailey are going to be taken care of by their grandmother who is fairly well off as she runs a store in town. Marguerite describes her experiences of deep southern racism and how she struggles both externally and internally growing up black in a world made for white people. The story is at times infuriating, at times enlightening, and at other times inspiring as Marguerite overcomes violence, misrecognition, familial struggles, and her own insecurities and doubts to ultimately become a strong assured teenage mother in San Francisco.

The book is titled *I Know Why the Caged Bird Sings* and was published in 1969 in the heat of the civil rights movement in the United States. In 1983, Angelou also wrote a poem called "Caged Bird" that contains these stanzas.

> But a caged bird stands on the grave of dreams
> his shadow shouts on a nightmare scream
> his wings are clipped and his feet are tied
> so he opens his throat to sing.
>
> The caged bird sings
> with a fearful trill
> of things unknown
> but longed for still
> and his tune is heard
> on the distant hill

Lori Gruen, *Empathy* In: *Philosophy for Girls*. Edited by: Melissa M. Shew and Kimberly K. Garchar, Oxford University Press (2020). © Oxford University Press. DOI: 10.1093/oso/9780190072919.003.0020.

> for the caged bird
> sings of freedom.

For Angelou, the caged bird is a metaphor for the confinement of anti-black racism and the desire she has, for all black people, to be free to live their lives as they choose, on their own terms.

Scholars who have studied Angelou's work noted that there was an earlier poem that inspired the title for her book, written in 1899 by one of the first widely recognized Black poets, Paul Laurence Dunbar, the son of freed slaves. Its final stanza is:

> I know why the caged bird sings, ah me,
> When his wing is bruised and his bosom sore,—
> When he beats his bars and he would be free;
> It is not a carol of joy or glee,
> But a prayer that he sends from his heart's dee core,
> But a plea, that upward to Heaven he flings—
> I know why the caged bird sings!

This Dunbar poem is titled "Sympathy" and though it never mentions racism, it is an obvious reflection on the terrible suffering that slavery and its aftermath have caused. Dunbar, like Angelou, was interested in helping others to understand the multiple ways that oppression operates. One potent tool for communicating experiences of all sorts, from joyous, defiant, and proud to depressing, humiliating, and excruciating is through what Dunbar called "sympathy" and I will call "empathy."

In this chapter I will look at the powerful role that empathy can play in understanding the different experiences of others. I also want to reflect on caged birds, and the use and confinement of other animals, as more than metaphors. But let's begin with thinking about how sympathy is different from empathy.

19.1 Sympathy and Empathy

Sympathy and empathy are often thought of as moral emotions, and they are also ways of attending to others through expressions of care and concern. But sympathy and empathy are really quite distinct perspectives. As philosopher

Heidi Maibom puts it, someone sympathizes with an other when she feels sad for that person as a result of perceiving something bad happening to that person, whereas someone empathizes with an other when they try to feel what it's like to be that other (Maibom 2014). Sympathy is a response to something unfortunate or unpleasant happening to someone else in which the individual sympathizing retains all of her attitudes, beliefs, and feelings. So when a young child gets lost in a store and starts to cry, a sympathetic observer will recognize the fear and attempt to comfort the child and find the person who is taking care of them. Or when a friend is upset about the fact that they didn't win the prize they really wanted to, a sympathetic person might try to cheer that person up (but could even feel secretly glad they didn't win the prize). In cases of sympathetic engagement, the sympathizer needn't try to understand or feel what the child or the friend feels from their point of view. There is usually no feeling *with* the other. Rather the sympathizer identifies the unpleasant or unfortunate event as unpleasant or unfortunate for the individual experiencing it, but does not experience it herself.

Sympathy involves maintaining one's own attitudes and adding to them a concern for another. Sympathy for another is felt from the outside, what we can call the third person perspective. I can feel sympathy for your situation, even pity, but still have some distance from you and your situation. For example, I might think "Oh, isn't that sad" when I see on the news a migrant woman and her child struggling at the US border, but I might not be moved to do anything about it.

Empathy, however, builds connection with others through a process in which the person empathizing attempts to understand the circumstances of the other. This understanding may never really be complete and often is in need of revisions, but the goal is to try to take in as much about another's situation and perspective as possible. Empathy does not involve abandoning one's own attitudes, perspectives, and commitments when feeling with the other and provides an important point from which to assess the features of a situation and to ask appropriate questions.

What might be good questions to ask oneself in order to try to determine what sort of attention and reaction empathy requires? We might want to ask how our own attitudes differ from those of the person or being we are empathizing with. We might ask how our social, cultural, racial, religious, gendered, familial, economic, educational, and embodied experiences differ and how that may impact our attitudes and choices differently than those we are empathizing with. We might also want to know if people like me tend to do better or worse empathizing with different others and what that might mean for working to understand the situation they are in.

For a long time, people used the word sympathy to refer to something more like empathy. That may have been what was going on with the title of the Dunbar poem. The use of the term "empathy" is relatively new, just over a hundred years old. The first systematic analysis of empathy is often linked to Theodor Lipps's theory of Einfühlung. Writing in the early 1900s, Lipps suggested that empathy was a specific perceptual way of understanding the world and others in it. In the last couple of decades it has gained increasing attention in ethics and in the last few years empathy has been discussed in greater detail in animal ethics.

19.2 Different Forms of Empathy

We empathize in different ways at different times. One type of empathy that lots of people and many animals share involves what is called "affective resonance." This is a spontaneous, somewhat reflexive, response to the feelings of another. Anyone who has lived with dogs will be familiar with this type of response. Many dogs are emotional sponges—they often become stressed when their person is stressed, sad when their person is sad, joyful when their person is joyful.[1] Though this is sometimes called "empathy" it is a kind of embodied response to other individual(s) in one's immediate environment and does not require any reflection or conceptualization or even understanding. Rather it involves the direct perception of the emotions of others.

I've always been quite fascinated by what psychologists have called "storied empathy," which is less automatic than affective resonance but it also doesn't involve understanding the actual situation of another. Here is why—this form of empathy doesn't apply to actual others. The most common examples are when children identify with the characters in stories and when the narrative indicates that the characters are suffering or scared, the child will empathize with the character. Unlike more autobiographical stories, like that of Maya Angelou, that also evoke empathic reactions, storied empathy applies to fictional characters. When storied empathy is operating, the empathetic individual often does not distinguish between reality and fiction. When parents tell their distressed child "this is just a story" and the child isn't consoled, we might say that they are involved in storied empathy. When they are able to recognize the difference between fiction and reality, they can limit their empathetic experiences to real others, and use their empathy toward fictional characters as a way of honing their empathetic capacities without doing any real person (or animal) any harm.

But even when one is considering actual others, there is a process in which the empathizer may substitute their own feelings for that of the other. Rather than recognizing that the other may have a different, and distinct, perspective, there is a type of projection that occurs. The idea that you put yourself into the position of the other is a common way that empathy is discussed. But when you put yourself into the position of the other with your own attitudes and beliefs rather than trying to understand the other you may end up overlooking their situation and replacing it with your own. This is often referred to as projection, but as we'll see next, not all empathy involves projection.

For these types of empathy usually the empathizer doesn't distinguish his or her own feelings or mental states more generally from those of another. I knew a chimpanzee named Sarah who was involved in a study in which researchers were trying to figure out whether chimpanzees have what is called "a theory of mind." That is the ability to recognize that others may have feelings or beliefs that are different from one's own. Sarah was asked to help a human solve a set of problems and she was often successful. But researchers were worried that maybe she was just putting herself in the position of the human trying to solve the problem rather than distinguishing herself from them. The researchers were actually worried that she might be "empathizing" with the human. I wouldn't be worried about that at all because it would still be a remarkable thing for Sarah to be doing. These researchers presented her with a set of problems that one of the people she really liked was trying to solve and a set of problems that a person she didn't really like was trying to solve, and they found that she helped the person she liked more than helping the person she didn't like. This led the researchers to conclude that Sarah wasn't empathizing but did have a "theory of mind." I think she could have been both empathizing and have a theory of mind, though, because some forms of empathy require being able to separate one's own attitudes form another.

When we differentiate between ourselves and others, when we can knowingly simulate or take the perspective of another being, a different form of empathy, sometimes referred to as "cognitive empathy," can occur. This sort of empathy involves a reflective act of imagination that puts us into the other's situation and/or frame of mind, with that other's attitudes. Empathy of this sort enables the empathizer to not only grasp the other's preferences or interests, but also the features of the situation that affect the being one is empathizing with and information about what led her to be in that situation in the first place.

I have developed a form of empathy that I believe is important for ethics called "entangled empathy." Entangled empathy goes beyond feeling what others feel and imagining ourselves in their shoes, as it were. It encompasses a process of developing and refining caring perception and involves a recognition that we are in relationships with all sorts of others and are responsible in these relationships. Following feminist philosopher of science, Karen Barad, I use the term "entanglement" to capture the ways that we are coconstituted by our social and material relations. Social entanglements often extend beyond the human and far beyond our geographical location. Material entanglements involve all sorts of relations, including our socioeconomic opportunities and limitations, our consumer choices, what we eat, and the safety of our physical environment (e.g., water, air, particulate matter, toxic exposure, our changing climate), for example. These entanglements are complex, and include our relations to the child slaves who harvest cocoa for chocolate; the orangutans who are on the brink of extinction due to our consumptions of palm oil and palm products; those working in sweat shops who provide cheap clothing; our greenhouse gas emitting activities that are creating climate refugees. This all constitutes who we are. Our identities are not simply "socially constructed"; rather, we are who we are at any particular time as an expression of entanglements in multiple relations across space, species, and substance. (See Gruen 2014 for fuller discussion of entangled empathy).

19.3 Worries About Empathy

Some people have raised concerns, as I briefly mentioned, that we can't really ever understand another's perspective and situation, so empathy is just a type of "narcissistic projection" of our own interests and desires onto others. This is a serious worry. Even when individuals are genuinely attempting to take the perspective of another, when they are mindful of the dangers of substituting their own frame of reference, their own interests, desires, or beliefs about the good for those with whom they are empathizing, there is always the possibility that they have not adequately distinguished their own view from that of the other. I do think this concern can be overcome, or at least minimized. Distinguishing one's own interests from those of an other may be more subtle or complex in practice, but merely substituting one's own interests, fears, hopes, and ideology for an understanding with the plight of those being empathized with amounts to empathetic failure that can and should be corrected. Asking good questions about the situation of the other is a good place to start.

Another worry that I have heard about empathy is that it reinscribes stereotypical gender divisions of emotional and ethical labor. This type of objection has also been raised against certain versions of care ethics because there is an assumption that there is a natural capacity for those who are thought to be women to be nurturing and caring. Constructed binary gender roles have allowed those who identify as women and certain "others" to develop and explore empathy; indeed, binary gender norms presume that women should care more and develop their empathetic capacities. Cis-gendered men are prevented or encouraged to truncate such engagement. Those men who tend to be more caring are thought to be "effeminate" and women who do not empathize the way they are expected to often are thought to be defective or dangerous.

I think it is important to acknowledge that at its root, the ability to empathize is a central skill that most social animals have, whatever gender they might be thought to be. In its basic form (as I discussed earlier) empathy allows social beings to successfully navigate interactions in their groups. It is a particularly important skill in the absence of language. Being able to empathize in the most basic affective ways with others in one's group allows one to learn what is expected, what is prohibited, and the safest way to interact with others. Empathy is important for understanding group norms. Those norms may come to be understood as gendered, but the capacity to empathize itself is not.

Another worry that has been expressed about cognitive empathy and entangled empathy is that they require the maintenance of the self/other dualism. The problem with dualisms is that they become limitations to our thinking and relating. When dualisms become "value dualisms"—distinctions that elevate one side of the dualism and diminish the other, as is the case with familiar dualisms such as nature/culture, gay/straight, black/white, female/male, animal/human—they also provide the conceptual bases for exploitative and oppressive practices. This has led some to argue that we ought to rid ourselves of all dualisms including the self and other dualism.

264 SECTION IV: CONTEMPLATION IN ACTION

I think it is easier for those who have not struggled to develop and maintain a self to be ready to dissolve it. For many whose subjectivity, agency, and experiences have been undermined, questioned, or denied, the maintenance of a self-identity is an achievement and not one we should readily give up. The distinction between self and other need not be one of distance, need not require dominance and subordination and thus can be maintained in ethical ways. Indeed, it is centrally important that one has a balanced and clear self-concept to be able to engage empathetically with others. Denying differences can be just as morally problematic as maintaining dualisms. Empathetic engagement with different others is a form of moral attention that not only brings into focus the claims that the more than human world make on us but also helps to shift our moral attention. We can recognize animals, for example, as creatures with whom we share a way of being in the world, but if we think we experience the world in the same ways, we are much more likely to engage in narcissistic projections and miss what is important and valuable to them from their point of view. As the late ecofeminist philosopher Val Plumwood puts it:

> The strength of this awareness of difference and the resulting tension between like and unlike can make experiences of contact with others in nature particularly powerful ones . . . I see the snake by the pool about the same time as it sees me. We are both watching the frogs, but with different aims . . . our interaction involves shared expectations (and hence recognition of the other as alike in being a center of needs and striving), but also recognition of difference: recognition of the other as a limit on the self and as an independent centre of resistance and opacity. (Plumwood 1993, 156–157)

The self/other distinction can help to make vivid both the durability and the fragility of the self in relation to others.

The self/other distinction is also important in responding to some of the most powerful objections to empathy—that when we empathize we are inevitably biased toward those who are like us or those who are near and dear to us. We feel more toward people who are similar and feel that those who are different are not as sensitive or important or worthy of our attention. The same is true for those who are near versus those who are far. The self/other distinction that is central for entangled empathy urges us to reflect on our own situation as distinct from that of others, and once we begin that reflection, we can also reflect on the ways our own biases and preferences may be distorting our responsiveness. Having a sense of oneself is for many, as I've suggested, an achievement, something we work at, we think about, we critically reflect on. That process continues with the process of empathizing with others, we come to re-examine our own perspectives and may very well change ourselves after empathizing. I know in my own case, my empathic relationships with other animals have fundamentally changed who I am.

19.4 Caged Birds

I spend a lot of time with animals who live in sanctuaries, places of refuge for them after they have been rescued from various dangerous environments, often industrial farming or biomedical research laboratories. I have been able to build relationships with many chimpanzees, and I have also spent time with cows, sheep, goats, chickens, emus, turkeys, and parrots. The chimpanzee sanctuary that I visit most frequently, Chimp Haven, in Shreveport, Louisiana, continues to be a site that deepens my empathy not just for chimpanzees, but for other nonhuman animals and humans as well. There is a sanctuary in Springfield, Vermont, called VINE Sanctuary that has also provided me with opportunities to build empathy for very different others and has taught me a lot about birds. (I also learned I'm a little bit frightened by cows. They are so big!) VINE sanctuary started when Pattrice and Miriam Jones were living in the Delmarva peninsula, home to the highest concentration of chicken producers. One estimate suggests that more that 600 million chickens were killed there in 2018. Miriam and Pattrice saved one chicken who fell off a truck taking her and hundreds like her to be slaughtered. After rescuing her they rescued more chickens, including fighting roosters, and when they moved from Maryland to Vermont they were able to rescue other formerly farmed animals as well as birds who were kept in cages as pets.

Sanctuaries are designed to make the animal residents' interests the top priority. They are much better places than institutions where animals are used for human ends. Sanctuaries like VINE allow animals to interact with others, both of their own kind and of different species, including humans, to build friendships and community. But the animals are still captive in sanctuary and while this sort of captivity is worlds better for most animals, there are some animals who suffer from captivity regardless of the good intentions of the rescuers. Miriam Jones recalls her experience with a wild rooster they named Albert to illustrate the problems of captivity, even when the animals are respected and well-cared for. At VINE, wild birds often join the ranks of those who are rescued as it was clearly a safe, enjoyable place to be. One year, when neighbors threatened to kill the wild chickens, the people at VINE decided to put up a stockade fence to keep them out of the neighbors' yard and harm's way. While the fence was being built, they kept Albert and about a dozen other chickens safe from the neighbors by cooping them up in a small barn. Albert hurt his leg while enclosed and no matter what they tried, wrapping the leg, massaging the leg, putting him on "cage rest," the leg did not heal. After six weeks in a cage, they thought he might do better out again. Miriam reports:

> Over time, Albert wandered about the yard more, and even interacted with some of the hens who lived there, but he was never the same as he had been when he was wild and living as he pleased with his wild friends. After a few months, we found Albert dead one morning in the coop. He had had no sickness or injury other than his chronic leg issue . . . he was young—a born-wild chicken who should have lived ten to fifteen years, easily. Why did he die? It was clear to me that once he finally accepted he would never walk well again—that he would never be free again—his life simply wasn't worth living, and so he died. (Jones in Gruen 2014, 91)

Captivity is a type of constriction, and in some instances, like in the case of poor Albert, that constraint can be unbearable. Conditions of captivity can vary considerably. Humans and nonhumans who are incarcerated—confined by bars, chains, cages, prisons, coops, or locked doors for which they do not have a key—are denied the most basic freedom. They often cannot move freely, cannot associate freely, and are not free to live the lives they might choose to live. Of course, very few of us are able to live exactly the kind of life we might want. But certain restrictions go beyond mere frustration, and can be just as limiting as being physically confined. Restrictions based on the genders we are assigned can be as unbearable as being cooped up if we don't see ourselves in ways that match our assigned gender. We are also restricted in an ableist society by various material and normative expectations. We are restricted by state power and other governmental and economic institutions. And in a society founded on slavery, like the United States, anti-black racism, as Angelou so powerfully illuminates, can be experienced as unbearably oppressive.

Philosopher Marilyn Frye, when considering oppression, particularly the oppression of those identified as women, notes that the experience of oppression is one of confinement. Oppressed people feel pressured to conform to systematic and purposeful expectations and are punished or blocked when they do not. And importantly, she says, they are denied movement in many directions. They are caged in. She uses the metaphor of a bird cage and points to the systematic structure of the cage as a way of understanding the interlocking forces that are at work holding the oppressed back.

> If you look very closely at just one wire in the cage, the bird cage, you cannot see the other wires. If your conception of what is before you is determined by this myopic focus, you could look at one wire up and down the length of it and be unable to see why a bird would not just fly around the wire anytime it wanted to go somewhere . . . It is only when you take a step back, stop looking at the wires one-by-one microscopically, and take a macroscopic view of the whole cage that you can see why the bird does not go anywhere. (Frye 1983, 18)

It isn't just one wire, not being able to dress a certain way, or act a certain way, or go to a particular part of town, or engage in a certain type of study, for example. It isn't one feature of one's situation, say being poor, being young, being black, being a girl that is holding her back. These forces, these wires, work together to build a cage. Sometimes it is an actual cage, as in the case of prisons or zoos, for example. But it is also a figurative cage in which all of the wires work together to systematically hold someone back from doing what they want to do and being who they want to be.

In order to empathize with others, humans and nonhumans alike, seeing what bars might be holding someone back, being mindful of the forces of oppression, is necessary in order to avoid the pitfalls I mentioned earlier. Entangled empathy urges us not just to think about the bird, or the black girl being laughed at in school, or the gender nonconforming person who doesn't seem to fit in, but to look to the forces that operate to impinge upon their flourishing. Finding out about the conditions of different others will not only help us empathize better, it can also help us reflect on our own entanglements, how we might inadvertently be upholding barriers that oppress others. Empathizing with others is a first step to trying to break down these barriers, and allow as many humans and nonhumans to live more satisfying, freer lives.

Note

1. This is a generalization, of course. My dog Taz, who is a retired racing greyhound, doesn't respond this way. Dogs who have been abused or had other traumatic early life experiences, do not respond to their people in these ways. Some breeds are not "tuned in" this way. Nonetheless, if the coevolution hypothesis of dogs and humans is correct, their being empathetically responsive to humans would enhance their chances for survival.

Bibliography

Angelou, Maya. 1969. *I Know Why The Caged Bird Sings*. New York: Random House.
Frye, Marilyn. 1983. *The Politics of Reality*. New York: Crossing Press.
Gruen, Lori. 2014. *Entangled Empathy*. New York: Lantern Press.
Jones, Miriam. 2014. "Captivity in the Context of a Sanctuary for Formerly Farmed Animals." In *The Ethics of Captivity*, edited by Lori Gruen. New York: Oxford University Press.
Maibom, Heidi (ed.) 2014. *Empathy and Morality*. New York: Oxford University Press.
Plumwood, Val. 1993. *Feminism and the Mastery of Nature*. London: Routledge.

20

Courage

Meliorism in Motion

Kimberly K. Garchar

Let's face it. We're undone by each other. And if we're not, we're missing something.

—Judith Butler[1]

Just remember that your real job is that if you are free, you need to free somebody else. If you have some power, then your job is to empower somebody else.

—Toni Morrison[2]

Harriet Tubman escaped American chattel slavery in 1849 when she fled across the Mason-Dixon line to Pennsylvania. Her escape meant that she was freer than she was while enslaved, but she was most certainly not free as we understand the concept. She was not guaranteed equal treatment under the law, she was not respected equally, and she was not fully autonomous, given that all her actions and choices still existed only in a framework of misogyny and white supremacy, even though she was no longer a slave.

Tubman could have built a quiet life in Philadelphia. Instead, her freedom, such as it was, was a catalyst for the Underground Railroad. She returned to the South over nineteen times, leading over three hundred slaves to what freedom could be had in the North. She is now perhaps the most well-known conductor of the Underground Railroad, and as she proudly explained to Frederick Douglass, she "never lost a single passenger."[3] Abolitionist John Brown once said that Tubman was "one of the bravest persons on this continent."[4]

Kimberly K. Garchar, *Courage* In: *Philosophy for Girls.* Edited by: Melissa M. Shew and Kimberly K. Garchar, Oxford University Press (2020). © Oxford University Press. DOI: 10.1093/oso/9780190072919.003.0021.

Tubman later served as a scout and spy for the Union Army in the Civil War, and after the war she was active in the women's suffrage movement. In any telling of her story, her actions are commendable and praiseworthy. She was indeed brave, loyal, generous, resilient, compassionate, and steadfast. She was incredibly smart. About her, Frederick Douglass said, "Excepting John Brown—of sacred memory—I know of no one who has willingly encountered more perils and hardships to serve our enslaved than [Tubman]."[5] She understood the suffering associated with oppression and acted to meliorate this suffering. Her care and sympathy and compassion, along with her sense of justice and fairness and equality, were made active. She put meliorism in motion. She was *courageous*.

20.1 Introduction

Simone de Beauvoir understood that our human values come into being only through conflict. If the world were perfect, or if we were perfect, we would know only perfection and thus know only goodness. There would be no sense of badness, wrongness, or evil, since our experience would be only of an uncomplicated and complete goodness. Beauvoir explains, "There is an ethics only if there is a problem to solve."[6] Our values develop and are shaped in disagreement, as we work through the many problems in our world. We attempt to articulate rightness and wrongness, morality and immorality, which actions should be applauded, and which actions should be condemned through the experience of difference and disagreement. We attempt to understand what makes a life good or bad, then pursue what is good and avoid what is not. This study and pursuit of a good life is the field of philosophy we refer to as ethics.

The ethical endeavor is not merely an individual one, though. Ethical relativism is, roughly, the doctrine of "to each her own" when it comes to the determination of good and bad. This kind of thinking consumes itself in the end, or dies the death of a logical contradiction. Absolute tolerance—the belief that each person may determine her own set of moral norms and we must accept each person's individual determinations—means that we must accept beliefs of intolerance and intolerant beliefs. Intolerant beliefs contradict and deflate the tolerant beliefs that supposedly give room for their existence. Beyond the logical problem of relativism, we are social creatures. The generative problems to which Beauvoir refers arise within a framework of unavoidable relations; we are always already bound to each other simply because we are human beings. The ethical project—the study and pursuit of a good life—is a human project and thus must itself be a relational project. What I believe to be good directly and indirectly affects others and their own pursuits of the good life, and their pursuits affect me. More importantly, my good life cannot exist in a sea of badness. I rely upon the flourishing of others to foster and cultivate my own flourishing. In her powerful collection of post-9/11 essays, contemporary philosopher Judith Butler emphasizes this connectivity when she writes, "For if I am confounded by you, then you are already of me, and I am nowhere without you."[7] In other words, if I am confused by you, in conflict with you, my confusion is evidence that you are fundamentally part of and tied to whoever I am. Further, I cannot extricate you from my own personhood without unraveling myself. Thus, our conflicts, rather than being instances of separation, are evidence of our relational nature and thus the instances where values are born.

There are many ways we can study and pursue good as we live and die together; there are indeed many ways to live a good life. In this chapter I focus on one particular theory and method of ethics, which is the training in and development of virtue.[8] In virtue ethics, one works to develop moral character and a good life by practicing, honing, and enacting virtue. I am here interested in the particular virtue of courage. As with any virtue, courage does not make all actions good, and courage alone certainly does not make an individual person good. It is difficult to isolate courage insofar as it overlaps and works in tandem with other virtues. Poet Maya Angelou understood the complex nature of courage when claiming, "Courage is the most important of all the virtues, because without courage you can't practice any other virtue consistently. You can practice any virtue erratically, but nothing consistently without courage."[9] She sees courage, as do I, as a grounding virtue, or perhaps an encompassing one. Courage is developed such that other virtues can be better practiced in the world. In this chapter I will reconceptualize and work to specify the virtue of courage; that is, I will identify qualities and characteristics important to courage and courageous acts. In so doing, I will demarcate courage from bravery, with which it is often conflated. Courage is empathy enacted and meliorism made manifest.

This reconceptualization of courage is warranted for several reasons. First, our world is broken. We need both the concept of courage and the work it does if we are to mend our world in any way. Second, a reworked courage will help us address stereotypically gendered assumptions and expectations about certain virtues and dispositions, including bravery (typically masculine) and care (typically feminine) as well as challenging the binary that generates the two stereotypes. While we cannot simply slip the binary gender norms woven through our culture, this development of courage will open a space where we can perhaps begin to undermine these assumptions. Courage, as proposed here, is a virtue that can and should be practiced by all people, regardless of gender.

20.2 Reclaiming Courage

The human condition, whatever else it may be, is relational. We should be able to agree that humans are known to make mistakes, too. People are sometimes simply wrong. We can no more escape our mistakes than we can shed our relations. Fallibility, that is, proneness to error, is another inescapable aspect of being human. Thus, we are tied to each other through our mistakes as well as through our kindnesses. These mistakes will exist in our ethical projects simply because ethical projects are human projects and humans are as broken (and as beautiful) as the world in which they live. Beauvoir insists that in ethics, "failure is not surpassed, but assumed."[10] Sadly, some of our mistakes will cause injury to others. Even when our mistakes are benign, their very existence is reason to remember that all human accomplishments are marred in some way and imperfect. Sometimes we will fail in our projects and these failures should be an impetus for reflection even through disappointment and possibly grief. Beauvoir insists, "The most optimistic ethics have all begun by emphasizing the element of failure involved in the condition of [people]; without failure, no ethics."[11] Failure follows us, like a gremlin, leaving sometimes a quiet wake (but a wake, nonetheless) and at other times complete chaos, destruction, and pain. The human condition, then, is relational and fallible, and these two aspects of our condition are bound to interact in explosive ways at times.

Nonetheless and importantly, ethics exists. We know that things— situations, interactions, environments—can be better or worse, even if imperfect. Goodness is possible and we are, minimally, obligated to work toward goodness, even as we work through arguments about what goodness actually is. Our responsibility is to become better even if we are incapable of becoming perfect. The Jewish concept of *tikkun olam*, which is translated as "repairing the world," is helpful here. It is an imperative to act for good and an aspiration to better our lives and the lives of others despite our tendency to foul things up in truly remarkable ways. This idea is expressed in the *Mishnah*: "Do not be daunted by the enormity of the world's grief. Do justly, now. Love mercy, now. Walk humbly, now. You are not obligated to complete the work, but neither are you free to abandon it" (Shapiro 1995, 41).[12]

I've painted a picture of humans necessarily tied together and bound to make mistakes. Let me return now to virtue ethics. Relatedness and fallibility will necessarily be present in any study or pursuit of virtue, again because our human characteristics are present in any of our projects or pursuits. Beyond a general admission that virtue is a trait that can be learned and practiced, virtue ethicists disagree on what virtue is, and thus they disagree on what it means to be virtuous. I follow Julia Annas, a contemporary philosopher who takes a number of philosophical cues from Aristotle, in understanding that virtue is a comportment, a way of presenting oneself to and responding in the world. Annas explains, "A virtue is a disposition to reason, feel, and act in certain ways, a disposition which is reliable in similar circumstances and persistent over differing circumstances, which is dynamic, always adjusting to new situations selectively and intelligently, and which continues to develop as it is exercised through the person's life."[13] To develop virtue means, among other things, to develop moral tendencies such that one will respond consistently and habitually as one encounters similar situations. Further, it is developing an awareness of what makes situations similar or dissimilar so that one's habitual response is appropriate. Virtue is about the way in which one approaches others and the world; it is one's bearing, one's character. It is as much about expectations as it is about previous experiences. Virtue is a way of being or, returning to Beauvoir, it is a way of "casting oneself into the world."[14] People do not passively float through time and space. Instead, persons actively move through this world, guided by what they have learned from previous successes and failures. The direction they chart is determined, in part, by virtue.

Historically, courage has often been conflated with the virtues of bravery and militarism and thus has often been thought of as fearlessness or perhaps fortitude in the face of danger.[15] I am undermining this association. Persons can and do act bravely and fearlessly, and we must recognize those actions as laudable when appropriate. We have the words and concepts to do that: bravery, fearlessness, fortitude, valor. Heroism may well be the most celebrated recognition of bravery and the term is often applied to soldiers, first responders, physicians, and others who knowingly place themselves in danger for the good of others. Courage must be something else. It is better described in terms of meliorism rather than militarism. When courage is conceptualized in a confrontational, aggressive, and militaristic way, especially in our patriarchal culture, it is a virtue reserved exclusively for those trained in confrontation and aggression. This is not usually a training that girls and women (and many others who challenge the gender norms of masculinity) regularly receive.[16] I am reclaiming courage such that courage requires first, a recognition of our related natures, especially when our relations cause pain and suffering, and second, an attempted meliorative response to the needs of others, including their suffering.

Certainly, courageous acts will overlap with and possibly contain other manifestations of virtue. Courageous acts may or may not include valor. The knowledge of potential failure may make courageous acts fearless. Courage will sometimes hurt. Not always, but sometimes. At other times one may feel righteous and justified, vindicated and strong when acting in courageous way. Importantly, courage is neither developed in isolation from other virtues nor is it practiced apart from other virtues. Nonetheless, courage is distinct from other virtues, including bravery, and deserves attention independently.

We know militarism and aggression will not heal the world. A quick look at human history is evidence of this. Similarly, empathy, as discussed in the next section, is not enough; empathy does not normally require action. Finally, while care and care ethics are powerful forces in the world, courage exceeds care. Care may not be the kind of response that is required in a courageous act. We need a concept of "repairing the world" that doesn't fall into the binary gender trap of bravery for men and caring for women. We need a way to think, practice, and prepare for acts that are challenging, difficult, and scary, without turning to battle or domination metaphors to describe them. We need a way to urge and applaud acts grounded in caring and compassion without employing the motherhood metaphor. We need ways to understand and teach active empathy, or meliorism in motion, which may or may not also include bravery, empathy, or care.

20.3 Empathetic Recognition

Girls are often the first to be taught to attune themselves to the needs of others. Historically, they have been taught to foster an awareness of others so very well that they learn to focus on the needs of others above and instead of their own needs. Further, girls' attunement, along with the normally pre-scribed associated caring responses addressed in the next section, begins to masquerade as something natural and innate instead of a learned and prac-ticed behavior. We come to expect girls to be empathetic and compassionate, focused selflessly on others, and caregivers, while boys and men are believed to be, naturally, something else.

This subtle but powerful social conditioning is an epistemological training in addition to an emotional training. It is true that empathy was originally understood as an emotion, and we still commonly know the term to mean something akin to "fellow feeling." An empathetic person was traditionally thought to feel what others feel. For example, if I observe a happy person, then I am myself happy empathetically. Beyond empathetic feelings, cog-nitive scientists now understand empathy in terms of mirror neurons and other neurological pathways, and we know emotions can themselves be sources of knowledge. I am borrowing from contemporary philosopher Lori Gruen, who develops the concept of entangled empathy and frames it as a process involving both emotional and cognitive activities. She explains, "Entangled empathy is a process that involves integrating a range of thoughts and feelings to try to get an accurate take on the situation of another and figure out what, if anything, we are called upon to do."[17] Knowing and feeling are bound together in Gruen's entangled empathy which is, like other virtues, a skill that can be learned and honed.

In outlining empathetic recognition, I am emphasizing the epistemolog-ical aspect of Gruen's entangled empathy without disregarding the emotional components. Girls are taught to see and hear, but these words mean more than perception. Their training is in understanding—that is, *knowing*—about the needs of others and especially of suffering in the world. But to truly understand neediness and suffering in others is to simultaneously under-stand one's own precarious nature and potential suffering. Further, the de-gree to which we rely on others, whether we want to or not, is brought to the fore in the empathetic recognition of suffering. Butler explains, "One insight that injury affords is that there are others out there on whom my life depends, people I do not know and may never know. This fundamental dependency on anonymous others is not a condition I cannot will away."[18] To deny the connections brought to light in moments of pain and suffering is to deny our humanity, both good and bad. My actions cause suffering in others and their actions cause suffering in me, which is even more evidence that we are ethi-cally bound together.

20.4 Response

Empathetic recognition is a necessary aspect of courage, and while difficult, it can be taught, learned, and practiced. Recognition is not sufficient for
courageous action, though. Courage requires an understanding of the pain
of others, a turning toward it, and *acting* in response to it. That is, courage
requires a *response* to the recognized suffering.

Learning and practicing appropriate responses to suffering are, admittedly, more difficult than cultivating the ability of empathetic recognition.
Courageous response requires a uniqueness that is determined and shaped
by the given situation and thus cannot be prescribed beforehand. Aristotle's
ethics teach that it is incredibly difficult to achieve virtuous action because
there are so many factors and variables at play in any situation; thus, getting
things exactly right is rare. This ought not discourage us, for it is rare that
we get anything exactly right and even experts continue a life-long practice
to hone their skills. We learn about appropriate responses through failure
and through retrospect reflection more often than anything else. That is,
we learn many things through trial and error. The entire discipline of science is, after all, one long series of trials and errors. Further, we work toward ideals in all aspects of our life. It would be strange if it were not also the
case in developing courage. Even though the task looms large, it does not
diminish our obligation to pursue it. Recall our responsibility as outlined in
the *Mishnah*: "You are not obligated to complete the work, but neither are
you free to abandon it."[19]

In an initial attempt to better theorize what these responses entail, even
while admitting the wide variety of content, we can conceptualize "response"
along two lines. First, responses might be thought of as a building or repairing
of relations that allow for human[20] flourishing. As a starting point, we can
think of these relations as caring relations and we can look to care ethicists,
who prioritize relationships, for inspiration here. Care ethics is a recent addition to the canon of ethical theory and its development of can be traced
to the 1980s, and especially the publication of Carol Gilligan's *In a Different
Voice*. Gilligan formalized the view that there are minimally two frameworks
through which a person could approach moral problem solving. The first
framework was dubbed the justice framework. Persons working within this
framework oriented themselves toward moral problems using somewhat abstract concepts such as justice, autonomy, individuality, and rights. This kind
of moral thinking is well represented in the history of Western philosophy.

The care framework, on the other hand, was new. Gilligan saw that a person could also approach moral problem solving by prioritizing connection, relationships, and intimacy. The care framework does not exist in opposition to the justice framework but rather is parallel to it. There has been an extended debate among philosophers as to whether this caring predisposition is or ought to be uniquely feminine, and I will not wade into that discussion here. It suffices for my argument to admit that care is a necessary and powerful dimension of the human moral experience and that it has been largely gendered in a binary way—that is, women have been primary caregivers—in the past. Nonetheless, care ethics is one model for the appropriate response to empathetic recognition that I envision.

Many human relations, though, are not necessarily relations of care. Indeed, many relations can actually be understood in terms of justice and fairness and we recognize broken or oppressive relationships as instances of injustice. Empathetic recognition and understanding of oppression, either one's own oppression or the oppression of others, is often the reason that the courageous action is required. The second line in conceptualizing the repair of broken relations then is justice, and a nebulous understanding of justice is swirling through and around this version of courage. I cannot here enter that discussion but rather paint a broad picture of justice in terms of fairness and fighting oppression while creating an environment in which humans and nonhumans can live flourishing lives and develop their various capabilities and capacities.

We can also imagine courageous responses that are formed through witnessing an affront to human dignity that is truly abominable. In this instance, we may find ourselves working through our own moral disgust at the given situation and acting to vindicate the respect and humanity of those in need. We know that, sadly, the same kinds of abuse occur in relations with nonhuman animals, too. It may well be that the courageous person acts to restore the dignity of nonhuman life, or life in general, as opposed to strictly the dignity of human life.

Regardless of how it comes about, Butler helps us envision the goal of courageous actions manifest as relational repair. She explains that we should be working toward "the possibility of community on the basis of vulnerability and loss" (Butler 2004, 20). We are constituted by our relations and marked by our fallibility, which means we are fundamentally vulnerable beings. Courage is manifest when we recognize pain, vulnerability, or oppression and work to meliorate said pain, vulnerability, or oppression. Courage is an empathetic recognition or attunement coupled with an active, meliorative response to the brokenness of the world.

20.5 Courage, Redux

Let's return to Harriet Tubman. Unquestionably, she was brave. She confronted and fought the dehumanizing institution of chattel slavery and the associated racism in America on many fronts. We can see her bravery quite literally in her work with the Union army. She was a soldier and a spy, and no doubt regularly found herself in dangerous and frightening situations. But she knew the oppression and suffering of others and responded empathetically. As she explained, "I had seen their tears and sighs, and had heard their groans, and would give every drop of blood in my veins to free them."[21] Her work was motivated by tears and sighs as much as it was by justice. She was courageous as I have outlined the virtue here; that is, she put meliorism in motion.

Let's consider several examples that perhaps further challenge binary gender norms, such as Imperator Furiosa in the film *Mad Max: Fury Road*. Furiosa is powerful and cunning, even in the midst of a raging, dystopian and (still) patriarchal future. She wields the power of a "war rig," challenging multiple armies, in order to save five young women. These women represent all girls and women, of course, which amplifies the consequences of Furiosa's actions. Consider further any number of fierce women characters from Wonder Woman, to Eowyn in *The Lord of the Rings*, to Rey and Princess Leia in the *Star Wars* films. Violence and aggression abound in all of these stories. These women are warriors, to be sure, but they are more than brave. They are not exclusively aggressive or fearless. They are not violent because they are "consumed" by violence, nor are they violent for abstract ideologies such as nationalism. Their aggression is driven by the fact that others, sometimes millions of others, are oppressed and suffering. They are attuned to the needs of others and respond appropriately. These characters sometimes fight for ideals of justice and human dignity in caring ways and sometimes in ferocious ways. Regardless, they are courageous.

Finally, let us consider more explicitly caring expressions of courage. Bearing witness to the death of a loved one is, in my mind, one of the most difficult aspects of our mortality. It is difficult precisely because we *want* to fight death, insofar as we feel that is unfair. Death is—of course—utterly indifferent to human wants and desires. We may delay death's arrival but ultimately there are no effective weapons and no legitimate arena for battle. Once exhausted from the winless fight, we are left with care and devotion as potential responses, and these actions will always seem insufficient. Further, for a person who has honed her ability to empathetically recognize the needs of others, to hold the hand of the dying means to recognize that she, too, will have these same needs. Perhaps the most challenging aspect of helping another die, though, is to comfort despite the fact that one's comfort will not save. Holding vigil through the death rattles is perhaps one of the scariest and most courageous things a person could do. These witnesses turn toward the suffering of others instead of turning away. They know they cannot beat death but they can ease suffering. They are courageous.

20.6 Conclusion

I have suggested that courage should be conceptualized in terms of meliorism and I have laid out argument because we, and the world, need new ways to think about easing our suffering and working to repair our brokenness. This is perhaps the most frustrating juncture of the chapter because it seems I should have more to say. There is indeed much more to be said though I cannot say it alone, nor can it be said here. It seems natural to ask how, *exactly*, one ought to go about developing empathetic recognition and learning appropriate responses. I cannot prescribe a single or simple answer. There are indeed places where we can look for guidance in the development of empathetic recognition; those trained in nursing often receive extensive practice in empathetic recognition. Learning appropriate responses is more difficult because any response is unique to the given situation. Nonetheless, we must study and practice in order to pursue a good life. We must get down to doing the work of ethics.

There are many who can guide us. We can look to existentialists such as Simone de Beauvoir and her remarkable book, *The Ethics of Ambiguity*, cited earlier. We can look to pragmatist thinkers such as Jane Addams and Josiah Royce, care ethicists such as Eva Feder Kittay, and critical theorists such as bell hooks. We can look to the contributors of this book, including Lori Gruen, from whom I have borrowed the idea of entangled empathy, and who helps us better understand our relationships with nonhuman animals. Gillian Russell and Shanti Chu clarify the logic of institutional and systemic oppression so that we can better recognize injustice. Shannon Winnubst elucidates the ways in which race, while constructed, is about philosophical differences in kind and that these differences play out in cruel and predictable ways in the world. In fact, all of the contributors of this book implicitly ask us to think and act courageously in our lives and world. Acting courageously means to act knowing that one will never fix the world but is working to better it, nonetheless. Courage is the pursuit of a not-quite-lost cause. Insofar as we are related to and depend on each other and yet remain fallible beasts, we cannot eradicate error or injury from our world. But we are also capable of learning and we are sometimes truly impressive in our ability to become better, which gives me *profound* hope for our world.

Notes

1. Butler (2004, 23).
2. Toni Morrison, quoted by Houston (2003).
3. WGBH (1998).
4. Ibid.
5. Ibid.
6. De Beauvoir (1976, 18).
7. Butler (2004, 49). Emphasis added.
8. Virtue ethics has been explicated elsewhere in this book. For additional reading, see Aristotle (1999), MacIntyre (2007), and Annas (2011).
9. Maya Angelou quoted in Graham (2006, 224).
10. De Beauvoir (1976, 13).
11. De Beauvoir (1976, 10).
12. This is Rabbi Rami Shapiro's interpretive translation of Rabbi Tarfon's work on the Pirke Avot 2:21. The text is a commentary on Micah 6:8.
13. Annas (2011, 282).
14. De Beauvoir (1976, 41).
15. Consider, for example, the core values of the United States Army: loyalty, duty, respect, self-less service, honor, integrity, and personal courage. Personal courage is defined as the ability to "face fear, danger, or adversity (physical or moral) . . . [and] Personal courage has long been associated with our Army" (https://www.army.mil/values/). This definition is more akin to bravery than to courage. We can also look at any number of essays on courage in journals such as the *Journal of Military Ethics*. For example, Zavaliy and Aristidou maintain that "*courage consists in overcoming the fear of significant harm for a worthy cause*" (2014, 174, emphasis in original).
16. It is certainly the case that persons who happen to not be men are capable of bravery and have acted bravely. Nonetheless, the image of male soldier, leader, and superhero are only recently being challenged, and those challenges are not necessarily welcome.

Consider, for example, the recently reenacted ban against transgendered persons serving in the US military.
17. Gruen (2014, 50).
18. Butler (2004, xii).
19. Shapiro (1995, 41).
20. I see this argument being easily extended to include other-than-human animals and possibly other aspects of our environment.
21. WGBH (1998).

Bibliography

Addams, Jane. 2009. *20 Years at Hull House*. Scotts Valley, CA: CreateSpace Independent Publishing Platform.

Annas, Julia. 2011. *Intelligent Virtue*. London: Oxford University Press.

Annas, Julia. 2015. "Book Forum on *Intelligent Virtue*." *Journal of Value Inquiry* 49: 281–288.

Aristotle. 1999. *Nichomachean Ethics*, trans. Terence Irwin. Indianapolis: Hackett Publishing.

Butler, Judith. 2004. *The Precarious Life*. London: Verso Press.

De Beauvoir, Simone. 1965. *A Very Easy Death*. Trans. Patrick O'Brian. New York: Pantheon Books.

De Beauvoir, Simone. 1976. *The Ethics of Ambiguity*. Trans. Bernard Frechtman. New York: Citadel/Kensington Books.

De Beauvoir, Simone. 2011. *The Second Sex*. Trans. Constance Borde. New York: Vintage.

Gilligan, Carol. 2016. *In a Different Voice*. Harvard, MA: Harvard University Press.

Graham, Stedman. 2006. *Diversity: Leaders Not Labels*. New York: Free Press.

Gruen, Lori. 2014. *Entangled Empathy*. New York: Lantern Books.

hooks, bell. 2003. *Teaching Community: A Pedagogy of Hope*. Philidelphia: Routledge.

hooks, bell. 2006. *Outlaw Culture: Resisting Representations*. Philidelphia: Routledge Classics.

Houston, Pam. 2003. "Toni Morrison Talks Love." *O, The Oprah Magazine*, November. http://www.oprah.com/omagazine/toni-morrison-talks-love/4.

Kittay, Eva. 1999. *Love's Labor: Essays on Women, Equality, and Dependency*. New York: Routledge.

Kittay, Eva. 2010. "The Personal is Philosophical is Political: A Philosopher and Mother of a Cognitively Disabled Person Sends Notes From the Battlefield." *Metaphilosophy* 40, nos. 3–4: 606–627.

Kittay, Eva, and Ellen K. Feder. 2003. *The Subject of Care: Feminist Perspectives on Dependency*. Totowa, NJ: Rowman and Littlefield.

MacIntyre, Alasdair. 2007. *After Virtue* Notre Dame: University of Notre Dame Press.

Mad Max: Fury Road. 2015. Dir. George Miller. Warner Bros. Pictiures. Film.

Royce, Josiah. 1995 [1908]. *The Philosophy of Loyalty*. Nashville, Tennessee: Vanderbilt University Press.

Royce, Josiah. 2001 [1912]. *The Sources of Religious Insight*. Washington, DC: Catholic University of America Press.

Shapiro, Rami. 1995. *Wisdom of the Jewish Sages*. New York: Harmony/Bell Tower.

Star Wars (original trilogy). 1977-1983. Dirs. George Lucas, Irvin Kershner, Richard Marquand. 20th Century Fox. Film.

Star Wars (sequel trilogy). 2015-2019. Dirs. J. J. Abrams, Rian Johnson, J. J. Abrams. Walt Disney Studios Motion Pictures. Film.

The Lord of the Rings (trilogy). 2001-2003. Dir. Peter Jackson. New Line Cinema. Film.

WGBH, Public Broadcasting System. Last modified 1998. "Africans in America: Harriet Tubman." http://www.pbs.org/wgbh/aia/part4/4p1535.html.

Zavaliy, Andre G., and Michael Aristidou. 2014. "Courage: A Modern Look at an Ancient Virtue." *Journal of Military Ethics* 13, no. 2: 174–189.

Index

philosophical questioning, 53, 54, 56–57, 59–60, 61–62, 105–6, 116, 126, 132–33, 201. *See also* epistemological curiosity

Plumwood, Val, 80, 88–89, 90–92, 264. *See also* dualism; feminist logic

Pope, Alexander, 174, 175–76

(post)colonialism, 185, 186–90, 191, 204, 207–8, 210–11

Poussaint, Alvin, 168

pride
  as absolute, 45–47, 48–50
  as group-based, 49
  as relative or comparative, 45–47, 48, 49–50
  as vicious, 39, 40–44, 47–48, 65, 67–68
  as virtuous, 40–44, 47–48, 49–50 (see also *Jane Eyre*)

Pride and Prejudice, 175, 177–78

projection. *See* empathy: objections

race
  concept, 181–82, 185–87, 188–90, 191, 205–6, 211–12, 240
  fetishization, 209–10
  misperception, 207, 208–9, 210–11, 221, 237–38, 257
  multiraciality, 205–14 (*see also* Kahlo, Frida: multiracial identity)
  and queerness, 205, 211–13, 214
  systemic racism, 131–32, 139–40, 168–70, 183–84, 185–91, 207–8, 209, 220–21, 226–27, 228–29, 232–41, 257, 258, 266, 278 (*see also* science: racist practices; white privilege)
  racial otherness, 205, 206, 207–8, 209–13, 214

Radice, Adrianna, 157–58

rage. *See* Medusa: women's anger

reflection. *See* knowledge: of the self

religion
  discussion of, 6, 8, 29–30, 32–33, 35–36, 64, 85, 129–30, 186–88, 189–90, 195–96, 199, 200, 248, 259–60
  during Enlightenment, 187–88 (*see also* Christianity)

respectability politics, 226–27. *See also* race: systemic racism

Roupenian, Kristen, 238

Sartre, Jean-Paul, 159–60. *See also* Beauvoir, Simone de: on self-doubt

science
  and art, 115, 117–18
  bias and objectivity, 119–23, 188, 197
  during Enlightenment, 112, 187
  gender imbalance, 112–13, 114, 115–16, 121–22, 123 (*see also* Morandi, Anna: as pioneer woman anatomist)
  Institute of Sciences, 112, 114–15
  methods, 112, 114–15, 118–19, 138–39, 188, 276
  neuroscience, 126, 196, 275
  philosophy of, 115–18, 120, 262
  pseudoscience, 118–19, 133–34 (*see also* craniometry)
  racist practices, 187–90, 191

self-trust. *See* knowledge: of the self

Sextus Empiricus, 106, 109

sexuality, 185–86

shame. *See* girl: oppression

Shelley, Mary. See *Frankenstein*

skeptical arguments
  from circularity, 101–2, 104–5
  from skeptical hypotheses, 101–2
  from regress, 101–2, 103–4

Slingerland, Edward, 106–7

Smith, Tara, 42–43, 45–46, 49–50

soundness. *See* philosophical argument: in logic

Spillers, Hortense, 184–85

Stanhope, Lord Philip, 167–68, 173–74

Stebbing, Susan, 80, 92–95. *See also* feminist logic

Steele, Claude, 171

Stein, Gertrude, 138–39

Stoljar, Natalie, 35

Stone, Sandy, 128

Striker, Gisela, 106

taboo, 254–55

Taylor, Gabriele, 40, 46–47

technology
  artificial intelligence (AI), 129–30 (see also *Frankenstein*)
  ethics of algorithms, 130–33
  and human nature, 126–27, 200–1
  philosophy of, 124–29, 130, 132–33, 134
  social media, 241–42

CPSIA information can be obtained
at www.ICGtesting.com
Printed in the USA
BVHW050843300423
663275BV00001B/1

9 780190 072926